THE
SIERRA CLUB
GUIDE TO
THE
NATURAL AREAS
OF FLORIDA

OTHER NATURAL AREAS GUIDES

Guide to the Natural Areas of California

Guide to the Natural Areas of Oregon and Washington

Guide to the Natural Areas of Colorado and Utah

Guide to the Natural Areas of New Mexico, Arizona, and Nevada

Guide to the Natural Areas of Idaho, Montana, and Wyoming

Guide to the Natural Areas of New England

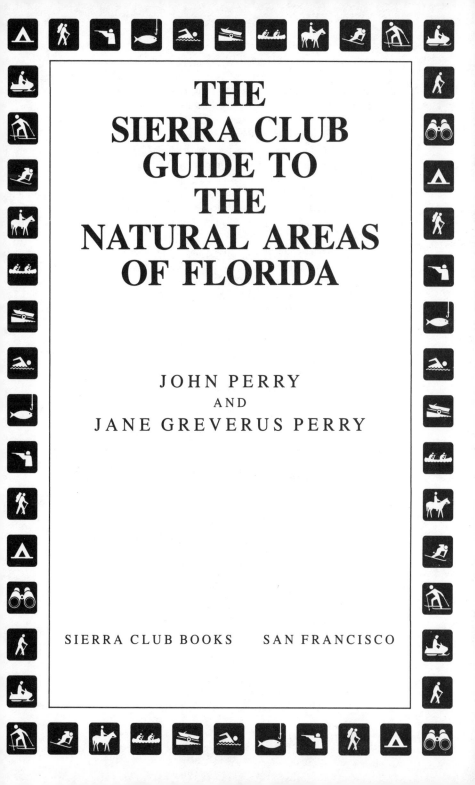

THE SIERRA CLUB GUIDE TO THE NATURAL AREAS OF FLORIDA

JOHN PERRY
AND
JANE GREVERUS PERRY

SIERRA CLUB BOOKS   SAN FRANCISCO

The Sierra Club, founded in 1892 by John Muir, has devoted itself to the study and protection of the earth's scenic and ecological resources — mountains, wetlands, woodlands, wild shores and rivers, deserts and plains. The publishing program of the Sierra Club offers books to the public as a nonprofit educational service in the hope that they may enlarge the public's understanding of the Club's basic concerns. The point of view expressed in each book, however, does not necessarily represent that of the Club. The Sierra Club has some sixty chapters coast to coast, in Canada, Hawaii, and Alaska. For information about how you may participate in its programs to preserve wilderness and the quality of life, please address inquiries to Sierra Club, 730 Polk Street, San Francisco, CA 94109.

Library of Congress Cataloging in Publication Data

Perry, John, 1914–
The Sierra Club guide to the natural areas of Florida / John
Perry, Jane Greverus Perry.
p. cm.
Includes bibliographical references and index.
ISBN 0-87156-551-X
1. Natural areas — Florida — Guidebooks. I. Perry, Jane Greverus.
II. Title.
QH76.5.F6P47 1992   333.78′09759—dc20   92-905
CIP

Production by Robin Rockey

Cover illustration by Bonnie Smetts

Book design by Abigail Johnston, based on concept by Lily Langotsky

Maps by Hilda Chen

Printed in the United States of America on acid-free paper
containing a minimum of 50% recovered waste paper of which
at least 10% of the fiber content is post-consumer waste.

10 9 8 7 6 5 4 3 2 1

TO THE RANGERS,

FORESTERS, NATURALISTS,

WILDLIFE BIOLOGISTS,

AND OTHER MEN AND WOMEN

WHO CARE FOR OUR FORESTS,

PARKS, AND PRESERVES

CONTENTS

INTRODUCTION

THIS IS A GUIDE TO FLORIDA'S QUIET PLACES, where flowers bloom, birds sing, and the signs of man are few. Many of these places are unknown to tourists, unfamiliar to most Floridians.

Florida's Division of Tourism says nearly 40 million visitors come to Florida each year. Most of these congregate at theme parks and on the beaches—few are aware of the natural Florida. Should they visit a State Park, most visitors see only the clusters of campsites, picnic tables, swimming beaches, and rest rooms. We describe the larger backcountry.

When waiting lines are long at EPCOT and beaches are crowded, one can walk in solitude through many a subtropical wonderland or drift in a canoe down a wilderness river, seeing cypress trees and mangroves, bromeliads and Spanish moss, roseate spoonbills, frigatebirds, manatees, armadillos, and alligators. One can even find an isolated ocean beach where sea turtles lay their eggs in summer. These are the places we have selected.

A REFUGE FROM SNOW SHOVELS

The climate of Florida's northern tier is temperate, with an occasional dusting of snow. In the southern Keys, it's tropical. Most of the state has subtropical weather. Summers are long, warm, and humid. Temperatures seldom rise much above 90°F, but humidity persuades some Floridians to have summer cottages in the Great Smokies.

Winters are usually mild, thanks to latitude and the Gulf Stream. In central Florida, brief killing frosts every few years distress citrus and strawberry growers, as well as vacationers. Spring and fall are seasons when screened windows and doors can be open day and night.

Resorts along the Panhandle's Gulf Coast are most popular in summer, uncrowded after Labor Day. Yet summer heat waves occur more often in the north, because peninsular weather has the moderating influence of the surrounding seas. The north is cooler in winter, but only by an average of 10° F. In central and southern Florida, the visitor season begins in December.

"Florida enjoys abundant rainfall," says the National Climatic Center. Sometimes. As we write, our home region is in the fourth dry year. Water-use restrictions are in force. Restrictions will become severe in coastal counties unless the weather breaks. Now some people actually wish for a hurricane, because Florida's average annual rainfall is 50 to 65 inches and hurricanes have been known to bring more than 30 inches in a single day.

Summer is the rainy season. Summer weather forecasts are often monotonous: "daytime temperatures in the low 80s, nights in the high 60s or low 70s, 30 percent chance of afternoon thundershowers." In summer, Florida earns its unofficial title as "lightning capital of the world." Television repair workers do a rushing business after each storm.

Winter is usually the dry season. Patterns of precipitation differ somewhat between northern and southern Florida, chiefly in the transition months. October is a dry month in the northwest; in the far south, it's the last month of the rainy season.

The hurricane season begins in late August. Then supermarket shopping bags are printed with instructions on how to prepare, newspaper charts track each tropical storm, and sales of plywood and duct tape increase.

The average number of tropical storms that touch some part of Florida in a year is 1.7, the range from 0 to 5. The chance of hurricane-force winds striking in a year ranges from 1 percent at Jacksonville to 14 percent at Miami and the Keys. The Gulf Coast is hit less often than the east.

Films and books have dramatized what a hurricane could do to condominiums and homes built at the edge of the sea. A higher risk is that storm winds and high tide may combine to cause massive flooding. Tens of thousands of homes are located on fingers of land extending into the Gulf and on artificial canals and islands. They stand only a few feet above normal high tides.

One fall we were driving home in a downpour. Minutes after we passed by, a tornado crossed our route, destroying a school, a factory, and mobile homes. Funnel clouds and tornados are reported 10 to 15 times a year, most often in spring. Tornado paths are usually short.

Few Florida residents have ever seen a hurricane or tornado. Their chief complaint about weather is that last year's frost damaged some shrubs or that a July day was too hot for lawnmowing. Most complaints about flooding come from people who bought land from speculators in dry periods.

More often than not, Florida weather is gorgeous!

UP FROM THE SEA

Florida is unique among the United States and surprisingly young. At various times in its geologic history, the peninsula has been submerged, an island chain, or twice its present width. In the Pleistocene epoch, the sea was as much as 270 feet above and more than 230 feet below the present level. Its general shape today is only a few thousand years old.

Florida's highest point is only 345 feet above sea level. The sand ridge forming the peninsula's spine is generally about 200 feet above sea level. Even a modest melting of the polar icecaps will again diminish the land.

Underlying Florida are several thousand feet of limestone rich in marine fossils. Alternately rising and falling seas inundated and exposed a great plateau. Much of that Florida Plateau is now beneath shallow water in the

Gulf of Mexico. In the Florida Panhandle, the plateau has been dissected by many rivers and streams.

The coastal areas are low-lying, indented by bays, tidal creeks, and marshes. Along the 1,200-mile coast lie long chains of barrier islands. Other islands are scattered offshore. Off the Florida Keys are many coral islands and reefs. No place in the state is more than 70 miles from salt water.

A WET LAND

Most Florida terrain is flat, and most of it was wet when Europeans arrived. Slow-moving rivers had extensive floodplains. Swamps, sloughs, marshes, and floodplains deterred for many years construction of roads and railroads. The Tamiami Trail across southern Florida, completed only in 1928, was considered an engineering feat. When Thomas Edison, Henry Ford, and Harvey Firestone built houses at Fort Myers, people and building materials got there by boat.

Okeechobee is the largest of several thousand lakes whose surface areas total almost 3 million acres. Almost all these lakes are natural, originating by dissolution or erosion of the limestone. More dramatic products of dissolution are the sinkholes that appear when the land surface collapses into an underground cavern. Near our home a sinkhole suddenly swallowed two lanes of a major road and undercut the corner of a restaurant. Recent sinkholes have engulfed automobiles and expanded to undermine houses. Florida's only waterfall (at Falling Waters State Park) is inside an old sinkhole.

Florida has only one large dry cave, at Florida Caverns State Park. Elsewhere, cave divers have explored and mapped extensive submerged caverns and passageways.

GET RID OF THE WATER!

In 1850 the federal government deeded to the State of Florida about 22 million acres of "swamp and overflowed lands," wetlands deemed unfit for cultivation or development. That was 58 percent of the state's land area! The State gave some to railroad promoters. An entrepreneur offered to drain 12 million acres in exchange for title to 6 million. He bought 4 million acres for 25 cents each. Lately the State has bought back some of this land for as much as $10,000 per acre.

For decades, "ditch and drain" was the land management doctrine. As drainage progressed, roads and railroads opened the peninsula to development and tourism. Florida's population grew on a steepening curve, doubling each 20 years.

Hundreds of miles of dikes and canals were built to protect burgeoning southeastern cities from floods. The meandering Kissimmee River was confined to a big ditch. Housing developments were built on filled-in wetlands. About three-fourths of the original wetlands have been altered.

Now the cry is "Save the wetlands!" Water is drained away so quickly that less seeps underground to replenish the aquifers on which Florida communities, farms, and industries depend. The headwaters of most rivers are wetlands, and much wildlife depends on wetlands.

THE COLONISTS

Emerging from the sea into a subtropical climate, the islands that became a peninsula were colonized by plants and animals. Some species migrated southward from the mainland. Others arrived from the Bahamas, the Caribbean, and beyond. Colonization continues. Storm winds and sea currents often carry exotic species, of which some become established. These and exotics introduced by human agency occasionally multiply and spread, displacing older immigrants now called "native."

When Europeans arrived, most of the state was forested. In the early years of the twentieth century vast areas of pine, oak, and cypress were logged. Today about half of the state is commercial forest, but few old-growth stands remain. Commercial forest occupies three-fourths of northwest Florida, less than one-fourth of the peninsula.

At first glance, a visitor might think most of Florida is piney woods. In fact, the natural Florida was and is a fascinating mosaic of plant associations, each providing habitat for a community of animals. Some species are at the northern limits of their ranges, others at the southern. Some are seen nowhere else in the world.

ENDANGERED LANDS

By 1970 warning signs were everywhere. Explosive growth threatened water supplies. State and local governments were falling behind needs for roads, schools, prisons, sewage treatment, and social services. Solid waste disposal was in crisis. By 1990 a complex growth management scheme was in place. It remains to be seen whether the scheme works.

State and local ordinances are written to protect beaches, wetlands, and other critical areas, but enforcement is elusive.

The State of Florida and some counties have begun the nation's most ambitious and costly land salvage. Thousands of acres of beaches, mangrove coasts, lake and river floodplains, forests, wetlands, scrub, and other critical areas are being purchased for parks, public forests, wildlife areas, and reserves. Some abused land is being restored.

The largest State acquisition program, Preservation 2000, was adopted in 1990. It authorizes $300 million in land purchases each year for a decade—a total of $3 billion. A year later, however, legislators who voted for the plan were balking at providing the money.

We hope this book will be out of date before it is published. We have before us long lists of sites awaiting State acquisition but can't predict which will be purchased or when. Some would add to sites we have included. Most are priceless natural areas coveted by developers. Unless saved soon, they'll be gone forever.

FLORIDA HABITATS

Some people find pleasure in identification, attaching names to the birds and trees and flowers they see. For others, a greater pleasure comes from asking, "Why?" and learning to read landscapes, recognizing associations: trees and flowers and birds and insects commonly found together.

Plant communities in mountainous regions are influenced by elevation and exposure. Different tree species succeed each other as one ascends from valley to timberline. Plant associations on north slopes differ from those on south slopes.

In Florida, moisture is the chief influence. A plant association on a mountain slope may span a thousand feet or more of elevation. In Florida, a foot or two makes a difference. Floridians commonly use a few words less familiar elsewhere: *hydric,* "wet"; *mesic,* "intermediate"; and *xeric,* "dry."

There's much talk about aquifers, especially the Floridan Aquifer. Peninsular Florida depends on water pumped from underground. Aquifers are recharged by seepage from the surface. If withdrawals exceed recharge, the aquifer is depleted and the state's in trouble. Along the coast, depletion of the aquifer permits intrusion of salt water, contaminating wells.

Other terms used in this book name some of Florida's principal natural associations (described more fully and illustrated in the leaflet *Common Florida Natural Areas* – see REFERENCES):

Pine flatwoods are the most extensive natural community. They are usually dominated by longleaf and slash pines, often with palmetto in the understory. When natural forest fires are suppressed, oaks gradually replace the pines. Florida foresters use prescribed burns to restore pine forests.

Sandhills are sandy, rolling lands usually dominated by pines, often sand pine. *Scrub* is sandy and drier; rain water disappears quickly into its deep sand. As the name implies, scrub vegetation is a thick growth of brush and stunted oaks. Some species of flora and fauna are found only in these dry habitats. Most sandhill and scrub areas have been converted to farms or subdivisions.

Hardwood forests and hammocks are dominated by oaks, often with cabbage palm, magnolia, holly, and other trees. Live oaks are the largest and oldest trees of Florida. Tropical hardwood trees occur in south Florida hammocks. "Hammock" isn't equivalent to "hummock." Hammocks are sometimes tree islands in wetlands, but the term is also applied to flat hardwood forests.

Prairies are open grasslands, wet or dry. Fire and grazing have suppressed tree growth; soils and moisture may be unsuitable for trees.

Freshwater swamps, like Florida lakes, are usually depressions formed by the dissolution of limestone. Some are seasonally or occasionally dry. Cypress trees often grow here. The term *cypress dome* refers to the shape of the canopy where trees grow in a depression; the tallest arise from the deeper center, where moisture is more abundant.

Mangroves grow in wet places: swamps, along streams, in bays and estuaries, and on island shores. Red mangroves, recognized by roots depending from branches, grow in the water. Red mangroves that root on sandbars often develop islands. Black mangroves grow thickly near water, white mangroves on slightly higher land.

Coastal areas are diverse and highly productive. They include vegetated dunes, tidal flats, salt marshes, beds of sea grasses.

FLORIDA'S WILDLIFE

Mountains, deserts, rain forests—each has its special assortment of living creatures. Florida's includes species that occur in other states but has some all its own.

BIRDS

Ardent birders come to Florida to augment their life lists. A telephone hot-line quickly spreads the word when an unusual species is sighted, and resident birders flock to the place.

Florida's Birds (Herbert W. Kale, II, and David S. Mehr, *Florida's Birds*, Sarasota: Pineapple Press, 1990) provides the following list of specialties visiting birders usually want to see, "species that are either restricted to Florida or are easier to find here."

White-tailed Tropicbird	Snail Kite	Burrowing Owl
Magnificent Frigatebird	Short-tailed Hawk	Antillean Nighthawk
Great White Heron	Crested Caracara	Red-cockaded
Reddish Egret	Spot-breasted Oriole	Woodpecker
Roseate Spoonbill	Sooty Tern	Gray Kingbird
Wood Stork	Brown Noddy	Cave Swallow
Greater Flamingo	Black Noddy	Florida Scrub Jay
Mottled Duck	White-crowned Pigeon	Red-whiskered Bulbul
Masked Duck	Eurasian Collared-	Black-whiskered
Limpkin	Dove	Vireo
American Swallow-	Mangrove Cuckoo	Cape Sable Seaside
tailed Kite	Smooth-billed Ani	Sparrow

Each of our zone prefaces has a list of the common birds one might expect to see, and when. Entries mention species of special interest often seen there. Few of the specialties just listed are common anywhere, which is why birders seek them.

MAMMALS

Like birds, mammals depend on habitat. Because Florida has few caves, cave-dwelling bats are rare, but several species of tree-living bats are abundant. The gray squirrel seems to thrive in any forest, while the southern flying squirrel has an affinity for oaks. Manatees gather in winter at springs where water temperature is constant.

Loss of habitat is a major reason why many mammal populations have declined. Fragmentation of habitat is another. These creatures are less mobile than birds, less able to migrate in response to habitat disturbances. Conservationists hope to establish "wildlife corridors" connecting fragments.

Black bears have vanished from most of their former haunts. Coyotes, once unknown here, are now rare but increasing. Raccoons, far from shy, are attracted by garbage cans and picnic tables. Bobcats are still widespread and numerous. River otters are common: we often see them while canoeing.

The bottlenose dolphin is the marine mammal most often seen from beaches, causeways, and in the wakes of motor vessels. Pilot whales sometimes beach themselves. Seals and other species of dolphins and whales are less common but sometimes seen.

Most endangered of the large mammals is the Florida panther. Many sightings are reported but few are confirmed by tracks or other physical evidence. Oddly, many reports are of *black* panthers, but the Florida panther is not black. The few surviving panthers may range widely, but the only permanent, breeding population is in the wild area of the Fakahatchee Strand, Big Cypress, and Everglades National Park. So few remain that captive breeding has begun.

Driving south near Lake City at dawn one day, we saw a jaguarundi cross the road. Common from Mexico south, its U.S. range is limited to the extreme south of Texas and Arizona. We reported the sighting to a State wildlife biologist, who wasn't surprised. Other sightings had been reported. His verdict: the animal had been released or had escaped. (Although the jaguarundi is smaller than the panther, it has a black phase. People unfamiliar with the jaguarundi might well think it a panther.)

Releases, escapes, and other introductions have contributed many exotic species to Florida, especially the southern peninsula. Several species of parakeets are well established, as are walking catfish and fire ants. Of the mammals, the most widespread and destructive is the wild hog, whose rooting behavior destroys trees and shrubs. Most land managers would like to see the hogs eliminated, but hunters won't have it.

REPTILES AND AMPHIBIANS

Many visitors from the north are excited on seeing their first alligator. Poachers killing gators for their hides made them an endangered species by the 1960s. Killing violated Florida law, but a poacher had only to cross the State line to be home free. Once out of Florida, the hides could be sold openly and legally.

The Endangered Species Act of 1969 outlawed interstate traffic and the export trade. Alligator numbers increased rapidly. Not only is there now a legal, monitored trade, but the Florida Game and Fresh Water Fish Commission is often asked to remove nuisance alligators from golf courses and from people's yards and swimming pools.

When we saw a visitor urging his small child to hand-feed a wild alligator, we spoke to him, not politely. Feeding violates State law. The dangerous alligators are those that have been fed and thereafter approach people for food.

Unprovoked attacks are rare. Cases of bites are reported two or three times a year, fatalities rarely. We canoe, swim, and hike near alligators without concern. Small children and dogs are more at risk than adults. Make inquiries before letting children or dogs play at the edge of unfamiliar waters.

Florida has a splendid array of snakes, nearly all beneficial and nonpoisonous. Although we spend much time outdoors, we see poisonous snakes about once a year. Hunters bushwhacking through palmettos and swamps do well to wear snake boots or leggings. Reaching into a hollow log or stirring a brush pile is inadvisable. For most people, the risk is infinitesimal.

We have three species of rattlesnakes and the water moccasin. It is almost impossible to be bitten by the small-mouthed, rear-fanged coral snake. The copperhead is rare even in north Florida.

More entertaining are the anoles. Small lizards, green, brown, and black, they dart and climb, the males threatening each other and us by head bobbing, doing push-ups, and inflating bright red throat pouches. We have dozens around our swimming pool. They are usually shy, but when we rescue one from the water it clings to a hand or arm until it's warm again.

WHERE NATURE RULES

FEDERAL LANDS

Florida has two National Parks: Everglades and Biscayne, the latter a chain of small islands and coral reefs. There are two National Seashores: Gulf Islands and Canaveral. The Big Cypress National Preserve is a huge, wet wilderness. The National Park Service also administers several National Monuments.

In the 1930s, the federal government bought much Florida land that had been deforested and virtually abandoned. Some was transferred to the State, some added to the National Forest system. The three National Forests encompass more than a million acres.

The 26 National Wildlife Refuges (NWRs) range in size from 146,000 to 20 acres. All are chiefly wetlands or islands. All have great variety of bird life.

The U.S. Army Corps of Engineers administers several coastal and inland waterways much used for recreation.

Two of the largest federal sites are the Eglin Air Force Base and Avon Park Air Force Range. Large areas of both are open to public recreation, with some restrictions.

STATE LANDS

The Division of Recreation and Parks manages 113 parks, recreation areas, preserves, reserves, and historic sites, a total of over 400,000 acres. Many other state park systems we've studied emphasize development of playgrounds, ball fields, bathing beaches, even golf courses. Florida's system has an unusual and admirable mandate: "State park lands are managed to appear as they did when the first Europeans arrived."

Few Florida parks were pristine when the State acquired them. The history of each has been traced: its original characteristics and how successive land uses altered them. Each now has a plan to restore the original ecosystems. It may take years to attain the goal, but most of the parks appear natural now.

Visitor facilities are usually concentrated in a modest portion of each site. The typical State Park leaflet has a map of this intensive-use area that doesn't show the more extensive undeveloped land. If this is a subtle way to influence visitor behavior, officials won't admit it. You are free to hike in the natural areas, and rangers will gladly advise you.

State Recreation Areas (SRAs) usually have less undeveloped land, but management is no less concerned with preservation and restoration of natural areas.

Hunting is prohibited in State Parks and in State Recreation Areas. Regulated hunting is permitted in State Reserves.

Florida's 18 State Forests encompass 350,000 acres. Two large units, Blackwater River and Withlacoochee State Forests, comprise 87 percent of that total. We have included six others in our entries.

State Wildlife Management Areas total more than 4 million acres, but this figure requires explanation. Only about a million acres is State land, and this includes State Forests and other agencies's land where the Florida Game and Fresh Water Fish Commission manages hunting and fishing.

The 4 million acres includes National Forests, where the Commission manages hunting and fishing. The Commission has arranged for public hunting on almost half a million acres of privately owned land, most of it owned by timber companies. Some of these privately owned Wildlife Management Areas (WMAs) are open to visitors outside of hunting seasons.

The Commission publishes a leaflet with map for each WMA. Each begins with this statement: "Persons utilizing the wildlife management areas are required to have appropriate licenses, stamps, and permits."

That puzzled us. Surely a State agency could not require permits of all visitors to National Forests. It has puzzled others, too. Some hikers and birders have avoided the WMAs because of the apparent license requirement. Several State Forest rangers told us they aren't sure what the rule means.

We wrote to the Florida Game and Fresh Water Fish Commission and received an admirably clear reply from Frank H. Smith, Jr., chief of the Commission's Bureau of Wildlife Management:

> We agree that the wording in the first sentence . . . can be misinterpreted, if it stands alone. . . . However, if one reads further into this section, it becomes clear tht the information presented pertains specifically to hunters. . . .
> There are only two areas, the J. W. Corbett and Cecil M. Webb, where every person who enters the area must possess a wildlife management area stamp.

Smith also wrote that the bureau "will clarify the opening sentence of this section in our 1992–93 summaries."

Five regional Water Management Districts have bought several hundred thousand acres of land to protect watersheds. Much of this land is open to recreation, in some cases managed by county governments or other agencies.

The State owns navigable waterways. We have entries for many canoe trails.

COUNTY LANDS

We seldom included county parks in earlier volumes of this guidebook series. Officials of county systems told us their parks are for local residents; taxpayers would resent an influx of outsiders. Most of the county parks we saw featured ball fields, swimming pools, playgrounds, and such.

We found great variety among Florida's 67 counties. Some have vestigial park systems. A few have parks comparable to state parks, with large natual areas and excellent interpretive programs. Hillsborough County is adding thousands of acres to its park system with funds from a bond issues approved overwhelmingly by voters. As this was being written, a Pasco County official called to tell us about two new wilderness parks there.

We have entries for several fine county parks and may have missed a few.

PRIVATE PRESERVES

The Nature Conservancy has acquired some of Florida's most outstanding and endangered natural areas. We have entries for a few of these preserves. The Conservancy can't invite visitors to its other tracts until land stewards are on site.

THE FLORIDA NATIONAL SCENIC TRAIL

The Florida Trail Association (FTA) was founded in 1966 by hikers who dreamed of a foot trail across the entire state. Its more than 4,000 members have planned and developed over 600 miles of trail, each segment maintained by a group of volunteers. Through State, federal, and private lands, the Florida Trail—most of it now designated a National Scenic Trail—

provides foot access to many of Florida's wildest and most scenic areas. In addition to the border-to-border trail, which still has gaps, the FTA has developed loops off the main route.

Private landowners that give FTA permission to develop the trail across their properties may limit trail use to FTA members.

Our entries note trail segments. We suggest that hikers join the FTA and obtain its guidebook, *Walking the Florida Trail*. Membership is $23 for individuals, $28 for families; the guidebook is $12.95 plus postage. A public trail guide is scheduled for publication late in 1991. The address is P.O. Box 13708, Gainesville, FL 32604; (904) 378-8823.

HOW TO USE THIS BOOK

This book is arranged so that readers can quickly see what natural areas are near their temporary or permanent residences. Many delightful places are open only by day. Some have special features such as a grove of giant trees or a spring run favored by manatees. We have entries for many hiking and canoe trails through subtropical wildernesses.

If we were staying at Daytona Beach, we'd consider a quiet hike in Tiger Bay State Forest, only five miles away. We wouldn't drive there from Lake Wales, not with Tiger Creek Preserve so close. Wherever you live or stay in Florida, you'll find many day-visit natural areas nearby.

MAPS AND ZONE PREFACES

Every traveler should have the 128-page *Florida Atlas and Gazetteer* (Freeport, ME: DeLorme Mapping Company, 1989), available at Florida bookstores, sporting goods shops, and many newsstands. Its 103 large maps show details no single road map can. Each of our entries notes its DeLorme *Atlas* map number and coordinates (for example, "Map 32, C-1.")

We divide the state into four zones: (1) Panhandle, (2) north Florida, (3) central, and (4) south. Each zone is briefly described in a preface. Each zone preface has a locator map and list of sites arranged by map number.

WHAT THE ENTRIES INCLUDE

Below each site name is shown the name of the federal, state, or county agency responsible for site management.

Routing directions are to the principal entrance. We urge the reader to use a map.

Symbols show what activities are available. Most are self-explanatory:

With the pack, backpacking opportunity.

Without pack, day hiking only.

This symbol of the Florida Trail indicates that the site includes a segment of the Trail.

The symbol indicates that motorized craft can be launched and used. Some sites have horsepower restrictions. Many prohibit airboats.

Horse riding is permitted. A few sites have special horse trails. Even fewer have corrals and horse camps. None have on-site liveries.

FEATURES are described: springs, sinkholes, marshes, ravines.

WILDLIFE is characterized, noting the best seasons for birding and species of special interest, the mammals most likely to be seen, and some of the reptiles and amphibians.

Birds. Many sites provide checklists of the birds one might see there. Everglades National Park lists 347 species. To list even the common species for each site would be repetitious and tedious. Our good friend Chuck Geanangel, leading environmentalist, expert on Florida's birds, and compiler of several checklists, has prepared lists of the common birds of each zone and the seasons when they are present. These lists appear in the zone prefaces.

Entries note if a site is a birding "hot-spot" or has species of special interest for birders.

Mammals. Some sites also provide checklists of mammals. Their abundance is more site-specific than regional, so we mention them in entries.

Plants. Habitats are likely to include several hundred plant species. Wildflower watchers will understand the problem. Florida has more than 3,500 native plants. Some sites have had comprehensive inventories of plant species made by professional botanists. The lists are long and seldom published for visitors. Sometimes shorter lists are compiled by seasonal volunteers who can identify wildflowers only when they're in bloom. *Florida Wild Flowers and Roadside Plants* (see References) illustrates and describes 500 species, using a zone system much like ours, showing blooming seasons, and stating where they occur.

INTERPRETATION includes visitor centers and museums, exhibits, campfire talks, guided walks, and other ranger programs.

ACTIVITIES are visitor opportunities:

Camping is usually restricted to designated campgrounds. Primitive campsites, accessible on foot or by canoe, are available in some sites. Permits are usually required. The exceptions are National Forests, where one can camp almost anywhere except in the November–January hunting season, and on some canoe trails, where informal camping on sandbars and beaches is allowed. Many Wildlife Management Areas (WMAs) have primitive campgrounds available only to hunters.

Hunting, where permitted, is managed by the Florida Game and Fresh Water Fish Commission, even in National Forests. The Commission publishes a leaflet for each WMA stating the seasons and rules for that site.

Fishing opportunities, including salt water, rivers, and hundreds of lakes, extend far beyond the scope of this Guide. Licenses are now required for saltwater as well as freshwater fishing. The Florida Game and Fresh Water Fish Commission publishes leaflets describing fishing opportunities on some of the popular lakes.

Boating opportunities are limitless. Florida has 7,800 lakes, 115 of them

THE NATURAL AREAS OF FLORIDA

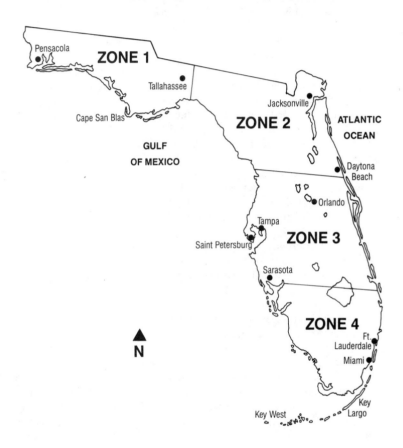

larger than a thousand acres; many navigable rivers; and thousands of miles of tidal waterways. Our entries note ramps and other boating facilities.

Canoeing is one of the best ways to see Florida's natural areas. We have entries for canoe trails, many passing through wildlands accessible in no other way. We urge canoeists to seek current local information before launching. High water, low water, blowdowns, and other changes can make a trip difficult.

Much riparian land is privately owned. Don't go ashore unless you know it's publicly owned land.

Major canoeing rivers are served by outfitters who provide canoes, shuttles, and camping gear for trips of a few hours or more than a week. A list of outfitters and the rivers they serve can be obtained from the Florida Association of Canoe Liveries and Outfitters, P.O. Box 1764, Arcadia, FL 33821.

Although few Florida rivers flow at more than 3 miles per hour, most canoeists prefer not to paddle upstream. Unless an outfitter provides the service, shuttling requires two cars. We have solved this problem with an electric fishing motor. It clamps at the stern with no bracket. Going upstream, we lower the shaft, lock it in position, switch on, and forget it. The thrust just offsets the stream flow, and we paddle normally. A charged marine battery lasts 5 or 6 hours.

Swimming opportunities bring many visitors to Florida. Entries note whether sites have designated swimming areas or if swimming is prohibited. We have entries for several Atlantic and Gulf beaches that are seldom crowded.

RULES AND REGULATIONS

All sites have rules. Parks and wildlife areas have the most rules, forests the fewest. Most rules are printed in site leaflets and posted on location. We note special local rules and warnings.

Concerning dogs, the State of Florida has more stringent rules than any of the 48 other states where we've hiked and camped. Furthermore, there are often discrepancies between official policies and local applications.

Florida is one of a very few states that prohibit dogs in State Park campgrounds. Camping with dogs is permitted in some State Forest campgrounds, not in the more developed ones. Dogs are permitted in National Park and National Forest campgrounds and in almost all commercial campgrounds.

Dogs are permitted on trails in some State Parks, prohibited in others. One State Park where we once hiked with our dog now forbids it. State headquarters assured us that hiking with a dog on leash is permitted in State Forests and Wildlife Management Areas except in hunting season. However, Florida Game and Fresh Water Fish Commission signs at entrances say, "No dogs, guns, or trapping devices allowed without proper authorization." We have been stopped at entrances by Commission employees who told us hiking with a dog on leash is prohibited. We wrote to the GFC and hope for clarification.

Dogs on leash are almost everywhere permitted on trails in National Forests (although you may see the same Commission signs) and National Wildlife Refuges, prohibited on trails in National Parks and National Seashores. Dogs are everywhere prohibited on swimming beaches, but are usually permitted in picnic grounds.

PUBLICATIONS are those reported by the site as available for distribution. We don't include outside publications, such as the many books about the Everglades.

HEADQUARTERS is the responsible administrative office, local or regional.

WHAT THE ENTRIES DON'T INCLUDE

The entries do not provide information about:

- *Entrance fees.* Required at many sites.
- *Campsite hookups.* Standard campground directories provide full information.
- *Picnicking.* Possible almost anywhere. Most parks and recreation areas have picnic tables; some have shelters.
- *Bicycling.* Popular in many parks. A few State Parks and State Recreation Areas have paved bicycle trails. Present and planned rails-to-trails projects provide for bicycling.
- *Cabins.* Available in a few State Parks.
- *Group camps and shelters.* Available at many sites by reservation.
- *Historical and archeological features.* Many of the sites for which we have entries include Indian mounds, ruins, and other artifacts. Many have been vandalized, few stabilized and protected. Rangers are glad to inform visitors with special interests.
- *Playgrounds, ball fields.*
- *Snack bars, restaurants.*
- *"Aquatic preserves."* Florida has thus designated some coastal waters to provide special protection.

REFERENCES

Many books have been written about Florida. Each time we look in bookstores and visitor centers, we see new ones. Here are a few to enjoy reading before a visit or to make visits to natural areas more interesting.

Derr, Mark. *Some Kind of Paradise.* New York: William Morrow, 1989. An entertaining social, economic, and environmental history, with a comprehensive bibliography.
Florida Atlas and Gazetteer. Freeport, ME: DeLorme Mapping Company, 1989. Maps plus lists of botanic gardens, golf courses, museums, historical sites, and more.
Marth, Del, and Martha J. *Florida Almanac,* 1990–91. Gretna, LA: Pelican

Publishing, 1990. This is the eighth edition, so there will probably be others.

Kale, Herbert W., II, and David S. Mehr. *Florida's Birds*. Sarasota: Pineapple Press, 1990.

Bell, C. Ritchie, and Bryan J. Taylor. *Florida Wild Flowers and Roadside Plants*. Chapel Hill, NC: Laurel Hill Press, 1982.

Tarver, David P., John A. Rodgers, Michael J. Mahler, and Robert L. Lazor. *Aquatic and Wetland Plants of Florida*. Tallahassee: Florida Department of Natural Resources, 1986.

Stiling, Peter D. *Florida's Butterflies and Other Insects*. Sarasota: Pineapple Press, 1989.

Brown, Robin C. *Florida's Fossils*. Sarasota: Pineapple Press, 1988.

Greenberg, Idaz. *Guide to Corals and Fishes of Florida, the Bahamas, and the Caribbean*. Miami: Seahawk Press, 1986.

Voss, Gilbert L. *Coral Reefs of Florida*. Sarasota: Pineapple Press, 1990.

Common Florida Natural Areas. The Florida Conservation Foundation. 1251-B Miller Ave., Winter Park, FL 32789. Illustrated folder ($1).

Myers, L., and John J. Ewall, eds. *Florida Ecosystems*. Gainesville: University of Florida Presses, 1990. Comprehensive scientific descriptions.

We found no popular field guide to Florida trees available in bookstores. A standard U.S. or eastern field guide will do nicely.

HOW WE GATHERED INFORMATION

Questionnaires were sent to all sites. From state and regional headquarters, we collected site histories, inventories, maps, annual reports, and management plans. The collection of documents occupies 15 shelf feet, reference books 5 more.

We're often asked if we visit every site. Not all, but most; in Florida, about 150 of them. At least as important are notebooks and cassette tapes recording interviews with people who know the sites more intimately than we ever could: their managers, rangers, biologists, wildlife offices, foresters, and other specialists. We're grateful to all of them.

Each entry was sent to the appropriate headquarters to be checked for accuracy. We pursued nonrespondents by mail and telephone. The final tally: about 90 percent response.

THE
SIERRA CLUB
GUIDE TO
THE
NATURAL AREAS
OF FLORIDA

ZONE 1
THE FLORIDA PANHANDLE

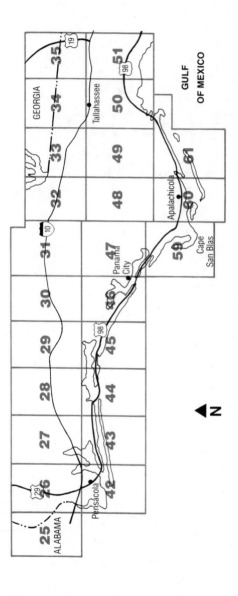

ZONE 1
THE FLORIDA PANHANDLE

0 _____ 35 miles

ENTRIES IN ZONE 1

The number preceding the natural area entry refers to the map number in the DeLorme *Florida Atlas & Gazetteer*.

25 Perdido River Canoe Trail	46 St. Andrews State Recreation
27 Blackwater River State Forest	Area
27 Blackwater River State Park	48 Apalachicola Bluffs and
27 Coldwater Creek Canoe Trail	Ravines Preserve
27 Sweetwater and Juniper	48 Apalachicola National Forest
Creeks Canoe Trail	49 Lake Talquin
28 Blackwater River Canoe Trail	49 Lake Talquin State
28 Eglin Air Force Base	Recreation Area
28 Rocky Bayou (Fred Gannon)	49 Ochlockonee River (Lower)
State Recreation Area	Canoe Trail
28 Yellow River Canoe Trail	50 Edward Ball Wakulla Springs
29 Shoal River Canoe Trail	State Park
30 Choctawhatchee River	50 Joe Budd Wildlife Manage-
30 Holmes Creek Canoe Trail	ment Area
30 Ponce de Leon Springs State	50 Ochlockonee River State Park
Recreation Area	50 St. Marks National Wildlife
31 Econfina Creek Canoe Trail	Refuge
31 Falling Waters State	50 Tallahassee–St. Marks
Recreation Area	Historic Railroad State Trail
32 Apalachicola River	50 Talquin Wildlife Management
32 Chipola River Canoe Trail	Area
32 Florida Caverns State Park	51 Aucilla River Canoe Trail
32 Lake Seminole	51 Aucilla Wildlife Management
32 Three Rivers State Recreation	Area
Area	51 Big Bend Wildlife Manage-
32 Torreya State Park	ment Area
34 Ochlockonee River (Upper)	51 Hickory Mound Unit, Big
Canoe Trail	Bend Wildlife Management
42 Big Lagoon State Recreation	Area
Area	51 Wacissa River Canoe Trail
42 Gulf Islands National	59 St. Joseph Peninsula State
Seashore	Park and Wilderness
42 Perdido Key State Recreation	Preserve
Area	60 Cape St. George Island
45 Grayton Beach State	60 St. Vincent National Wildlife
Recreation Area	Refuge
46 Pine Log State Forest	61 St. George Island State Park

ZONE I, THE FLORIDA PANHANDLE, extends eastward from the Alabama border to the Big Bend of the Gulf Coast, where the peninsula begins. From the northern border, adjoining Alabama and Georgia, the land slopes gently to the Gulf of Mexico, drained by creeks and rivers that offer many fine canoe trails.

The Panhandle is the most heavily forested part of Florida. The state's largest remaining stands of longleaf pine are here. Zone 1's three largest tracts of publicly owned land are the Blackwater River State Forest, Apalachicola National Forest, and Eglin Air Force Base. Most of the base is forest, maintained in natural condition, and open to visitors.

The Gulf Coast is fringed by barrier islands and peninsulas. Behind the outer islands are bays, sounds, and marshes cut by tidal creeks, all attractive to boaters and fishermen. Gulf Islands National Seashore is the largest public recreation area on the coast. There are also State Parks and State Recreation Areas as well as congested resorts.

Unlike southern Florida, the coast's busy season is summer. By Labor Day, some resort businesses have closed. In September we found the weather delightful and the crowds gone. "It's cold here in winter," someone complained, but the average winter minimum temperature is only 10 degrees cooler than that of southern Florida.

The Panhandle has many points of interest: Florida's highest hill, its only waterfall, its only cavern, several National Wildlife Refuges, and large Wildlife Management Areas.

The northern Panhandle has an extraordinary diversity of flowering plants. Many species are at the southern limits of their ranges. Some birds, too, seldom venture farther north. The Gulf islands are birding hot-spots during spring migrations.

COMMON BIRDS OF ZONE 1
by Chuck Geanangel

The Panhandle is a transition region for avian life. Some bird species seldom venture further south. For some it's the northern limit of their ranges.

The Gulf islands are birding hot-spots during spring migrations. In winter, Florida Caverns State Park is a place to see winter wrens, juncos, brown creepers, and several sparrow species. From Torreya State Park and nearby Apalachicola Bluffs, one can often see Mississippi kites. Wakulla Springs has many limpkins. St. Marks National Wildlife Refuge offers closeup views of waterfowl, plus some rarities. The more compact Hickory Mound also has many waterbirds. To see the Snowy Plover, try St. George Island State Park.

Lists like these are at best a rough guide in trip planning. "Winter residents" will almost certainly be present in winter, but fall arrivals and spring departures vary from species to species and year to year. It was tempting to mention specialties and rarities that attract birders from afar, but one can't be sure of seeing them. When you visit a park or refuge, ask for a bird list. Then ask for the news: What special birds are present? When and where can they be seen?

WATER HABITATS, FRESH, BRACKISH, AND SALT
Permanent residents, here all year

Pied-billed Grebe	Snowy Egret	Greater Yellowlegs
Double-crested	Wood Duck	Lesser Yellowlegs
Cormorant	Common Moorhen	Spotted Sandpiper
Great Blue Heron	Killdeer	Laughing Gull
Great Egret		

Permanent residents of the coastal region

Brown Pelican	Piping Plover	Sanderling
Clapper Rail	Willet	Dunlin
Black-bellied Plover	Whimbrel	Royal Tern
Semipalmated Plover	Ruddy Turnstone	Sandwich Tern

Transients, spring and fall

Common Tern	Semipalmated
	Sandpiper

Winter residents, fall to spring

Common Loon	Redhead	Dowitcher
Horned Grebe	Ring-necked Duck	Common Snipe
American White	Lesser Scaup	Bonaparte's Gull
Pelican	Bufflehead	Ring-billed Gull
Green-winged Teal	Ruddy Duck	Herring Gull
Mallard	Sora	Forster's Tern
Northern Pintail	American Coot	Red-breasted
Blue-winged Teal	Western Sandpiper	Merganser
Northern Shoveler	Least Sandpiper	Belted Kingfisher
American Wigeon		

Summer residents, spring to fall

Green-backed Heron	Least Tern	Gray Kingbird
White Ibis	Black Tern	

LAND HABITATS

Permanent residents, here all year

Turkey Vulture
Red-shouldered Hawk
Red-tailed Hawk
Northern Bobwhite
Rock Dove
Mourning Dove
Eastern Screech Owl
Great Horned Owl
Barred Owl
Red-headed
  Woodpecker
Red-bellied
  Woodpecker
Downy Woodpecker
Northern Flicker

Pileated Woodpecker
Blue Jay
American Crow
Fish Crow
Carolina Chickadee
Tufted Titmouse
White-breasted
  Nuthatch
Brown-headed
  Nuthatch
Carolina Wren
Marsh Wren
Blue-gray Gnatcatcher
Eastern Bluebird
Northern Mockingbird

Brown Thrasher
Loggerhead Shrike
European Starling
White-eyed Vireo
Pine Warbler
Common Yellowthroat
Northern Cardinal
Rufous-sided Towhee
Red-winged Blackbird
Eastern Meadowlark
Boat-tailed Grackle
Common Grackle
Brown-headed
  Cowbird
House Sparrow

Transients, spring and fall

Broad-winged Hawk
Ruby-throated
  Hummingbird
Yellow-bellied
  Sapsucker
Eastern Wood Pewee

Tree Swallow
Bank Swallow
Gray-cheeked Thrush
Swainson's Thrush
Veery
Wood Thrush

Yellow Warbler
Prairie Warbler
Hooded Warbler
Rose-breasted
  Grosbeak

Winter residents, fall to spring

Northern Harrier
Sharp-shinned Hawk
American Kestrel
"Empidonax"
  Flycatcher
Eastern Phoebe
House Wren
Ruby-crowned Kinglet
Hermit Thrush
American Robin

Gray Catbird
Water Pipit
Cedar Waxwing
Orange-crowned
  Warbler
Yellow-rumped
  Warbler
Black-and-white
  Warbler
American Redstart

Northern Waterthrush
Chipping Sparrow
Field Sparrow
Vesper Sparrow
Savannah Sparrow
Song Sparrow
Swamp Sparrow
White-throated Sparrow
Northern Oriole
American Goldfinch

Summer residents, spring to fall

Cattle Egret
Black Vulture
Yellow-billed Cuckoo
Common Nighthawk
Chuck-will's-widow
Chimney Swift
Great Crested
  Flycatcher

Eastern Kingbird
Gray Kingbird
Purple Martin
Northern Roughwing
  Swallow
Barn Swallow
Red-eyed Vireo
Northern Parula

Yellow-throated
  Warbler
Prothonotary Warbler
Summer Tanager
Blue Grosbeak
Indigo Bunting
Orchard Oriole

APALACHICOLA NATIONAL FOREST

U.S. Forest Service
563,668 acres; 631,260 acres within boundaries.   Maps 48–51.

South and west from the outskirts of Tallahassee to the Apalachicola River.

The Forest extends 54 miles west from Tallahassee. It is almost bisected by the Ochlockonee River. Most inholdings are in the river valley. Total visitor-days per year is about 475,000, divided almost equally between recreation centers and undeveloped area. The concentrated visitor use is in recreation areas near Tallahassee. Even on peak season holidays and weekends one can find quiet places to camp, hike, and canoe.

Except near Tallahassee no U.S. highway crosses the Forest. Entirely south of SR 20, it is crossed by State routes 65, 67, 375, and 267. About 580 miles of National Forest roads were built chiefly for logging. Most are unpaved. Their condition ranges from good to poor. Except in Wilderness Areas, most points are less than four miles from a Forest road.

The Forest is within six watersheds. Its principal rivers are the New and Ochlockonee in the central area, the Sopchoppy and Lost Creek on the east. Largest of the rivers, the Apalachicola, draining the western portion of the Forest, is outside the boundary except for six miles in the south. The Forest has many streams, small lakes, ponds, and wet prairies. Average annual precipitation is about 60 inches.

The area is almost flat. Elevations range from 10 feet in the south to 100 feet near Tallahassee. This highest ground, the Lake Munson Hills, has sand ridges and many sand-bottomed lakes and ponds.

Plants: The original forest was clear-cut between 1910 and 1930. Fires were frequent, overgrazing common. The federal government began acquiring the land in the 1930s. Today 71 percent of the area is forest suitable for timber management, chiefly pinelands with lesser tracts of pine/hardwoods, hardwoods, and pine/titi. Throughout the forest, controlled burning is used to suppress undergrowth and sustain ecological conditions produced originally by natural wildfires.

Other communities include hardwood swamps, savannahs, pure titi areas, live oak hammocks, and dry ridges.

Much of SR 65 is on a low embankment. Driving south from Hosford we passed pine plantations with open understory, clear-cut areas, and unevenage stands with dense understory. More mature trees are on river banks and in hardwood swamps.

Hiking on Forest roads and the Florida Trail in October, we found two dozen species of wildflowers blooming. No checklist is available, but rangers said something is blooming in any season.

Birds: Headquarters has a list of 190 species that lacks indication of abundance, seasonality, or habitat. Many species of waterfowl and shorebirds have been recorded, but suitable habitats are limited. However, the 21 species of wood warblers and 8 species of woodpeckers do indicate both good variety and seasonal abundance of upland species, including several uncommon in southern Florida.

Mammals: 47 species have been recorded, including panther, no longer a permanent resident. The list includes nine bat species, a dozen species of rats and mice. Also included are marsh and cottontail rabbits; gray, fox, and flying squirrels; beaver, red and gray foxes, black bear, raccoon, long-tail weasel, mink, spotted and striped skunks, river otter, bobcat, feral hog, whitetail deer.

Reptiles and amphibians: A long list of amphibians and reptiles indicates the presence both of many species and of dedicated observers. No less than 13 salamander species appear, and an equal number of tree frogs; 17 turtles, tortoises, and terrapins; half a dozen skinks. The 37 snakes include water and upland species. Venomous species include the copperhead, here at the southern limit of its range, as well as the coral snake, cottonmouth, and diamondback and pygmy rattlesnakes. Alligators are common.

FEATURES

The *Apalachicola Wildlife Management Area* includes virtually the entire Forest. By agreement, the Florida Game and Fresh Water Fish Commission is responsible for wildlife management, including administration of hunting and fishing regulations.

Bradwell Bay Wilderness, 24,602 acres, is in the southeastern sector of the Forest, bounded by Forest Roads 13, 348, 329, and 314. The Wilderness is a large, shallow basin with several hundred acres of slash pine, blackgum, mixed hardwoods, and titi. A rare stand of old-growth slash pine lies deep inside. A 10-mile section of the Florida Trail crosses the Bay Wilderness on the higher ground. Along the way, seasonally, one may see orchids, lilies, bladderworts, and pitcher plants.

Mud Swamp–New River Wilderness, 8,018 acres, is a more recent addition to the Wilderness system. In the southwest sector, it is bounded by Forest Roads 182, 120, 120B, and 114. The terrain is flat, the swamp a few feet lower than surrounding sandy flatwoods. New River flows into the swamp and loses its identity until it consolidates again at the southern edge.

No marked trails cross the Wilderness. When river flow is sufficient, it can be crossed by canoe.

Lakes and ponds are scattered through the Forest. Those with picnic and camping areas are the Forest's principal recreation centers. They include:
- *Silver Lake,* a 23-acre spring-fed lake 8 miles west of Tallahassee, is the most popular center. It has a sand beach, nature trail. Lost Lake is nearby; no camping there. Also nearby is Trout Pond, developed for the handicapped but open to all April–September, by reservation October–March. It has a nature trail, fishing pier, no campground. Wood Lake is in the south, just east of the Ochlockonee River.
- *Camel Lake, Hitchcock Lake, Whitehead Lake,* and *Wright Lake* are west of the Ochlockonee River, scattered.
- *Ochlockonee River,* dividing the Forest, flows from Lake Talquin to Ochlockonee Bay, offering a 67-mile canoe run with 5- to 14-mile segments. See entry, Ochlockonee River (Lower) Canoe Trail.
- *Apalachicola River* is west of the Forest boundary except in the far south, but its wide floodplain extends well inside, with numerous creeks and marshes. Trip planners should note there is no bridge or ferry to cross the river in the 50 miles between Bristol and Apalachicola, a 150-mile circuit by road. The river, part of the Inland Waterway, is more suitable for power boats than canoes. In the south, White Oak Landing, Cotton Landing, and Hickory Landing are campsites on short tributaries. (White Oak Landing has no facilities.)
- *Leon Sinks Geological Area,* off US 319 south of Tallahassee, has five major sinkholes. Trail, boardwalk, observation decks.

Apalachee Savannahs National Forest Scenic Byway is a loop combining SRs 12, 379, and 65. A brochure and wayside exhibits are in preparation. It passes through longleaf pine flats, prairie savannahs, cypress swamps. We also enjoyed unhurried exploration of lightly traveled Forest roads.

ACTIVITIES
Camping: 9 developed campgrounds; 8 primitive camps. Silver Lake, Camel Lake, and Wright Lake have modern rest rooms. In a National Forest, one can usually camp anywhere unless posting forbids. Here camping is limited to designated sites during the November–January hunting season.
Hiking, backpacking: 66 miles of the Florida Trail. (Best to have the FTA guidebook [*Walking the Florida Trail*]. We found one trailhead overgrown, the route unclear.) Vinzant Riding Trail is available to hikers. Many miles of Forest roads and unmarked jeep trails.
Hunting: See regulations of Game and Fresh Water Fish Commission. Rated *good:* deer, fox; *fair:* turkey, bear, gray squirrel, quail, waterfowl; *poor:* fox squirrel.
Fishing: Bass, bream, warmouth, catfish.
Swimming: Supervised only at Trout Pond.
Boating, canoeing: Chiefly on the Ochlockonee River. Ramps at Pine Creek and Mack landings, and private sites.
Horse riding: Vinzant Riding Trail; 30 miles, three trails, two loops. From

SR 20, south on Forest Road 342 to SR 267, for horse trailer parking. Riding also on Forest roads.

Pets must be leashed in developed areas; not allowed on beaches. Off-road vehicles (ORVs) are prohibited in Wildernesses, restricted to designated roads in some areas. See the Forest travel map.

PUBLICATIONS
Forest map. $2.
Silver Lake Recreation Area.
Vinzant Riding Trail.
Apalachicola Shooting Range.
Canoeing the Apalachicola National Forest.
Canoe brochure and map. $3. (Includes Ocala National Forest.)
Hunting and fishing regulations. Florida Game and Fresh Water Fish Commission.
Ochlockonee River (Lower) Canoe Trail. Division of Recreation and Parks; Department of Natural Resources.

HEADQUARTERS: National Forests in Florida, 227 N. Bronough St., Tallahassee, FL 32301; (904) 681-7265.

RANGER DISTRICTS: Wakulla R.D., Route 6, Box 7860, Crawfordville, FL 32327; (904) 926-3561. Apalachicola R.D., P.O. Box 579, Bristol, FL 32321; (904) 643-2283.

APALACHICOLA RIVER
103 miles.   Maps 32, 33, 48, 60.
From Lake Seminole to the Gulf of Mexico.

It's Florida's eighth longest river but ranks first in average flow. Partly because of controlled releases from Seminole Dam, its flow is variable, from less than 8,000 cubic feet per second to over 100,000. The level varies by as much as 20 feet in the north, 10 feet in the south. On an October visit we found the level far down, but the banks showed evidence of recent flooding.

The river has carried commercial traffic since the steamboat era. Seminole Dam and locks extended navigation far into Georgia. Power boaters use the river, especially its lower reaches, but few canoeists. Land access is limited by its wide floodplain, but there are about 20 marinas and ramps.

APALACHICOLA BLUFFS AND RAVINES PRESERVE
The Nature Conservancy
6,300 acres; 4,500 in main tract.   Map 48, A-3

From I-10, Exit 25 (SR 12) (Map 33, D-2) southwest about 20 miles to Garden of Eden Road, north of Bristol. Turn right on this dirt road to a small parking area.

The range of elevations here is almost 200 feet, extraordinary in Florida. The state's largest exposed geologic formation, Alum Bluff, overlooks the Apalachicola River 180 feet below. The sandy uplands are cut by deep ravines, unlike other areas of Florida.

Most of the uplands were logged before The Nature Conservancy's purchase. However, the longleaf pine/wiregrass community is being restored, and TNC scientists identified many endangered plant and animal species here.

The site is partially forested, species including northern and southern hardwoods and several rarities: the Florida torreya (see entry for nearby Torreya State Park), Florida yew, pyramid magnolia, and Ashe magnolia. Among the many species of flowering plants are star anise, silver bell, flowering dogwood, yellow jessamine, trillium.

A self-guided 3½-mile trail loop from the parking area traverses upland, ravine, and floodplain habitats and includes the bluff overlook. A map is available at the trailhead.

Wildlife: No bird list has been compiled. It would be similar to Torreya State Park's list of 140 species. Swallow-tailed and Mississippi kites have both been seen.

Mammals often seen include opossum, gray and fox squirrels, armadillo, raccoon, and whitetail deer. Bobcat, coyote, and red and gray foxes are present but seldom seen.

Pets are prohibited.

PUBLICATION: Trail map.

HEADQUARTERS: The Nature Conservancy, Northwest Florida Land Steward, 515A North Adams St., Tallahassee, FL 32301; (904) 222-0199.

AUCILLA RIVER CANOE TRAIL
19 miles.   Map 51, B-3.

Begins at US 27 bridge, one mile southeast of Lamont.

The river flows through cypress/gum swamps, at times between high limestone banks. Trees on higher ground include live, water, and laurel oaks; sweetgum; loblolly, slash, and longleaf pines; spruce; and pond cypress.

The first take-out point is at a bridge on County Road 257, 13 miles downstream from the put-in. The end of the designated trail is at a logging road near Cabbage.

Skill rating is intermediate to technical, difficulty moderate to strenuous, because of shoals and remains of two dams. The run is more hazardous at low water.

About 3 miles below the put-in, the river enters a 9-mile strip of land owned by the Suwannee River Water Management District, managed by the Division of Forestry. Up to a mile wide, this strip has unimproved roads suitable for hiking. Dogs on leash are permitted here.

After passing County Road 257, the river flows through the Aucilla Wildlife Management Area (see entry). About 12 miles farther downstream, near US 98, the Aucilla meets the Wacissa River. (See entry, Wacissa River Canoe Trail.)

Wildlife: Often seen: deer, bobcat, squirrel, opossum, raccoon, gopher tortoise, wild turkey, wood duck, many species of owls, hawks, woodpeckers, warblers.

PUBLICATIONS

Aucilla River Canoe Trail. Leaflet with map. Division of Recreation and Parks.

Middle Aucilla River Tract. Suwannee River Water Management District.

AUCILLA WILDLIFE MANAGEMENT AREA
Florida Game and Fresh Water Fish Commission
75,110 acres.   Map 51, D-1, 2.

South of US 98: between the St. Mark's River and SR 14. North of US 98: from SR 59 east across the Wacissa River.

Much of the property is owned by St. Joe Paper Company, leased to the Commission for hunting. The company uses its land for wood fiber production. We were told the company permits hiking, fishing, and nature study outside hunting seasons. The 14,000 acres known as the Wacissa River–Aucilla Sinks is State-owned. The State portion is managed for recreation.

The area is flat, the highest elevation 50 feet. Communities include pine/palmetto flatwoods, cypress/gum swamps, mixed hardwood hammocks, pine/oak uplands, and, in the south, cabbage palm hammocks. Many woods roads provide routes for hunters and hikers. Two canoe trails, the Wacissa and Aucilla (see entries), cross the site. There are numerous sinks and shallow ponds.

Hunting is the principal visitor activity. Deer and turkey are the principal game species.

PUBLICATION: Hunting regulations with map.

HEADQUARTERS: Florida Game and Fresh Water Fish Commission, Northeast Region, RFD 7 Box 440, Lake City, FL 32055; (904) 758-0525.

BIG BEND WILDLIFE MANAGEMENT AREA

Includes three units: Hickory Mound in Zone 1, Spring Creek and Tide Swamp in Zone 2. See those entries.

BIG LAGOON STATE RECREATION AREA

Division of Recreation and Parks
699 acres.   Map 42, B-2.

10 miles southwest of Pensacola, off SR 292.

The site, close to a major city, has almost two miles of swimming beach. One would expect it to be heavily impacted. When the State acquired it in 1977, it had been abused: slashed by jeep trails, paths, and ditches; cluttered with old cars, appliances, and other junk; excavated for sand; and piled with dredging spoil. Significant remnants of natural coastal communities remained, which the Division has preserved. Nature and management are repairing the damage.

Visitors come, about 90,000 per year, a relatively low number because of the many other beaches nearby, including Gulf Islands National Seashore. Most come in summer and congregate along the shore. On weekends and holidays, some may not find picnic tables. From fall to spring, the site is uncrowded. When we visited one sunny morning in early fall, we were alone.

Plants: Headquarters has a long list of the site's native plants. Over 300 acres are sand pine scrub, a fragile community becoming rare in Florida. Even foot traffic damages the delicate ground cover. The community depend on periodic fires, now provided by controlled burning. The 185 acres of wet flatwoods also depend on periodic fires, lest increasingly dense ground cover provide fuel for a catastrophic canopy fire. The site's grassy tidal marshes support such species as shrimp, crab, oyster, and numerous fishes.

Birds: 113 species have been recorded. Of special interest to birders are common loon, magnificent frigatebird, Mississippi kite, ruddy turnstone, black skimmer.

Mammals: Although there is considerable development along SR 292A nearby, swamp forest lies to the north. Thus it is not surprising that the mammals recorded at Big Lagoon include beaver, striped skunk, raccoon, gray fox, and whitetail deer.

ACTIVITIES
Camping: 75 sites. Telephone reservations accepted.
Swimming: Three beach areas.
Boating: Ramp.

INTERPRETATION
Nature trails pass through the several land habitats.
Amphitheater, seating 500, is an unusual facility. The complex includes stage, meeting rooms, and large kitchen.

PUBLICATION: Leaflet with map.

NEARBY: Perdido Key State Recreation Area (see entry) is a satellite.

HEADQUARTERS: 12301 Gulf Beach Highway, Pensacola, FL 32507; (904) 492-1595.

BLACKWATER RIVER CANOE TRAIL
31 miles.   Map 28, A-1.

Put-in at Kennedy Bridge. From Baker (Map 27, A-1), northwest on SR 4, crossing Cotton Bridge (a put-in or take-out at mile 11). Continue to right turn on first paved road, Forest Road 47. At next paved road, Forest Road 31, turn right. In about two miles turn right on dirt road (see Hurricane Lake sign), Forest Road 24 to Kennedy Bridge.

The water is tannin-stained but pure, with white sandbars. The current is moderate, difficulty rating "easy" except after heavy rains. Canoes can navigate even at low water.

The trail is through Blackwater River State Forest, ending at Blackwater River State Park (see entries). Although no established campgrounds are along the way, camping is permitted at any suitable place, and many who make the run, including outfitter parties, do camp, often on sandbars.

Especially in the upper reaches, cedar, maple, and cypress trees shade the river. Some sections are between high bluffs. Deer, turkey, and bobcat are often seen. Numerous bird species include the Mississippi kite.

Alternate put-in or take-out points are at miles 6, 11, and 23.
Several outfitters serve the route with canoes, shuttles, and overnight trips.
See list in the main preface.

PUBLICATION: *Blackwater River Canoe Trail.* Division of Recreation and
Parks.

BLACKWATER RIVER STATE FOREST
Division of Forestry
183,155 acres.   Map 27, A-3.

From Milton, NE on SR 191.

The Forest adjoins the Conecuh National Forest in Alabama. Together they
have the largest remaining stand of longleaf pine, a species once dominant
in much of Florida. The Blackwater has other northern affinities. Its vast
assortment of wildflower species is typical of the southern Appalachians,
and many of its bird species are here at the southern limit of their ranges.

Finding one's way around the Forest isn't easy. The DeLorme *Atlas* map
doesn't show Forest boundaries or private inholdings. "Entering" and "leaving" signs are on SRs 191 and 4, the two main roads crossing the Forest.
Some sections of Forest boundaries are marked by white bands on trees,
white slash marks showing the direction of Forest land. The 600 miles of
roads maintained by Forest personnel have been assigned route numbers,
but these numbers are posted only on main roads. For the stranger, pathfinding requires a Forest map, dividers or a substitute, and close attention to
your car's odometer.

We admire the Forest and its staff. Their dedication, skill, and patience
have built a new forest on the ruins of the old. By the middle 1920s, this
area was a wasteland, logged off, burned, abandoned by owners. Most of
it was acquired by the federal government in the 1930s. Not much happened
until it was transferred to State ownership about 1955.

Our chief disappointment at Blackwater is that management has not closed
and naturalized a block of the old logging roads, eventually to establish at
least one wilderness area. On the whole, management objectives are admirable, and practices seem consistent with objectives.

The Forest is also a Wildlife Management Area (WMA), and the Florida
Game and Fresh Water Fish Commission participates in shaping the Forest
plan. Rookeries, other nesting areas, live oak clumps, scrub, and other critical

habitats are protected, as well as natural food-producing areas. Red-cockaded woodpeckers require old trees with cavities for nesting; almost 200 such trees have been mapped and marked for protection. Management is considering closing roads in wildlife-sensitive areas for part of each year.

No clear-cutting is permitted unless funds are available to convert slash pine plantations to natural longleaf stands. Overstory cuts are scheduled where longleaf seedlings are established. The objective is regenerating the longleaf/wiregrass ecosystem. Recreation areas are given special attention. Historical and archeological sites are cataloged and protection considered.

Elevations range from under 100 to over 250 feet. Terrain includes flatwoods, rolling hills, and swamps. Its four major streams, Blackwater River and Coldwater, Juniper, and Sweetwater creeks are chiefly sand-bottomed and clear. All four watersheds are largely within the Forest, so there is no industrial, agricultural, or municipal pollution. Clear-cutting and most commercial logging is prohibited within 50 yards of these streams. The Blackwater is one of the nation's purest rivers. The four streams are canoeable in all seasons, and canoeing is increasingly popular, attracting one-fifth of the Forest's visitors.

Five artificial lakes lie within the Forest boundaries: Krul (6 acres), Bear (107 acres), Karick (58 acres), Hurricane (350 acres), and Bone Creek (8 acres). More may be built to promote fishing.

Plants: Longleaf pine is the principal tree species, dominant on three-fourths of the Forest acreage. Other forest types are oak, gum, cypress, and oak/hickory. Species include blackjack and turkey oaks, red oaks, sweetgum, bay, blackgum, dogwood, and pines: slash, loblolly, sand, and juniper. Most trees are 50 to 75 years old. The sustained yield plan calls for a 60-year rotation; the actual cycle is somewhat longer. We were told the average diameter of standing commercial timber is over 14 inches.

No list of flowering plants is available, but it would be a long one, with some blooming at every season.

Birds: No list is available. The list compiled for the nearby Eglin Air Force Base (see entry) has some relevance, except that Eglin has salt marshes, estuaries, and Gulf frontage, while Blackwater has higher ground.

Mammals: Species observed include opossum, cottontail and marsh rabbits, gray and flying squirrels, raccoon, gray and red foxes, beaver, nine-banded armadillo, whitetail deer. Reported infrequently: black bear, panther, bobcat, weasel, striped skunk.

ACTIVITIES

Through roads intersecting at Munson in the heart of the Forest make visitor counts unreliable. About four-fifths of the visitors are Floridians, most of them living nearby. Hunting and fishing are their chief interests, followed by swimming, camping, and canoeing.

Camping: 9 campgrounds, 357 sites. The Krul Recreation Area is largest, best-developed, most popular. Bear Lake, Hurricane Lake, and Karick Lake also have facilities. Other campgrounds are primitive. Campgrounds are likely to be full during spring school vacations, crowded in summer.

Hiking, backpacking: Publicity given to the 21½-mile Jackson Trail, a section of the Florida Trail, is increasing the number of hikers. At present, trailside camping is permitted almost anywhere. The rule is under review.

Hunting: Judged good for deer, turkey, quail.

Fishing: Chiefly in Hurricane, Bear, and Karick lakes; stocked with large-mouth bass, bluegill, channel catfish, shellcracker.

Swimming: Krul and Bone Creek lakes, several other locations.

Canoeing, boating: The four principal streams are delightful canoe trails: 31 miles on Blackwater River, 18 on Coldwater Creek, 13 on Sweetwater and Juniper creeks. Several outfitters provide canoes, shuttle service, overnight trips. (See entries.)

Horse riding: Coldwater Recreation Area has stables, other facilities, access to several riding trails. Riding is permitted on Forest grounds. Reservations are required for use of stables.

Pets are prohibited in the Krul and Bear Lake Recreation Areas. At present they are permitted on leash in other campgrounds and elsewhere, but this rule is under review.

Off-road vehicles must stay on established roads.

PUBLICATIONS

Forest map with general information.
Coldwater Horse Trails.
From Florida Game and Fresh Water Fish Commission:
  Hunt map and regulations.
  Fishing maps and regulations for Hurricane, Bear, and Karick lakes.
From Division of Recreation and Parks:
  Blackwater River Canoe Trail.
  Coldwater Creek Canoe Trail.
  Sweetwater/Juniper Creeks Canoe Trails.

HEADQUARTERS: Route 1, Box 77, Milton, FL 32570; (904) 957-4201.

BLACKWATER RIVER STATE PARK
Division of Recreation and Parks
590 acres.   Map 27, C-3.

From Milton, northeast on US 90 to Harold, then north to Park.

The Park is on the south edge of Blackwater River State Forest (see entry) and has many of the same qualities. It has 7,800 feet of shoreline on the Blackwater River, one of the purest in the nation, and is the end of the Blackwater River Canoe Trail (see entry). Large white sandbars at river bends are fine sites for boaters' picnics.

Terrain is hilly, with large stands of white-cedar, sandhill, and pine flatwoods, and an extensive river swamp with numerous oxbow ponds.

Wildlife: Includes wild turkey, red-shouldered hawk, bluebird, bobcat, river otter, gray fox, deer, snapping turtle, gopher tortoise.

ACTIVITIES

Camping: 30 sites. No reservations.
Hiking: Two nature trails. Also trails and roads in adjoining Forest.
Fishing: Bass, bream, catfish, pickerel, shellcracker, speckled perch.
Swimming: White sand beaches.
Canoeing: Take-out for river trips. Outfitter services are available nearby.

PUBLICATION: Leaflet with map.

HEADQUARTERS: Route 1, Box 57C, Holt, FL 32564; (904) 623-2363.

CAPE ST. GEORGE ISLAND

Division of Recreation and Parks
2,300 acres.   Map 60, D-2.

Barrier island south of Apalachicola. Visitors must provide their own transportation.

The management priority here is protection and preservation. Visitors will be welcome unless their impact becomes adverse. The rules hadn't been written when we gathered information, but it's clear that access will be by boat only and that few if any facilities will be provided.

The Island is within the Apalachicola National Estuarine Research Reserve. Apalachicola Bay is enclosed by a chain of barrier islands. Much of St. George Island, about 19 miles long, accessible by road, has been commercially developed. St. George Island State Park (see entry) is at its east end. Cape St. George Island is separated from the larger island by a pass. On the west, St. Vincent Island (see entry) is a National Wildlife Refuge.

The Cape is about nine miles long, from one-quarter to one mile wide. Its western and eastern ends are low-lying pine flatwoods, occasionally inundated by storm surges. Highest point of the central section is 26 feet, but most dunes are less than half that high. The central section offers a variety of environments including flatwoods, scrub, hammock, and swale wetland. About half of the island is forested. The rest is beach, berm, maritime grassland, and salt marsh.

Birds: The island is a birding hot-spot, a crossroads of migration routes, and has a substantial winter population. Occasionally spring migrants crossing the Gulf meet rain and strong winds pushed by a cold front. In great numbers they "crash" on the Preserve, their first landfall, resting and feeding until conditions improve. The island also attracts many shorebirds, wading birds, and waterfowl.

Camping: Primitive camping at designated sites. Check with the Research Reserve Office first.

HEADQUARTERS: Apalachicola National Estuarine Research Reserve, 261 7th St., Apalachicola, FL 32320; (904) 653-8063.

CHIPOLA RIVER CANOE TRAIL
52 miles.   Maps 32, B-1, to 48, B-1.

Put-in at bridge on SR 167, one mile north of Marianna.

The designated trail begins at Florida Caverns State Park (see entry), but the first mile, an old log chute, is hazardous, so the bridge on SR 167 is recommended. From there to the take-out at Scotts Ferry, near the intersection of SR 71 and CR 392, it's an easy run except for a few low-water shoals, one of which, below SR 274, may require portaging.

Although the run is not through publicly owned land, there is little riverside development. For the most part the river flows through swamps and hardwood forests, with occasional limestone bluffs. The canoeist will see many birds as well as alligators, turtles, sometimes beaver or raccoon.

Alternate put-in or take-out sites are at miles 11, 21, 29, and 39. Numerous informal campsites are along the way.

Beyond the designated take-out at mile 52, one can continue through Dead Lake to Dead Lakes State Park (see entry). Snags, fallen trees, and other obstructions make this extension inadvisable in bad weather.

Several outfitters serve the river.

PUBLICATION: *Chipola River Canoe Trail.* Division of Recreation and Parks.

CHOCTAWHATCHEE RIVER
100 miles in Florida.   Map 30, A-2.

First put-in is at Curry Ferry. From Caryville on I-10, north about 11 miles on SR 179 to Izagora, then left.

We haven't canoed this river. Some who have think it should be a State Canoe Trail. No outfitter is on the river. However, it's a scenic route, largely undeveloped, canoeable, with several State, county, and private ramps.

The Choctawhatchee begins in Alabama 70 miles from the border. It flows south to the crossing of SR 20, then west to Choctawhatchee Bay. Several springs and creeks feed the river, which flows through wetlands with occasional stretches of upland forest. It has the second largest floodplain in Florida. No large towns are on the river.

Below the state line, the banks are high and heavily wooded. Exceptionally large sandbars make good picnic and camping sites. Downstream are a few houses and fish camps. Canoeing is said to be more popular on the upper river. The segment closest to the bay is considered the most scenic, least disturbed.

The Northwest Water Management District owns much of the land between Caryville and the mouth. The Nature Conservancy owns 2,760 acres adjoining the bay, where the river becomes a complex of salt marsh islands and tidal channels.

Unless the State publishes a canoe trail leaflet or an outfitter adopts the river, a newcomer must explore. The private campground at Caryville should be a good information source.

COLDWATER CREEK CANOE TRAIL
18 miles.   Map 27, A-2.

Put-in at bridge over Big Coldwater Creek, on SR 4 between SR 87 and SR 191; north of Milton.

Spring-fed, cool even in summer, the creek flows rather swiftly over a white sand bottom. The route is through pine and hardwood forests. The upper portion of the run is through the Blackwater River State Forest (see entry).

Camping is available at the Coldwater Recreation Area 4 miles downstream. Informal camping is possible at other points.

Several outfitters serve the route with canoes, shuttles, and overnight trips.

PUBLICATION: *Coldwater Creek Canoe Trail.* Division of Recreation and Parks.

ECONFINA CREEK CANOE TRAIL
22 miles.   Map 31, D-2 (put-in).

From Fountain (Map 47, A-2), 4 miles north on US 231, then left on
Scott's Road to Scott's Bridge. (The leaflet says "US 341," an apparent
error.)

"Expect the unexpected," says the Division of Recreation and Parks leaflet.
Then it spoils the surprise by warnings: Check the depth gauge at Scott's
Bridge; if level is above 4.0 or below 2.0, try another canoe run. Also, the
upper river is for skilled paddlers only: narrow, tight curves, chutes; pullovers and log jams at low water. Alternate put-ins are at miles 10, 15, and
16. The lower section, now called Econfina River, fed by springs just above
and below SR 20, is slower, easy going.

Although the river flows through privately owned land, little development
is seen on the run. Limestone walls, sand bluffs, and forest make it a scenic
route. Wildlife is abundant.

Camping at the 10-mile point, Walsingham Bridge, requires a permit from
the Washington County tax collector.

Beyond the take-out at the SR 388 bridge, the river flows into Deer Point
Lake, which leads into North Bay at Lynn Haven.

PUBLICATION: *Econfina Creek Canoe Trail.* Division of Recreation and Parks.

EDWARD BALL WAKULLA SPRINGS STATE PARK
Division of Recreation and Parks
2,862 acres.   Map 50, C-2.

From Tallahassee, south on SR 61. Left on SR 267. Entrance on right.

Open 8 A.M. to sunset.

The spring, one of Florida's largest, was a privately owned tourist attraction until 1986, when the State acquired it, assisted by the Florida Nature
Conservancy and Northwest Florida Water Management District. The 27-
room lodge, restaurant, and conference center are now operated by the
Florida State University Center for Professional Development.

A fence controls access to the waterfront. The fence gate was still locked
at 9 A.M. when we visited.

For 50 years the previous owner, Edward Ball, had strict rules protecting the site's wildlife. Visitors could not enter the woodlands except on a nature trail. Hunting, fishing, and diving were prohibited.

The Division of Recreation and Parks intends to continue this protection, with minor modifications. Visitors can picnic, swim, take the glass-bottomed boat tours, and walk the nature trails. They can patronize the restaurant and lodge. Private boats may not enter from the river. Planned changes include a hiking trail, primitive walk-in camp, additional nature trail, and more picnic tables.

The 36-acre area around the waterfront, lodge, and picnic tables is landscaped, with lawns and walks. The undisturbed part of the site has old-growth hardwood forests, upland pine forest, old-growth stands of bald cypress. The hardwood forests include three State Champion trees, but visitors won't see them because about one-fourth of the area is open water, sloughs, swamps, and floodplain forest.

The spring: The main spring is huge. The average flow is almost 3,000 gallons per second. Its highest recorded flow is over 14,000 gallons per second, the state record. When the water is clear, visitors can see the bottom, 95 feet down.

Scuba divers have discovered a complex of aquatic tunnels and a large cavern, 150 feet wide with a 100-foot arched ceiling. In the cavern is a 300-foot-long fossil bed.

Wildlife: The Park supplies a lengthy bird list that appears to be for the Tallahassee region. Species often seen include white ibis, limpkin, osprey, purple gallinule, anhinga, and bald eagle. We saw a large river cooter digging a nest in front of the lodge. Told of this, the Park naturalist secured the site.

Old records note a number of species that were former visitors. A few manatees are seen downstream each year, but in 1883 they were recorded in the spring.

INTERPRETATION
  Guided river tours, daily.
  Glass-bottomed boat tours when the water is clear.
  Nature walks and *slide presentations* are offered occasionally.

PUBLICATIONS
  Leaflet.
  Site map.
  Bird list.

HEADQUARTERS: One Spring Drive, Wakulla Springs, FL 32305; (904) 222-7279.

EGLIN AIR FORCE BASE
U.S. Air Force
464,000 acres.   Maps 27, 28, 29, 44, 45.

Between I-10 and US 98. Crossed by SRs 87, 85, 285, 20.

Open 1 ½ hours before sunrise to 1 ½ hours after sunset.
Everyone must have a permit. Permits are issued Monday–Friday (7 A.M. –
3:15 P.M.) at the Natural Resources Branch on SR 85 in Niceville. General
recreation permits cost $3 and are good for the fiscal year. Special per-
mits are needed for camping, hunting, and fishing. Call (904) 882-4164
for information.

In 1979 we were asked not to include Eglin in a guide we were preparing
then. "A large influx of outside visitors would be undesirable" was the explanation. Today 273,000 acres, three-fifths of the reservation, are open
to the public.

Eglin is the largest Air Force base. On Eglin, 99 percent of the acreage
is undeveloped. More than 85 percent of the area is forest, managed much
like national and state forests. Buffer zones are maintained around active
ranges, and the commander can close any area to visitors, but such changes
rarely interfere with visitors' plans.

Why bother with a site that requires permits and has special rules? Because it's one of Florida's largest and most diverse natural areas, extending
from coastal barrier islands to high sandhills. Its 780 miles of pristine streams
arise from 1,200 perennial springs. It has 30 miles of rivers, with fine backcountry canoe trails, 32 small lakes, over 26,000 acres of wetlands, 57 miles
of estuarine shoreline, 20 miles on the Gulf of Mexico. Elevations range
from sea level to 295 feet. Terrain is gently rolling.

Even were a permit not required, a stop at the Natural Resources Branch
office would be essential. The *Outdoor Recreation, Hunting and Fishing
Map* is indispensable. The area is so huge one needs advice on where to
go. The base measures 51 miles west–east, 19 miles north–south. The map
shows many trails. Which are the most interesting? Points of interest include Weaver Creek, old-growth longleaf pines in the Roberts Pond area,
and red-cockaded woodpecker colonies.

Several municipalities are within the outer boundaries of the base, including
Fort Walton Beach, Ocean City, Shalimar, Valparaiso, Niceville, and
Freeport.

Portions of Santa Rosa Island and Okaloosa Island are owned by the base.
SR 399, Santa Rosa Boulevard, and US 98 traverse these barrier islands,
which have fine beaches. The 14-mile stretch of Okaloosa Island, just across

the bridge from Destin, is open to visitors without permits; other beach accesses are along the routes.

Plants: Almost 80 percent of the base is classified as sandhills, where longleaf, slash, and sand pines predominate. Other associations include longleaf pine/mixed oak, mixed oak/pine, and bottomland hardwoods: oak/hickory and oak/gum/cypress. Canoeists will see red maple, sweetbay, titi.

Coastal sand dune plants include sea oats, sea rocket, sea purslane, beach morning glory, rosemary. Freshwater marshes: red maple, alder, willow, greenbrier. Salt marshes: sawgrass, black rush, wax myrtle. Bogs: titi, sweetbay, pitcher plant.

Birds: Eglin's bird checklist includes an astonishing 335 species. However, it is built from observations dating from 1885, including many records from the early 1900s. It also includes accidentals—species seen only once or twice. Seasonality and abundance are noted, but without indication of how recently these judgments were made. The copy we obtained in 1990 is identical with one we received in 1979.

These qualifications aside, Eglin is a prime area for birding because of its extensive, diverse, relatively undisturbed habitats.

Mammals: Include eastern coyote, beaver, armadillo, oppossum, southern pocket gopher, bobcat, striped skunk, whitetail deer, rice rat, cotton mouse, beach mouse, raccoon, eastern harvest mouse, eastern gray and eastern fox squirrels, hispid cotton rat, wild pig, eastern cottontail, gray and red foxes, black bear.

Reptiles and amphibians: Our correspondent wrote, "Eglin AFB is also very unique in that it has over 120 species of native amphibians and reptiles. As a result, Eglin is considered to be one of the most diverse herpetological areas in the southeast."

ACTIVITIES

Camping: 16 primitive campgrounds. Each can accommodate up to 50 campers. A camping permit is required.

Hiking, backpacking: The Outdoor Activities map shows trails, but no printed trail guides are available. We suggest seeking advice from the Natural Resources Branch office. Backpacking is allowed, using one of the 16 campgrounds for overnighting.

Hunting is a major public use. Special rules and seasons for coyote, deer, fox, raccoon, bobcat, opossum, wild turkey, wild hog, waterfowl, dove, migratory game birds.

Fishing: Surf and stream. Species include largemouth bass, bluegill, redear sunfish, channel catfish.

Canoeing: Seven canoe trails of 2 to 26 miles, totaling 55 miles. The Canoe Trail Guide makes choice difficult: "A beautiful canoe trail with clear water and numerous white sandbars"; "a twisting clear-water creek"; "a dark-water stream that winds through Eglin's forests." The longest trail overlaps with the State's Yellow River and Shoal River Canoe Trails (see entries).

Boating: Most boating is in the estuaries and bayous. The recreation guide indicates no public ramps on the base, but there are many ramps and marinas in the area.

Swimming: Gulf beaches and fresh water, at your own risk.

Because this is an active air base, many rules and regulations govern public use. We cannot summarize them here. They are provided when you obtain a permit.

PUBLICATIONS
Outdoor Recreation, Hunting and Fishing Map.
Bird checklist.
Canoe Trail Guide.

HEADQUARTERS: Natural Resources Branch, 3200 SPTW/DEMN, Eglin AFB, FL 32542; (904) 882-4164.

FALLING WATERS STATE RECREATION AREA
Division of Recreation and Parks
155 acres.   Map 31, C-1.

From I-10 near Chipley, south on SR 77, then east on SR 77A.

Florida's only waterfall pours down into a sinkhole and vanishes. With so much underlying limestone, sinkholes are common in the state. Occasionally one develops suddenly, swallowing a car, part of a house, or a section of road. Falling Waters is a special place because of the waterfall, the number of sinkholes close together, and their cylindrical shape.

From the parking and picnic area, it's a short walk to the sinkhole trail—much of it boardwalk with wooden stairs—which passes the principal sinkholes. Trees growing inside them attest to their ages. Falling Waters Sink is 15 feet in diameter, 100 feet deep, with smooth vertical walls. Steps lead down to a viewing platform below the top of the falls. We were there just after a heavy rain. The cluster of sinkholes is in a mature hardwood hammock.

Short trails lead to a small lake.

ACTIVITIES
Camping: 24 sites. No reservations.
Swimming: Lake.

PUBLICATION: Leaflet with map.

HEADQUARTERS: Route 5, Box 660, Chipley, FL 32428; (904) 638-6130.

FLORIDA CAVERNS STATE PARK
Division of Recreation and Parks
1,783 acres.   Map 32, B-1.

From US 90 at Marianna, north on SR 167.

Open 8 A.M. to sunset.

Florida's most accessible caverns aren't far from Florida's only waterfall (see entry, Falling Waters State Park). Other known caverns are submerged, as at Wakulla Springs. These caverns, a series of connecting rooms, have massive and delicate calcite formations like those of such larger caverns as Mammoth Cave.

Above ground, the park has pine forest, hardwood hammock, river swamp, and the Chipola River, which disappears, then rises a short distance downstream.

Plants: Trees include American beech, southern magnolia, white oak, and dogwood. The many wildflower species include a number common to the Appalachians, here at the southern limit of their ranges.

Birds: A list was compiled between 1944 and 1972. Our copy has handwritten changes. Relative abundance is not noted.

Mammals: Caves attract bats, and the 1944–1972 list includes five species. Also recorded: opossum, eastern mole, eastern cottontail, beaver; gray, fox, and southern flying squirrels; raccoon, whitetail deer.

Reptiles and amphibians: The same-vintage list includes American alligator, 9 turtle species, 6 lizards, 14 snakes, 8 salamanders (including cave species), and 13 frogs and toads.

ACTIVITIES
Camping: 32 sites. Telephone reservations accepted.
Hiking: The Park leaflet doesn't show them, but there are about 7 miles of trails.
Fishing: Bass, bream, catfish.
Swimming: Blue Hole isn't a first-magnitude spring but it's good for swimming.
Canoeing: First put-in for the Chipola River Canoe Trail. The first section of the trail requires skill. See entry.

INTERPRETATION
Guided cave tours are offered daily. Fee.
Visitor center has audiovisual program and exhibits.

PUBLICATIONS
Park leaflet with map.
Vertebrate list.

HEADQUARTERS: 3345 Caverns Road, Marianna, FL 32399; (904) 482-9598.

GRAYTON BEACH STATE RECREATION AREA
Division of Recreation and Parks
1,179 acres.   Map 45, B-2.

From US 98, south on SR 283.

Open 8 A.M. to sunset.

Because of its location, between Pensacola and Panama City, Grayton Beach isn't heavily impacted. Other beaches along the hundred-mile strand are closer to both cities. The Division's visitor statistics puzzled us. In 1989, this SRA had more visitors in March and April, before the swimming season, than in June or August. We can confirm the sharp decline in October. We visited on a warm, sunny day and had the place to ourselves.

It's a splendid mile of sand beach, but that is only one of the site's attractions. Back of the beach are fine barrier dunes. What seem to be shrubs protruding from the dunes among the sea oats are the tops of trees, slash pine and magnolia, buried by shifting sands.

The SRA leaflet shows only the developed area. Camping is east of the entrance station. The road then crosses an arm of Western Lake, turns to run back of the dunes, passes one picnic area, and ends at another, near the bathhouse. Beyond is an area of pine flatwoods.

Western Lake, 80 acres in size, is the larger of two freshwater bodies, separated from the Gulf of Mexico by a sand barrier. Occasionally the lake's water level rises high enough to reopen a channel. The lake becomes tidal and brackish until drifting sand again fills the gap. Western Lake is ringed by marshes.

We had no map of the entire site when we visited, and the attendant at the entrance station had none. The developed area shown on the leaflet amounts to about 350 acres. The attendant couldn't tell us about or direct us to the other 820 acres.

We have since learned that about 530 acres are across SR 30A. Western

Lake extends into this tract. No development is planned. Birding is probably good there.

The remaining acreage is on the Gulf between the town of Grayton Beach and the Gulf Trace subdivision. No parking is available, and access is therefore difficult. The unit has 1,900 feet of beachfront. The State is considering a lease to Walton County of the beach and enough upland for parking.

Birds: A checklist in production includes 146 species, noting their abundance and seasonality. Of the 146, 58 are permanent residents, 54 winter residents. Only 17 are noted as transients. This differs surprisingly from other Gulf sites, which report great numbers of spring migrants.

ACTIVITIES
Camping: 37 sites. Telephone reservations accepted March 1 through Labor Day.
Hiking: Barrier dune nature trail; extension loop through pine flatwoods. We found birding good along the entrance road.
Fishing: Surf and lake.
Boating: Ramp on lake. No access to Gulf.

PUBLICATIONS
Leaflet with map.
Grayton Beach Nature Trail.

HEADQUARTERS: Route 2, Box 6600, Santa Rosa Beach, FL 32459; (904) 231-4210.

GULF ISLANDS NATIONAL SEASHORE
National Park Service
Land area in Florida: 9,367 acres;
total: 28,976 acres.
Land area in Mississippi: 10,078;
total: 69,150 acres.   Maps 42, 43-B.

Florida visitor center: entrance on US 98 southeast of Pensacola.

Authorized by Congress in 1971, the National Seashore extends along 150 miles of Gulf Coast, from West Ship Island in Mississippi to Santa Rosa Island in Florida. The authorization states that the Seashore was established

> To conserve and manage the wildlife and natural resources.
> To preserve as wilderness any area within the Seashore found to be suitable . . .
> To recognize, preserve, and interpret the national historical significance of Fort Barrancas Water Battery, Fort Barrancas and the Advanced Redoubt of Fort Barrancas, . . . Fort Pickens on Santa Rosa Island . . .

It includes six offshore islands and three mainland tracts. The Mississippi and Florida units are more than 50 miles apart. This entry describes the Florida unit, with references to some Mississippi features.

In Florida, the Seashore includes portions of Santa Rosa Island and Perdido Key, the Naval Live Oaks area on US 98 east of Gulf Breeze, and the Fort Barrancas and Advanced Redoubt at the Pensacola Naval Air Station. Most visitor facilities are in the Fort Pickens area at the west end of Santa Rosa Island and at Johnson Beach on Perdido Key.

The Gulf beaches are splendid. Visitation is increasing, but even the principal beach sites are seldom crowded because other public beaches are nearby. June–August is the busy season, December–January the slowest.

Barrier islands are rapidly changing landforms, first shaped by variations in sea level over the past million years. As the polar icecaps increased and melted, sea level fluctuated. At times it was as much as 200 feet higher than at present and most of present-day Florida was submerged. As recently as 18,000 years ago, Florida's land area was more than double its present size. Gulf barrier islands appeared as the sea level rose.

Their shapes change continuously as sand is moved by wind, wave, littoral current, and storms. The Gulf islands are being moved westward and narrowed. Hurricanes have inundated low-lying islands, sometimes cutting one in two.

On the Gulf side of the islands are beaches of white quartz sand. The front dunes, most exposed to wind and storm, are partially stabilized by salt-tolerant vegetation, chiefly sea oats. Picking or disturbing this vegetation is forbidden.

The inner dunes are older, higher, and vegetated with palmetto, scrub live oak, and slash pine. The area between the fore and inner dunes is low. Rain collects in freshwater marshes. Fringing the bay shores are salt marshes and beds of submerged grasses.

We suggest going first to the visitor center on US 98 near Gulf Breeze. Rangers, exhibits, audiovisual programs, and an array of special leaflets will help you plan a day visit or a two-week vacation.

Plants: An excellent folder classifies "common or conspicuous plants" by habitat and season. Common on the fore dunes: sea oats and sea rocket. Dunes and swale: jointweed, yellow-eyed grass, balduina, woody goldenrod, golden aster, rockrose, evening primrose, bladderwort, rustweed, sundew, arrowleaf morning glory, meadow beauty, sea pink. Forest and marsh: lizard's tail, sawgrass, cattail, conradina.

Birds: A checklist of 280 species is keyed for seasonality and abundance. Spring is the best season for birding, especially for migratory species. Summer is the slowest season, but even then 54 species are rated "common."

Mammals: No large terrestrial mammals are common here. Small mammals on the islands include eastern cottontail, wood rats, raccoon, skunk, fox, old-field mice.

Endangered species: Special programs are seeking to reestablish several endangered species. Nests and decoys have been built to attract brown pelicans. Between 1985 and 1989, 42 bald eagles were released on Horn Island (Mississippi) with the hope they would return to nest. Captive-bred red wolves have been released on Horn Island; their offspring will be used to reestablish a wild population in North Carolina. The Perdido Key beach mouse, extirpated in Florida by a 1979 hurricane, has been reintroduced and is thriving.

FEATURES

Naval Live Oaks. At the visitor center. Live oak timber was highly prized by early shipbuilders. To assure a supply for warships, the government set aside a reservation. On a peninsula sheltered from salt spray by Santa Rosa Island, Naval Live Oaks has a great diversity of plant species. Trees include live oak, southern magnolia, southern redcedar, hickory; and slash, sand, and longleaf pines. In the understory: titi, sweetbay, holly, myrtle, blueberry. Hiking on the beach and nature trails.

Santa Rosa Island. SR 399 crosses Santa Rosa Sound on a toll bridge. On the island, turn left 7 miles to the *Santa Rosa Day Use Area,* 7½ miles of beach. Swimming, with lifeguard in summer, picnic sites, rest rooms and showers, concession. Miles of beachcombing. To the east, beyond Navarre Beach, is a beach owned by the Eglin Air Force Base (see entry).

On the island, turn right toward Fort Pickens. Beyond the entrance station are several parking areas for beach access.

Fort Pickens was built between 1829 and 1834, one of the fortifications designed to protect the Navy depot at Pensacola. Preserved, the fort is open to visitors, with an interpretive program.

The Fort Pickens area is the Seashore's principal recreation center in Florida. It includes an information station, museum, auditorium, campground, campground store, amphitheater, nature trails, fishing pier, snack bar, and swimming beach.

Perdido Key Area: Johnson Beach. Open 8 A.M. to sunset. From Pensacola, southwest on SR 292. The central area has lifeguards in summer, nature trail, rest rooms and showers, picnic shelters, small-boat launch, and snack shop. Swimming in the Gulf and Big Lagoon. Roadside parking is permitted. The island continues for 5 miles beyond the end of the paved road. Access is by foot or boat only. Primitive camping is permitted here, but a ranger must be informed if a car is parked overnight.

ACTIVITIES

Camping: Fort Pickens area: 200 sites; no reservations. Primitive hike-in camping on Perdido Key; notify a ranger. In Mississippi, primitive camping is permitted on East Ship, Horn, and Petit Bois islands. Inquire.

Hiking: Trails and beaches. Keep off the dunes.

Fishing: From shore except in swimming areas. Fishing pier at Fort Pickens.

Swimming: In summer, swimming in protected areas is recommended. Rip tides can occur.

Boating: The only small-craft ramp is at Davis Bayou, in Mississippi.

INTERPRETATION

Visitor centers are at Naval Live Oaks, Fort Pickens, Fort Barrancas. Guided walks, auditorium programs, exhibits, literature.

Museum at Fort Pickens.

Nature trails at Naval Live Oaks, Fort Pickens, Fort Barrancas, Perdido Key.

PUBLICATIONS

Seashore leaflet with map.

The Gulf Islands Barnacle. Seasonal activities information. Activities schedules.

Camping on a Wilderness Island.

Area information pages:

Naval Live Oaks.

Santa Rosa.

Fort Barrancas.

Advanced Redoubt.

Concrete Batteries.

Fort Pickens.

Fort Pickens camping information.

Perdido Key Area.

Natural history pages:

Nature Trails.

Wildflowers and Barrier Island Plants.

Birds.

Insects: Masters of Survival.

Saving Endangered Species.

HEADQUARTERS: 1801 Gulf Breeze Parkway, Gulf Breeze, FL 32561; (904) 934-2600.

HICKORY MOUND UNIT, BIG BEND WILDLIFE MANAGEMENT AREA

Florida Game and Fresh Water Fish Commission

14,427 acres.   Map 51, D-3.

From Perry, about 10 miles west on US 98. See sign. South 6 miles.

Just west of the Unit boundary, SR 14 ends at a fish camp on the Econfina River. Beyond is the St. Marks National Wildlife Refuge. Between the Unit and the Gulf of Mexico is the marsh buffer of the Big Bend Aquatic Preserve.

The chief attraction of the WMA is the 1,600-acre Hickory Mound impoundment, to the right at the end of Cow Creek Road in from US 98. This, we were told, is the largest brackish impoundment on the Gulf Coast, attracting large numbers of migratory waterfowl in season as well as many wading and shorebirds, spring through summer. Crabbing is excellent in the impoundment.

Before visiting call headquarters to make sure the impoundment isn't in a drawdown phase.

PUBLICATION: Leaflet with map.

HEADQUARTERS: Florida Game and Fresh Water Fish Commission, Northeast Region, RFD 7 Box 440, Lake City, FL 32055; (904) 758-0525.

HOLMES CREEK CANOE TRAIL
16 miles.   Map 30, C-3.

From SR 79 north in Vernon, take dirt road ¼ mile east to Vernon Wayside Park.

Spring-fed Holmes Creek meanders between high sandy banks and through scenic hardwood swampland. Most of the bordering land is undeveloped or agricultural. Gentle curves don't tax a paddler's skill, but the slow-moving current doesn't offer a free ride.

Alternate take-outs or put-ins are at miles 9 and 10. Or one can launch at Cypress Springs, 3 miles upstream. The run ends at Live Oak Landing, 2½ miles from New Hope. Holmes Creek joins the Choctawhatchee River.

It's a beautiful river but plagued by pollution: inadequately treated sewage from four towns and runoff from cropland and hog farms.

PUBLICATION: *Holmes Creek Canoe Trail.* Division of Recreation and Parks.

JOE BUDD WILDLIFE MANAGEMENT AREA
Florida Game and Fresh Water Fish Commission
7,383 acres.   Map 50, A-1.

From I-10 west of Tallahassee, exit west on US 90. In 2.1 miles, turn left on CR 268. In 2.4 miles, turn left on High Bluff Road (see sign).

This WMA is popular with hunters because of its high deer population. Budd Pond (20 acres) attracts fishermen. Few nonconsumptive visitors use the site, a situation the Commission hopes to change.

Most of the site was owned by the Florida Power Company. The Budd family had hunting, fishing, and grazing rights and owned 794 acres adjoining. The power company had leased timber rights to the St. Joe Paper Company. Notified that the State would acquire the site in 1977 when their lease expired, the paper company logged off almost everything but young pine plantations. Six small natural hardwood tracts remained. Under State ownership, the Division of Forestry undertook reforestation with slash and longleaf pine. The Commission manages wildlife.

The WMA is on the north shore of Lake Talquin (see entry). Its west boundary is Little River. From the lake shore at 70 feet above sea level, the land rises steeply to about 115 feet. The terrain is then gently rolling, the highest point about 150 feet. Several small creeks drain the area. Most of the hardwoods are along these drainages.

Few hikers and birders use the site. Except at Budd Pond, it is usually deserted outside hunting seasons. Little has been done to publicize it or to provide on-site information. An environmental center was built at Budd Pond, but it has been used chiefly for hunter safety courses and administrative purposes. A hiking trail built by volunteers was abandoned for lack of use. No ramp or other facilities are at the lake shore.

We were told recreation leaflets will eventually be prepared for most WMAs. Such a leaflet with a good map, recognizable boundary markers, and hiking trails would make the site more attractive to visitors.

ACTIVITIES

Camping: A primitive camp at High Bluff Road landing is jointly managed with Gadsden County. The Commission plans to close the site to camping except in hunting season. No other camping facility is proposed.

Hiking: Unpaved roads, old logging roads, and hunter trails.

Hunting: Deer, hog, squirrel, quail, rabbit.

Fishing: Bluegill, largemouth bass.

PUBLICATION: Hunting leaflet with map.

HEADQUARTERS: Florida Game and Fresh Water Fish Commission, Northwest Region, 6938 Highway 2321, Panama City, FL 32409; (904) 265-3676.

LAKE SEMINOLE
U.S. Army Corps of Engineers
37,500 water acres.   Maps 32, 33.

From Chattahoochee, west on US 90 to SR 271, then north.

The Jim Woodruff Lock and Dam was built on the Apalachicola River just below the junction of the Chattahoochee and Flint rivers. The project made the Chattahoochee and Flint rivers, now comprising portions of the Inland Waterway, navigable by commercial vessels from the Gulf of Mexico to Columbus and Bainbridge, Georgia.

Only the western half of the impoundment is in Florida. All access to this side is from SR 271. Looking at a map before our visit, we wondered why there was so little development between SR 271 and the lake. Driving the route told us. From the Three Rivers State Recreation Area (see entry) until it turns away from the lake, SR 271 is on an embankment with wetlands on both sides: open water, potholes, sloughs, shallows studded with snags, grass and cattail marshes, and swamp forest. Most of the Corps property, leased to the Florida Game and Fresh Water Fish Commission, is the 7,952-acre Apalachee Wildlife Management Area.

A wide strip of maintained grass is on both sides of the highway embankment. One can pull off the right-of-way to picnic, fish, or hike. Traffic is light and the birding good.

ACTIVITIES

Camping: At Three Rivers State Recreation Area and Corps accesses: Parramore Landing, Buena Vista Access Area, and Neal's Landing.

Hiking: Along the embankment. Entrances to the WMA are marked, and unimproved roads offer hiking routes.

Hunting: Deer, small game, some waterfowl.

Fishing: The lake offers excellent fishing for largemouth, hybrid, striped, and white bass, plus catfish, crappie, bream.

Boating: Ramps at Three Rivers SRA, U.S. Army Corps accesses. A fish camp at Parramore Landing has boat rentals, supplies.

PUBLICATIONS

U.S. Army Corps of Engineers brochure.

Apalachee WMA hunting leaflet (Florida Game and Fresh Water Fish Commission).

HEADQUARTERS: U.S. Army Corps of Engineers, P.O. Box 96, Chattahoochee, FL 32324; (909) 663-2291.

LAKE TALQUIN
8,850 acres.   Maps 49, A-3; 50, A-1.

West of Tallahassee. South shore access from SR 20.

The lake was formed in 1928 by damming the Ochlockonee River. Its northern shoreline is irregular, the impoundment having drowned numerous streams. The lake is shallow except at the old river channel, where depths range up to 50 feet. The dam broke in 1957 and was rebuilt. In the late 1940s water hyacinths spread over 3,000 acres. Chemicals were used to suppress their growth.

The lake is used chiefly by fishermen. The fishery is managed by the Florida Game and Fresh Water Fish Commission, which has eliminated "undesirable" fish species and stocked the lake. Game species include largemouth bass, bluegill, crappie, and striped bass.

As in many man-made lakes, dead vegetation and silt accumulate on the bottom, water quality declines, aquatic vegetation dies, and fishing suffers. In 1983 and again in 1990 the Commission dropped the water level about 17 feet, exposing much of the lake bottom. As the muck dried, it was seeded and the lake gradually refilled.

Surrounding public lands provide opportunities for camping, hiking, hunting, horse riding, and nature study. At several points where we hiked through forests toward the lake, we came to bluffs. Between them and open water is a wide band of wetlands.

Land ownership around the lake is a mixture of State, county, and private holdings. Lake Talquin State Forest has 13,280 acres. Overlapping are several Wildlife Management Areas (WMAs). The Commission leaflet shows the locations of eight public ramps and fish camps, four on each side of the lake. Sites on the south side are easier to find, all on side roads off SR 20, most of them marked at the highway. Those on the north are on secondary roads, paved and unpaved, off SRs 26 and 268. The Commission's Lake Talquin leaflet has the best map of the area we've seen.

See the entries for the Lake Talquin SRA and the Talquin and Joe Budd WMAs. Other publicly owned sites include the following:

- *Coe's Landing,* off SR 20, 7 miles from Tallahassee. A Leon County park with campground, picnic area, fishing pier, boat ramp. No swimming.
- *Williams Landing,* off SR 20, 11 miles from Tallahassee. A Leon County park with camping, ramp, dock, fishing, pier, picnic area.
- *Hall's Landing,* off SR 20, 14 miles from Tallahassee. A Leon County park with primitive campsites (no RVs), picnic area, observation boardwalk, ramp, fishing pier, picnic area.

- *Hopkins Landing,* on the north shore. From SR 20 west of the Ochlockonee River, north 2½ miles on SR 267, right on Hopkins Landing Road. Camping, ramp, dock, picnic area. A Gadsden County park.

PUBLICATION: *Lake Talquin.* Leaflet with map. Florida Game and Fresh
  Water Fish Commission, Northwest Region, 6938 Highway 2321, Panama
  City, FL 32409; (904) 265-3676.

LAKE TALQUIN STATE RECREATION AREA
Division of Recreation and Parks,
Division of Forestry
19,600 land acres.   Map 49, A-3.

From SR 20, 12 miles west of Tallahassee, north on Jack Vause Road.

The Division of Recreation and Parks manages only River Bluff, a small
tract off Jack Vause Road. Most of the site is managed by the Division of
Forestry, with the Game and Fresh Water Fish Commission managing the
wildlife.

River Bluff has a nature trail, observation boardwalk, fishing pier, and
picnic area. It is open 8 A.M. to sunset.

The 19,600 acres are part of a 640,000-acre block of public land. On the
south is the Apalachicola National Forest (see entry). On the northeast is
the Joe Budd Wildlife Management Area (see entry), on the west the Robert
Brent Wildlife Management Area. Nearby, northwest of the lake, is the 465-
acre Bear Creek SRA, not yet open to the public.

The Lake Talquin SRA has no boat ramps. (See Lake Talquin entry for
lake access points.) Indeed, there are few places where a hiker could reach
the lake shore dry-shod. Except at River Bluff, the SRA has no trails or
other recreational facilities. No maps have been published, so hikers must
find their own way on old woods roads and hunter trails.

At first glance the Lake Talquin SRA looks like many other cut-over sites
with regenerating forests. However, it has special qualities the planners are
considering. The terrain is gently rolling, with stream-cut ravines that widen
near the lake. Other physical features include bluffs, shoreline slopes, and
floodplain. Together with a number of soil types, these support 21 distinct
biological communities. In the planning process, state biologists have studied
the flora and fauna of each.

Sandhill communities occupy 5,924 acres of the Talquin SRA. Most have
been logged and planted with slash pine. Development of pine forest depends

on periodic fires to reduce hardwood competition. For some time, fires have been suppressed.

Upland hardwood forests occupy 2,273 acres. These are typically young and in poor condition.

Slope forests, rare in Florida, occupy 2,300 acres, chiefly at the edge of the lake or its floodplain. Parts of this intermediate zone between bottomland and upland forest have been damaged. Those remaining will be protected.

Floodplain hardwood forest, frequently inundated, largely pristine, occupies 1,435 acres along the river upstream from the lake.

Bottomland forest, also largely hardwoods, occupies 1,348 acres, what remains after the lake filled. This forest is also largely pristine.

Other communities of interest include bluff, mesic flatwoods, xeric hammock, baygall, floodplain swamp, basin swamp, dome, wet flatwoods, depression marsh, marsh lake, river floodplain lake, swamp lake, blackwater stream, seepage stream, and alluvial stream. Of these, bluff and seepage stream are rare in Florida and are marked for protection.

To enjoy the natural qualities of such a diversified area, one need not remember these names or learn their special characteristics. Walking along a forest trail, one can see the changing patterns of tree and understory species as soils, moisture, and slopes change. Each community has its special assortment of seasonal wildflowers, and each attracts and nurtures an array of birds and other wildlife. So far 154 bird species, 28 mammals, and 90 reptiles and amphibians have been observed.

We expect some development of recreation facilities and publication of a map within the next few years.

PUBLICATION: River Bluff leaflet.

HEADQUARTERS: Star Route 1, Box 2222, Tallahassee, FL 32310; (904) 576-8233.

OCHLOCKONEE RIVER (LOWER) CANOE TRAIL
63 miles.   Maps 49, 61.

First put-in at SR 20 bridge, 22 miles west of Tallahassee.

The lower Ochlockonee flows from the dam at Lake Talquin (see entry) to Ochlockonee Bay. The river is relatively pristine, almost entirely within the Apalachicola National Forest (see entry), although there are many inholdings. The final take-out is at Ochlockonee River State Park (see entry). We recommend carrying the National Forest map as well as the Canoe Trail folder.

No developed launch area is at the SR 20 bridge. Roadside parking is available, and it's an easy carry down.

Under normal conditions, it's an undemanding, quiet run. In two days on the river, spring and fall, we met no other boats and few of the cottages along the way were occupied.

The river meanders at two to three miles per hour through a variety of habitats: high bluffs with loblolly pine, magnolia, beech, and oak; pine flatwoods; cypress swamps; quiet sloughs. Wildlife is abundant, as are seasonal wildflowers.

Five take-outs or alternate put-ins are at intervals of 5 to 14 miles between SR 20 and the State Park. We camped at Pine Creek Landing, a National Forest campground at mile 13. It has a ramp. It's the only such campground on the trail, but one can camp anywhere in a National Forest, and numerous informal sites are available.

Because its flow depends chiefly on rainfall, the river's level varies more than if it were spring-fed. The current is swifter at high water, requiring somewhat more paddling skill. In periods of drought, sandbars and snags may require pullovers and portages. Water releases from the dam are not announced, but one can telephone for information: (904) 576-2572.

Nearing the State Park, the river widens and motor craft are encountered more often.

PUBLICATION: *Ochlockonee River (Lower) Canoe Trail.* Division of Recreation and Parks.

OCHLOCKONEE RIVER STATE PARK
Division of Recreation and Parks
392 acres.   Map 50, D-1.

From Sopchoppy, 4 miles south on US 319.

This small riverside park was once part of the adjoining St. Marks National Wildlife Refuge. It is bounded on three sides by rivers: the Ochlockonee and the Dead rivers, and Big Tide Creek. It is the end of the Ochlockonee River (Lower) Canoe Trail (see entry) and near the river's mouth. The site has oak thickets, small ponds, and bayheads. There is a short nature trail.

The park is a strategic base for fishermen with boats. They can run upstream for freshwater species, downstream to Ochlockonee Bay and the Gulf of Mexico.

ACTIVITIES
Camping: 30 sites. Telephone reservations accepted June 1 to Labor Day.
Hiking: River trail and nature trail.
Swimming: Beach.
Canoeing: Ochlockonee River, Dead River, and Tide Creek.
Boating: Ramp.

INTERPRETATION: *Guided walks* and *campfire programs* in summer.

PUBLICATION: Leaflet with map.

HEADQUARTERS: P.O. Box 5, Sopchoppy, FL 32358; (904) 962-2771.

OCHLOCKONEE RIVER (UPPER) CANOE TRAIL
26 miles.   Map 34, C-2.

Put-in at SR 12 bridge, 8 miles east of Havana.

We haven't made this run. The river flows from Georgia to Lake Talquin
through woodlands and cypress swamps, crossing US 27 between Havana
and Tallahassee. It is narrow, shallow, often silty, and so twisting it takes
26 river miles to travel 10 crow-flight miles. It's easy paddling, current moving at 2 to 3 miles per hour.

The leaflet advises that hunting occurs in season, especially from SR 12
to US 27. From Tower Road, just below US 27, to the take-out at US 90
the river is the west boundary of the Ochlockonee River Wildlife Management Area. It seems wise to canoe elsewhere in hunting season.

The segment just below the Georgia line has poor water quality because
of farm runoff and wastewater discharges in Georgia.

Alternate put-in and take-out sites are at miles 14 and 20. Campsites are few.

PUBLICATION: *Ochlockonee River (Upper) Canoe Trail.* Division of Recreation and Parks.

PERDIDO KEY STATE RECREATION AREA
Division of Recreation and Parks
247 acres.   Map 42, B-1.

15 miles southwest of Pensacola on SR 292.

Perdido Key is a long, narrow barrier island. Its eastern half encloses Big Lagoon. On its western half, the SRA has 1½ miles of shoreline on the Gulf of Mexico, another 1½ miles on saltwater Old River. The SRA is between resort developments.

The white sand Gulf beach is 100 to 170 feet wide. Along it are low vegetated dunes, the highest 25 feet above sea level. Back of the dunes are long strands of slash pine with live oak and wax myrtle. On the river side are tidal marshes, some with solid masses of black rush.

Before State ownership, the SRA site was unprotected, littered with junk and garbage, dune vegetation destroyed by off-road vehicles. Those abuses have been remedied, but trails through the dunes have been worn by visitors parking along SR 292.

The site offers good birding, especially during spring migration.

PUBLICATION: Leaflet with map.

HEADQUARTERS: c/o Big Lagoon State Recreation Area, 12301 Gulf Beach Highway, Pensacola, FL 32507; (904) 492-1595.

PERDIDO RIVER CANOE TRAIL
24 miles.   Map 25, B-3.

Three Runs put-in: From CR 99 at Bay Springs (Map 26, B-1) take CR 97A west and north 4½ miles. West 2½ miles on Pineville Road to first dirt road on left beyond Brushy Creek bridge.

The Perdido River is near the Florida–Alabama border. The river is clear, flowing at 2 to 3 miles an hour over a white sand bottom. It's easy paddling. Unless a log jam on the upper section has been cleared, one portage is necessary.

The river, joined along the trail by numerous creeks, flows through pine/cypress forest. It's remote, mostly forested, with little riparian development. Florida public lands along the route include the Perdido Key State Recreation Area (see entry), Muscogee Boat Ramp and Muscogee Landing, and La Floresta Perdida Wildlife Management Area.

Alternate take-outs are at miles 5 and 15. The final take-out is at Muscogee Bridge on CR 84.

No guns or dogs are allowed on the Alabama side.

PUBLICATION: *Perdido River Canoe Trail.* Division of Recreation and Parks.

PINE LOG STATE FOREST
Division of Forestry
6,911 acres.   May 46, A-1.

From US 98 at Panama City Beach, north about 7 miles on SR 79. Environmental Center and campground are in the northwest corner of the Forest.

The forest, flat to gently rolling, is drained chiefly by Little Crooked Creek and Pine Log Creek, tributary to the Choctawhatchee River.

When the site was acquired in 1936, it had been cut over and repeatedly burned. By 1940, a few small tracts were planted with pines. With more plantings in 1948–1950 and 1958–1961, most of the suitable land was in slash, sand, and longleaf pine. Other species present include turkey oak, blackjack oak, titi, cypress, red maple, sweetgum, blackgum, juniper, sweetbay, and magnolia.

Replanting completed, management was broadened to include wildlife, recreation, and education. Wildlife management became the responsibility of the Florida Game and Fresh Water Fish Commission. An environmental center with an open-air pavilion is staffed by a ranger. Recreation activities center around a cluster of small lakes in the northwest corner.

Visitation is light to moderate. About half of the visitors come from nearby. Camping and picnicking are their chief activities, hunting, hiking, and bird watching each representing about one-tenth of the visitor-days.

ACTIVITIES

Camping: 20 sites. No reservations. Seldom full.

Hiking, backpacking: Crossed by 8 miles of the Florida Trail. Also a 3-mile trail loop and Forest roads.

Hunting: Deer, turkey, quail.

Fishing: Bass, panfish, catfish.

Swimming: Lake.

Boating, canoeing: Ramp on Pine Log Creek. We haven't canoed here. The Forest map shows the creek to be intermittent, but headquarters staff told us the creek is canoeable to the Choctawhatchee River all year.

PUBLICATION: Leaflet with map.

HEADQUARTERS: Division of Forestry, 715 West 15th St., Panama City, FL 32401; (904) 872-4175.

PONCE DE LEON SPRINGS STATE RECREATION AREA
Division of Recreation and Parks
443 acres.   Map 30, C-1.

In the town of Ponce de Leon on SR 181A.

Open 8 A.M. to sunset.

More than half of this attractive small park is maintained as a natural area.
Swimmers dress at a bathhouse next to the parking area. The famous spring,
surrounded by a wall since 1926, gushes 14 million gallons of water per
day at a constant 68°F. Beside the spring-fed stream are two loop trails
through maturing forest, a mix of oak, pine, holly, magnolia, sweetgum,
and blackgum, some with 30-inch diameters.

The park leaflet says that catfish, largemouth bass, chain pickerel, and
panfish reward the "patient angler."

PUBLICATION: Leaflet with map.

HEADQUARTERS: Route 5, Box 660, Chipley, FL 32428; (904) 638-6130.

ROCKY BAYOU (FRED GANNON) STATE RECREATION AREA
Division of Recreation and Parks
357 acres.   Map 28, D-3.

From Niceville, 3 miles southeast on SR 20.

The site is on a peninsula separating Rocky Bayou from Choctawhatchee
Bay. Away from main traffic routes, the SRA has less than 40,000 visitors
a year, many from nearby Niceville. On a fine sunny day in October, we
were alone there.

From the bayou shore, the terrain slopes up to the 35-foot contour. Within
a relatively small area are several interesting natural communities. Most of
the visitor facilities are within the pine flatwoods. Adjoining are areas of
sand pine scrub and estuarine tidal marsh. The SRA has about 7,000 feet
of shoreline on the Bayou, 5,600 feet on Puddinhead Lake, a long narrow
impoundment formed by an old earth dam. The SRA adjoins the Eglin Air
Force Base (see entry).

ACTIVITIES
Camping: 42 sites. No reservations.
Fishing: Saltwater fishing in bayou, freshwater fishing at Rocky Creek.
Swimming: Unsupervised.
Boating: Ramp.

INTERPRETATION
Three nature trails visit the several habitats.
Guided walks and *evening programs* are offered occasionally.

PUBLICATIONS
SRA leaflet. (Out of print when we visited.)
Sand Pine Nature Trail guide.
Information pages:
  Seaweed.
  Nesting Shorebirds.

HEADQUARTERS: Route 1, P.O. Box 597, Niceville, FL 32578; (904) 897-3222.

ST. ANDREWS STATE RECREATION AREA
Division of Recreation and Parks
1,063 acres.   Map 46, C-3.

On the Panama City beach at the southeast end of SR 392.

The Panama City beach is a typical congested seaside resort, high-rise condos
and motels side by side, parking and beach access limited for day visitors.
This visual hullabaloo stops abruptly at the SRA entrance. To be sure, it's
one of the State's most popular parks, with over 30,000 summer visitors,
but skillful planning has maintained many of its natural qualities. Most visitors come to enjoy the beach, which is constantly renewed by tide and storm.
Once the swimming season ends, it's a quiet place, at least on weekdays.
   The SRA is on the tip of a peninsula that has the shape of a barrier island,
lying between the Gulf of Mexico and Grand Lagoon. Back of the white
sand beaches are rolling dunes, stabilized by sea oats, interspersed with pine
flatwoods and marshes. Older dunes farther inland are overgrown with sand
pine, scrub oak, rosemary, and other salt-tolerant plants.
   The entrance road curves back of the dunes, a short spur leading to one
beach area, a longer one to a second near the jetty on the inlet. Camping
is on Grand Lagoon.
Pine Flatwoods Nature Trail passes through the several habitats, including

good birding areas. Indicators of past activities here include a turpentine still and gun mounts.

Wildlife: Checklist of vertebrates includes 219 recorded bird species, noting seasonality and abundance. Relatively few mammals reside here, these including marsh and cottontail rabbits, squirrel, beaver, red fox, raccoon, striped skunk. The list includes whitetail deer, although we saw no signs and suitable habitat seems too limited. Also listed are numerous reptiles and amphibians.

ACTIVITIES
   Camping: 176 sites. Telephone reservations accepted.
   Fishing: One fishing pier on the Gulf, another on the lagoon. Also jetty and surf fishing.
   Boating: Ramp on Grand Lagoon.

PUBLICATIONS
   Leaflet with map.
   Wildlife checklist.
   Nature trail guide.

NEARBY: *Shell Island,* across the inlet, is undeveloped, with natural qualities similar to those of the SRA. A small passenger ferry operates occasionally from the SRA.

HEADQUARTERS: 4415 Thomas Drive, Panama City, FL 32408; (904) 234-2522.

ST. GEORGE ISLAND STATE PARK
(Also called Dr. Julian D. Bruce St. George Island State Park)
Division of Recreation and Parks
1,963 acres.   Map 61, C-1.

From US 98 at East Point, south across bridge and causeway.

Open 8 A.M. to sundown.

Approaching the island on the causeway, one is tempted to turn back. Ahead is a seemingly unbroken line of beach resort development. That ends, however, at the park gate. Like many Gulf beaches, the park attracts most of its visitors in summer. Although attendance figures show about 10,000 October visitors, none were present when we arrived on a sunny Wednesday.
   The 29-mile-long narrow barrier island, largest of the chain enclosing Apalachicola Bay and St. George Sound, is an accumulation of sands deposited

by wind and wave, ever changing. The park, occupying 8½ miles at the east end of the island, has more than 25 miles of undeveloped shoreline on the Gulf and Sound. The Gulf beach is relatively straight. On the Sound side are peninsulas, coves, two small islands, and reefs.

The park, one writer declared, "contains pristine examples of beautifully preserved natural domain." That's the way it looks, a reminder that barrier beach ecology is fragile but also resilient. Great storms sweep away past sins, giving nature another chance.

The island was a cattle ranch. Its trees were tapped for turpentine. It was used for military training in the early 1940s. The present park site was a bombing range. Developers arrived in 1954. Their demand for a causeway succeeded in 1965. Then dune buggies and 4-wheel-drive vehicles roamed the island, destroying dune vegetation. The state began land acquisition in 1973 in time to block development on the eastern end.

Back of the Gulf beach are low dunes, few more than 10 feet high. Older dunes, farther back, are 15 to 30 feet high and have more vegetative cover. Gap Point, a large peninsula, has elevations up to 21 feet, its plant communities including forests of pine and oak, rosemary scrub, and salt marsh.

Planners put the park road just back of the front dunes and designated most of the area beyond, especially on Gap Point, a protected zone. Here any development, including a foot trail, is planned so as not to promote erosion or disturb wildlife. The park's 17 biological communities have 13 rare species of flora and fauna.

Birds: An annotated checklist of 241 species is available. For spring migrants crossing the Gulf, St. George Island is first landfall after a long flight. Then and on their fall return, birding is outstanding. Occasionally there is a "crash," when the spring migration confronts rain and wind; thousands then alight on the island for food and rest.

Fewer birds are present in summer, but snowy plover and gray kingbird are among the 39 species known to nest here. During the winter large numbers of waterfowl can be seen in the waters around the park.

Other wildlife: The island attracts the largest numbers of nesting loggerhead turtles in the northern Gulf of Mexico. This is a management problem, since they nest during the height of the visitor season. Several strategies are used: erasing crawl marks to conceal nests; protecting nests; and moving eggs to safer locations.

Few mammals live in the park. Raccoons are an occasional campground nuisance. Otters have been seen occasionally, bobcat reported. Feral cats, which kill birds, are being eliminated.

Shells: This is one of the best State Parks for shelling. An annotated checklist is available. Shells are most abundant at low tide, especially following a storm. Live shells may not be collected.

ACTIVITIES

Camping: 60 sites. Telephone reservations accepted. Reservations are needed weekends and holidays.

Hiking, backpacking: A 2½-mile trail on Gap Point leads to a primitive camp. Miles of beach walking.

Fishing: Gulf and Sound; saltwater species.

Swimming: Fine Gulf beaches.

Boating: Ramps on the Sound side.

PUBLICATIONS

Leaflet with map.

Vertebrates checklists.

Shells of St. George Island State Park.

HEADQUARTERS: P.O. Box 62, St. George Island, Eastpoint, FL 32328; (904) 927-2111.

ST. JOSEPH PENINSULA STATE PARK AND WILDERNESS PRESERVE

Division of Recreation and Parks

2,516 acres.   Map 59, B-2.

From Port St. Joe on US 98, south on SR 30 and 30A, west on SR 30E.

This slender 14-mile peninsula was once a barrier island and could become one again in the next hurricane. The road from the mainland passes a beach owned by Eglin Air Force Base, then turns north. The Park facilities are clustered at Eagle Harbor, about 10 miles from the turn.

Traveling with our Labrador, we couldn't camp at the State Park and found an attractive commercial campground on the Gulf at the base of the peninsula. Next morning we walked for miles along the beach, exploring Cape San Blas, which projects below the peninsula's elbow. Unlike Robinson Crusoe, we saw no footprints.

The Cape is best known to fishermen. For decades they have made their way to the tip, slogging through sand in 4-wheel-drive vehicles or in light autos with deflated tires. Many camp near the dunes. Shark Hole is their shared secret. A county permit is required to drive on the beach.

Driving north, St. Joseph Bay is on the right, the Gulf beyond dunes on the left. We saw many places where one can pull off and park. This is one of Florida's best coasts for solitary beachcombing.

The developed Park area straddles a narrow neck between the Gulf and Bay. Marina, boat ramp, bathhouse, picnic shelters, cabins, and overlook are at the neck. Campground, nature trails, more picnic shelters, and more overlooks are north of the neck. In this part of the peninsula the dunes are high, sea oats abundant; sand pine provides limited shade back of the dunes.

In all, the peninsula has 16 miles of beach on the Gulf, plus 7 miles of "fishable" beach on the Bay. The accent is strongly on fishing. Many of the Park campers and day visitors bring rods.

More than half of the Park visitors come in summer, attendance peaking in July.

Wildlife: Birders come here, too. Like other barrier beaches along the Gulf coast, the peninsula attracts many birds, including waves of spring migrants. Well over 200 species have been recorded. Hawk watching is good in the fall.

Mammals observed include bobcat, striped skunk, gray fox, raccoon, and whitetail deer.

In the fall is the astonishing migration of monarch butterflies. We've watched them fluttering along, seemingly aimless and unhurried, sometimes gathering on trees to await a favoring wind.

WILDERNESS PRESERVE

The 1,650-acre wilderness preserve occupies the north end of the peninsula. Here are some of the state's largest sand dunes. Communities include sand pine scrub on old dunes, slash pine flatwoods, and small freshwater marshes.

It's a 5-mile hike to St. Joseph Point, or one can make the trip by boat. Beach driving is prohibited.

The Wilderness is limited to 20 visitors per day, or one group of not more than 40. All visitors must register.

ACTIVITIES

Camping: 119 sites. Telephone reservations accepted.

Hiking, backpacking: Primitive camping is permitted anywhere in the Wilderness except on sand dunes and in sand pine scrub.

Boating: Ramp and boat basin.

In summer, bring repellent.

INTERPRETATION

Nature trails are near the entrance station, picnic area, and camping area.

Campfire programs and *guided walks* are offered seasonally.

PUBLICATIONS

Park leaflet with map.
Wilderness leaflet with map.
Vertebrates checklist.

HEADQUARTERS: Star Route 1, Box 200, Port St. Joe, FL 32456; (904) 227-1327.

ST. MARKS NATIONAL WILDLIFE REFUGE
U.S. Fish and Wildlife Service
65,248 land acres;
32,000 acres of Apalachee Bay within boundaries.   Map 50, D-1, 3.

To visitor center: From US 98 near Newport, south on SR 59.

Open daylight hours.

The Refuge sprawls for about 40 crow-flight miles along Apalachee Bay, many more miles of actual shoreline. It extends from the Ochlockonee River on the west to the Aucilla River on the east. In few places is the boundary more than 3 miles inland. Established in 1931, it's one of the oldest federal wildlife refuges.

We suggest going first to the visitor center. Its dioramas and other presentations are a fine introduction not only to the Refuge but to the complex ecosystems of all such areas on the Gulf Coast.

SR 59, the road most visitors travel, passes the visitor center and ends after seven miles at St. Marks lighthouse, built in 1831 and still operational. Other roads that penetrate, cross, or skirt portions of the Refuge are—from east to west—SR 365, 367, and 367A; US 98; and SR 372, 372A, and 372B. Much of the Refuge is accessible only on foot, by bicycle, or by boat. Here it offers some of the most exciting and diversified hiking of any wildlife area in Florida.

Back of the extensive salt marshes are cypress and gum swamps, old-growth hardwood forests, beech/magnolia groves, cabbage palm and live oak hammocks, and forests of longleaf pine and turkey oak. Each of these habitats attracts and supports an array of wildlife. Salt marshes are a nursery for fish, shrimp, and shellfish. Hardwood swamps are nesting grounds for wood ducks and night-herons, shelter for black bears, otters, and raccoons. Whitetail deer, wild turkeys, fox squirrels, and pine warblers favor the pine forests. Freshwater impoundments produce fish and support waterfowl.

The Refuge has about 28,000 acres of salt marshes, 33,000 acres of forest land, 2,000 acres of artificial impoundments, and 1,000 acres of natural lakes and ponds. Of the woodlands, almost two-thirds are predominantly pine, one-third bottomland and upland hardwoods.

Part of the Refuge's marsh and forest communities are managed to enhance wildlife habitats. Miles of dikes impound fresh water for wintering waterfowl. However, on both sides of SR 59 are Wilderness Areas, totaling 18,000 acres, where all interference with nature is prohibited.

Mounds 2,000 years old are evidence of Indian settlements. Fort San Marcos de Apalachee, built by Spaniards in 1679, was at various times garrisoned by pirates, the British, and by both Confederate and Union forces in the Civil War. It is now a State museum. Still visible are the remains of salt vats used by the Confederates. Active for 150 years was the West Goose Creek Seine Yard, where mullet were seined from October through January; it was closed, perhaps temporarily, in 1991.

Plants: No plant list has been published, but exhibits and other information at the visitor center identify the trees and flowering plants the visitor may see.

Birds: St. Marks is noted for the great number of species that occur here, not for large populations of any species. Over 300 species have been recorded, more than 270 of them often enough to be considerd part of the region's fauna. Almost 100 species have nested on the Refuge.

Fall and spring are peak seasons for both variety and numbers. Waterfowl viewing is best from mid-November through December. Shorebirds are most abundant in late spring and early fall.

Ask rangers at the visitor center where to look for birds of special interest, such as red-cockaded woodpecker.

The *Calendar of Wildlife Events* tells, month by month, what to look for. For example, "JULY . . . Large flocks of white ibis, Eastern kingbirds and purple martins noted along Lighthouse Road. Wood storks are often seen in Headquarters Pond."

Mammals: Checklist notes abundance and preferred habitats. Of the 50 species occurring on the Refuge, 16 are rated common, 27 uncommon, others rare. A number of the common species are nocturnal. Mammals are best seen early and late in the day.

Reptiles: Checklist notes abundance, preferred habitats, descriptions, and in some cases habits. Of 18 turtle species, 12 are rated common; of 10 lizards, all but 1 are common; of 33 snakes, 26 are common.

Amphibians: Checklist notes abundance, preferred habitats, descriptions, and, in some cases, habits. Illustrations show a few species, tadpoles, and eggs the visitor might see. Of 33 species, 29 are rated common.

FEATURES

Freshwater pools, on SR 59 near headquarters. The dikes are open for hiking all year, daylight hours. Stoney Bayou trail is 6 miles. Deep Creek trail, 12 miles, is on the route of the Florida Trail.

St. Marks Lighthouse, at the end of SR 59, is open to visitors occasionally. Near the lighthouse are a mile-long nature trail, exhibits, observation tower, and 24-hour boat ramp.

Otter Lake Recreation Area is at the west end of SR 372A. Two primitive trails circle the lake, one 5 miles long, the other 9. Fishing; boat ramp; picnic area.

ACTIVITIES
Camping: None in the Refuge. Newport Park, a primitive State Forest campground, is on US 98 just east of SR 59; it is often full in hunting season. Ochlockonee River State Park (see entry) adjoins the Refuge on the west.
Hiking: A 35-mile segment of the Florida Trail crosses the Refuge. The guidebook of the Florida Trail Association, *Walking the Florida Trail,* has a detailed description. The Refuge is the southern terminus of the Tallahassee–St. Marks Historic Railroad State Trail (see entry), Florida's first rails-to-trails project. Many other trails; inquire.
Hunting: In designated areas, subject to special regulations. Consult headquarters.
Fishing: Freshwater, in areas designated by signs, subject to Refuge regulations; saltwater, commercial fishing and sports netting are prohibited in Refuge waters.
Boating, canoeing: Boats and canoes are permitted in Refuge pools from March 15 to October 15. Motors limited to 10 hp.
Ramps at Otter Lake, Wakulla Beach, lighthouse, Stoney Bayou Pool Number 1, and East River Pool.

Pets are permitted, on leash.

PUBLICATIONS
Refuge folder with map.
Calendar of Wildlife Events.
Bird checklist.
Mammals checklist.
Reptiles checklist.
Amphibians checklist.
Nature checklist for children.
Mounds Interpretive Trail guide.
Map of primitive walking trails.
Fishing regulations and map.
Nearby campground information.
St. Marks Lighthouse.
Lighthouse Road drive guide.

NEARBY: On the east, the Refuge adjoins the Aucilla Wildlife Management Area (see entry).

HEADQUARTERS: P.O. Box 68, St. Marks, FL 32355; (904) 925-6121.

ST. VINCENT NATIONAL WILDLIFE REFUGE
U.S. Fish and Wildlife Service
12,358 acres.   Map 60, C-1.

Island, southwest of Apalachicola. Private boat access only. Public ramp at Indian Pass, on Indian Peninsula, end of SR 30B.

Daylight hours only.

St. Vincent is one of several barrier islands enclosing Apalachicola Bay. In the 1940s a temporary bridge was built and much of the old-growth pine logged. In 1948 new owners introduced an array of exotic species: sambar deer, zebra, eland, blackbuck, ringneck pheasant, and Asian jungle fowl. All lived free. Some found the habitat suitable and reproduced.

We first saw the island when it was offered to and politely declined by the Smithsonian Institution. In 1968 The Nature Conservancy bought the island, acting for and later repaid by the U.S. Fish and Wildlife Service. Removal of the exotic wildlife was an initial objective, no easy task since junglelike second growth covered much of the island. A few sambar deer remain. Management policy is now minimum interference with natural processes.

The island is triangular, nine miles long, four miles wide at the east end. The highest elevation is 20 feet. Habitats include dense saw palmetto cover, pine flatwoods, scrub oak ridges, cabbage palm and magnolia hammocks, freshwater marshes. Two bayous, the larger three miles long, penetrate the east half of the island. Here also are a number of lakes and ponds, the largest two miles long. Fourteen miles of beaches are on the Gulf and Bay. The island is cross-hatched by 80 miles of unmaintained sand roads.

Two-thirds of the visitors come to hunt and fish. Even in the hunting and fishing seasons, few people are on the beaches. At other times it's a quiet place.

Birds: Over 183 species recorded, chiefly during spring migration. Checklist is available.

ACTIVITIES

Hunting: Managed hunts, in three 5-day periods. Permit required. Game species are whitetail and sambar deer, feral pig, raccoon.

Fishing: Freshwater season: May 15 to September 30.

Swimming: At your own risk.

Boating: Indian Pass crossing is ¼ mile. Access to freshwater bodies at east end is a 9-mile crossing from Apalachicola. Only electric motors are permitted on ponds; others must be dismounted and locked.

Pets are prohibited. All motor vehicles are prohibited. Camping is permitted only during managed hunts.

PUBLICATIONS
  Refuge folder with map.
  Hunting regulations.
  Fishing regulations.

HEADQUARTERS: P.O. Box 447, Apalachicola, FL 32320; (904) 653-8808.

SHOAL RIVER CANOE TRAIL
27 miles.   Map 29, B-1.

From US 90 west of De Funiak Springs, north 3½ miles on SR 285. Access at bridge.

The only major tributary of Yellow River (see entry), Shoal River drains some of Florida's highest land. The canoeist sees few intrusions on a natural area of forest and wetlands. Flowing at 2 to 3 miles per hour except at high water, the river meanders but demands no technical skill of paddlers. It's a sand-bottomed creek with clear tan water.

Above the I-10 crossing, the river has cut a deep valley. The channel is narrow and usually only a few feet deep. It widens as the river nears the Yellow.

Eglin Air Force Base borders the river for several miles.

PUBLICATION: *Shoal River Canoe Trail.* Division of Recreation and Parks. (Not available when we inquired.)

SWEETWATER AND JUNIPER CREEKS CANOE TRAIL
13 miles.   Map 27, B-3.

Put-in at bridge on SR 4, 1½ miles east of Munson. Munson is north of Milton on SR 191.

The creeks are in the Blackwater River State Forest (see entry). The run begins on Sweetwater Creek, narrow, winding, fairly swift. Intermediate skill is advisable here, plus checking conditions after a heavy rain. Juniper Creek is wider, slower. Water is somewhat tannin-stained, flowing over sandy bottom.

Possible take-outs or alternate put-ins are at the 2- and 7-mile points. Several outfitters serve the route with canoes and shuttles.

PUBLICATION: *Sweetwater/Juniper Creeks Canoe Trail*. Division of Recreation and Parks.

TALLAHASSEE–ST. MARKS
HISTORIC RAILROAD STATE TRAIL
Division of Recreation and Parks
16 miles.   Map 50, B-3, C-3.

From Tallahassee south of Capital Circle on SR 363 to St. Marks.

As railroad lines are abandoned, State and local governments, with organized citizen support, are converting them to recreation trails for hiking, biking, and horse riding. The Tallahassee–St. Marks route is the first in Florida. The legislature has authorized funds for more.

The trail is limited to the railroad's 60-foot right-of-way. Three-fifths of the trail adjoins SR 363. Railroad maintenance kept the right-of-way clear of trees and brush. In addition to the railroad's grade crossings, others may be mandated by surrounding development. Unauthorized use by motor vehicles is next to impossible to prevent.

Assets are that most of the surrounding area is, for now, undeveloped. Some is second-growth forest. For about 1¼ miles the trail adjoins the Apalachicola National Forest, and for two-thirds of that distance the forest is old-growth longleaf pine. A few short sections have a live oak canopy. The trail passes through one basin swamp, has 1,000 feet of frontage on the St. Marks River, and terminates in marshland. Management plans call for trees and other plantings to screen the trail from the highway.

The trail passes near the Wakulla Springs State Park (see entry).

TALQUIN WILDLIFE MANAGEMENT AREA
Florida Game and Fresh Water Fish Commission
2,993 acres.   Map 50, A-1.

North of SR 20, 3½ miles west of Tallahassee, just west of Geddie Road.

See entry for Lake Talquin. Most of the WMA is young pine/oak woodland with bottomland hardwoods along the lake shore, Ochlockonee River, and creek bottoms. A few beaver ponds are along the creeks. We passed one cattail pond. Hunting, chiefly for deer and turkey, is the principal visitor activity. A few hikers and birders come from nearby Tallahassee.

A box inside the marked entrance sometimes has leaflets. The interior roads are numbered and well maintained. Not shown on the map are dirt tracks and old logging roads now closed to vehicles but used by hunters and hikers.

Although the WMA has frontage on lake and river, we found no way to approach the shore without wading. Bluffs drop sharply to cypress swamp and other wet bottomlands.

Except in hunting season, it's a place for quiet, easy hiking and birding.

PUBLICATION: Leaflet with map.

HEADQUARTERS: Florida Game and Fresh Water Fish Commission, Northwest Region, 6938 Highway 2321, Panama City, FL 32409; (904) 265-3676.

THREE RIVERS STATE RECREATION AREA
Division of Recreation and Parks
683 acres.   Map 32, C-3.

From US 90 at Sneads, north one mile on SR 271.

This SRA has two miles of frontage on Lake Seminole (see entry). It occupies the highest terrain on the Florida side of the lake, rising 126 feet from lake level to the highest hills. Between the two hills and the lake are five steep-sided ravines.

The original forests were logged years ago. However, the SRA has not been cut over in the past three decades. Virtually the entire area is forested with mixed pines and hardwoods. The understory has a great variety of seasonal wildflowers.

This part of the lake is too shallow for swimming. We saw large patches of emergent vegetation 50 yards off shore.

Wildlife: No bird checklist has been published. Observations include a diversity of waterfowl, shorebirds, and upland species. Deer, fox, and bobcat are present but seldom seen. More common are squirrel, opossum, raccoon. Many reptiles have been recorded, including all the venomous species occurring in Florida. Boaters often see alligators and large snapping turtles.

ACTIVITIES
Camping: 65 sites. No reservations.
Hiking: 2-mile loop trail; nature trails.
Fishing: Fishing pier. The lake is a well-known bass fishery.
Boating: Ramp.

PUBLICATION: Leaflet with map.

HEADQUARTERS: Route 1, Box 15 A, Sneads, FL 32460; (904) 482-9006.

TORREYA STATE PARK
Division of Recreation and Parks
1,063 acres.   Map 32, D-3.

From Bristol on SR 20 (Map 48, A-3), northeast on SR 12; left on CR
1641.

The entrance road ends at a parking area. Directly ahead, on the river bluff,
is Gregory House, built by planter Jason Gregory in 1849. This was the
steamboat era on the Apalachicola, when upwards of 200 vessels carried
freight and passengers. Roads had yet to be built. The river, now also known
as the Inland Waterway, is still an important commercial navigation route.
(See entry, Apalachicola River.)

Gregory built his house across the river near his plantation landing. When
it was given to the State in 1935, the Civilian Conservation Corps moved
it here, board by board. Guided tours of the house are offered at 10 A.M.
on weekdays; at 10 A.M., 2 P.M., and 4 P.M. on weekends and holidays.

A view! Such vantage points are rare in Florida. From the Apalachicola
River bluff, we looked down at the river 150 feet below, then out to the
horizon over unbroken expanse of forest.

Hikers who complain Florida trails are too flat will find a modest challenge
here. The river is the western and northern park boundary. The high terrain is cut by deep ravines that are crossed by a 7-mile loop trail.

We had come at the best season, a ranger told us: October–December.
April and May are also good, and that's the best time for birds. Summers
are hot and buggy, winters "cold." The Division of Recreation and Parks
attendance figures show few campers in summer. Day visitors, three-fourths
of the total, show no pronounced seasonal pattern.

Plants: Also unusual is the Park's diversity of plant species. The ranger
smiled when we asked for a list. Botanists are developing one, he said, but
it's a huge undertaking. The botanists have identified over 1,000 species

thus far (hundreds are characteristic of the southern Appalachians, but unusual in Florida).

The Park was named for a tree of the yew family, the Florida torreya, and its discoverer, American botanist John Torrey. It occurs only here, along this river. Scientists are intrigued by the distribution of its close relatives. The California torreya, found only in the Torrey Pines State Reserve and on one offshore island, shares with a Florida species a sobriquet: "stinking cedar." Two other *Torreya*s are known, one in China, one in Japan.

The grounds around the house have many tall trees, chiefly pines, some with two-foot diameters.

Birds: A checklist of 140 species notes seasonality and abundance.

Mammals: The list of mammals observed includes bobcat, black bear, river otter, and whitetail deer.

Reptiles and amphibians: The long list includes, among others, 14 turtles and tortoises, 30 snakes, 19 frogs and toads. It doesn't list the alligator.

ACTIVITIES
Camping: 35 sites. No reservations.
Hiking, backpacking: The 7-mile loop is a section of the Florida Trail. Primitive campsites are along the trail for backpackers, who must register.
Boating, canoeing: No ramp or canoe access is in the Park. The river is fine for power boats, unattractive for canoeists because of rapid current and commercial traffic.

PUBLICATIONS
Leaflet with map.
Wildlife checklist.
The Gregory House.

HEADQUARTERS: Route 2, Box 70, Bristol, FL 32321; (904) 643-2674.

WACISSA RIVER CANOE TRAIL
14 miles.   Map 51, B-2.

Put-in at Wacissa Springs County Park. From Wacissa, south on SR 59. Where 59 turns west, continue straight.

This clear, spring-fed river calls for less paddling skill than the nearby Aucilla (see entry) and offers a campground at the 9-mile point. Almost all the surrounding land is swamp and hardwood hammock, much of it within the Aucilla Wildlife Management Area (see entry), giving canoeists a wilderness experience. Wildlife is abundant. The river has a large population of wading birds. Manatees are sometimes seen in the lower river.

Big Blue is the largest spring seen on the run, about 2 miles below the put-in. About 50 yards in diameter, it is one of the Wacissa Group, qualifying collectively as a first-magnitude spring with an average flow of 374 cubic feet per second.

The campground or rest stop is the Goose Pasture Recreation Area. Few people outside the county know it's there, but local residents make good use of it for camping and fishing, especially on weekends. At times the river corridor is heavily used for hunting, fishing, camping, boating, canoeing, and swimming.

The only tricky part of the run is finding the canal to the Aucilla junction. It's on the right, about a mile below Goose Pasture, almost hidden by willows. Take-out is at Nutall Rise Landing, a short but energetic paddle upstream on the Aucilla.

PUBLICATION: *Wacissa River Canoe Trail*. Division of Recreation and Parks.

YELLOW RIVER CANOE TRAIL
56 miles.   Map 28, A-2.

Put-in at Oak Grove, SR 2 bridge, 4½ miles west of SR 85.

This is one of the longest designated canoe trails in Florida. The distances between alternate take-outs are exceptionally long: 17, 19, and 20 miles. Although there is little State-owned land along the way, long sections are isolated and primitive with abundant wildlife. Eglin Air Force Base borders part of the Trail.

The Division of Recreation and Parks folder identifies no campsites, but since the run can't be made in one day canoeists improvise, remembering the banks are privately owned. Two fish camps and two local parks are on the route.

The river drains Florida's highest terrain, and its flow in the upper reaches is relatively swift, over three miles per hour, requiring some paddling skill. Here it flows between high sandy banks and hardwood forests. West of Crestview it slows and widens, meandering through cypress/gum swamps.

Southwest of Crestview, after passing under I-10, it is joined by the Shoal River (see entry, Shoal River Canoe Trail). Beyond this junction canoeists may encounter motor craft coming up from Blackwater Bay.

The last take-out, at the SR 87 bridge, is on the north boundary of Eglin Air Force Base (see entry). A permit is needed to enter the base.

PUBLICATION: *Yellow River Canoe Trail*. Division of Recreation and Parks.

ZONE 2
NORTH
FLORIDA

ZONE 2
NORTH FLORIDA

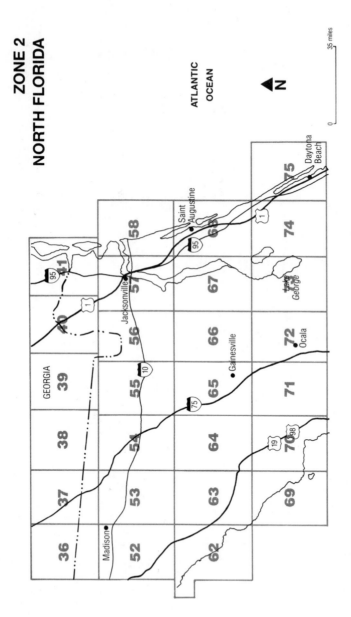

ATLANTIC OCEAN

N

0   35 miles

ENTRIES IN ZONE 2

The number preceding the natural area entry refers to the map number in the DeLorme *Florida Atlas & Gazetteer.*

37   Withlacoochee River (North) Canoe Trail
38   Suwannee River
41   Fort Clinch State Park
53   Allen Mill Pond
53   Christian Tract
53   Suwannee River State Park
54   Big Shoals Tract, Big Shoals Wildlife Management Area, Big Shoals State Forest
54   Mattair Spring Tract
55   Osceola National Forest
56   Cary State Forest
56   St. Marys River Canoe Trail
58   Guana River State Park, Guana River Wildlife Management Area
58   Little Talbot Island State Park, Amelia Island State Recreation Area, Big Talbot State Park, Fort George Island
62   Hagens Cove
62   Spring Creek Unit, Big Bend Wildlife Management Area
62   Tide Swamp Unit, Big Bend Wildlife Management Area
63   Jena Unit, Big Bend Wildlife Management Area
64   Andrews Wildlife Management Area
64   Ichetucknee Springs State Park
64   Ruth Springs Tract
65   Devil's Millhopper State Geological Site
65   O'Leno State Park, River Rise State Preserve

65   Paynes Prairie State Preserve
65   Santa Fe River Canoe Trail
65   San Felasco Hammock State Preserve
66   Camp Blanding Wildlife Management Area
66   Mike Roess Gold Head Branch State Park
67   Lake Ocklawaha (Rodman Reservoir)
68   Anastasia State Recreation Area
68   Beverly Beach
68   Faver-Dykes State Park
68   Fort Matanzas National Monument
68   Pellicer Creek Canoe Trail
69   Cedar Key Scrub State Reserve
69   Cedar Keys National Wildlife Refuge
69   Lower Suwannee River National Wildlife Refuge
70   Gulf Hammock Wildlife Management Area
70   Manatee Springs State Park
70   Waccasassa Bay State Preserve
72   Ocala National Forest
72   Silver River State Park
74   Bulow Creek State Park
74   Bulow Creek Canoe Trail
74   De Leon Springs State Recreation Area
74   Lake Woodruff National Wildlife Refuge
74   St. Johns River

ZONE 2 IS NORTH FLORIDA, from the Georgia line to just south of Daytona Beach. Along its Atlantic coast are Jacksonville, St. Augustine, and beach resorts. The north central and southwestern portions of the zone are largely wetlands. Much of the Gulf coast is fringed by swamps and salt marshes, a vast watery wilderness known as Gulf Hammock, with large timber company holdings inland. The zone has a diversity of uncrowded natural areas for camping, hiking, canoeing, and birding, as well as hunting and fishing.

The Suwannee River offers the state's longest canoe trail, an 8-day voyage from Georgia's Okefenokee Swamp to the Gulf of Mexico. One can canoe on two Withlacoochee rivers, through a wildlife refuge, or explore tidal creeks that meander through Atlantic coastal marshes.

The largest publicly owned tracts in Zone 2 are the Osceola and Ocala National Forests; the latter has many lakes and large springs. Along the north-flowing St. Johns River are several lakes, State Parks, and the Lake Woodruff National Wildlife Refuge.

Zone 2 has several of the longest sections of the Florida Trail, with primitive campsites for backpackers. Throughout the zone are opportunities for day hiking in solitude.

Barrier beaches extend along the Atlantic coast. We found a few uncrowded beaches. Rivers and salt marshes are back of the dunes.

Features of the zone include the Talbot islands; Devil's Millhopper, a huge sinkhole; giant live oaks at Bulow Creek State Park; and a prairie that became a lake that became a prairie.

COMMON BIRDS OF ZONE 2
by Chuck Geanangel

North Florida offers birders extraordinary variety at any season. It includes the least developed section of Gulf coast, mostly wetlands cut by tidal creeks. The Atlantic coast has a fringe of barrier islands. The Lake Woodruff National Wildlife Refuge is a huge freshwater marsh and hardwood swamp. Paynes Prairie attracts up to 2,000 Sandhill Cranes in migration. Cedar Key is noted for its rarities.

Lists like these are at best a rough guide in trip planning. "Winter residents" will almost certainly be present in winter, but fall arrivals and spring departures vary from species to species and year to year. It was tempting to mention specialties and rarities that attract birders from afar, but one can't be sure of seeing them. When you visit a park or refuge, ask for a bird list. Then ask for the news: What special birds are present? When and where can they be seen?

WATER HABITATS, FRESH, BRACKISH, AND SALT
Permanent residents, here all year

Pied-billed Grebe	Little Blue Heron	Killdeer
Double-crested	Tricolored Heron	Greater Yellowlegs
Cormorant	Wood Duck	Lesser Yellowlegs
Great Blue Heron	Mottled Duck	Spotted Sandpiper
Great Egret	Common Moorhen	Laughing Gull
Snowy Egret	Limpkin	

Permanent residents of the coastal region

Brown Pelican	Piping Plover	Sanderling
Clapper Rail	Willet	Dunlin
Black-bellied Plover	Whimbrel	Royal Tern
Semipalmated Plover	Ruddy Turnstone	Sandwich Tern
Wilson's Plover		

Transients, spring and fall

Common Tern	Semipalmated Sandpiper

Winter residents, fall to spring

Common Loon	Redhead	Common Snipe
Horned Grebe	Ring-necked Duck	Bonaparte's Gull
American White	Lesser Scaup	Ring-billed Gull
Pelican	Bufflehead	Herring Gull
Green-winged Teal	Ruddy Duck	Forster's Tern
Mallard	Sora	Red-breasted
Northern Pintail	American Coot	Merganser
Blue-winged Teal	Western Sandpiper	Belted Kingfisher
Northern Shoveler	Least Sandpiper	
American Wigeon	Dowitcher	

Summer residents, spring to fall

Green-backed Heron	Least Tern	Gray Kingbird
White Ibis	Black Tern	

LAND HABITATS
Permanent residents, here all year

Turkey Vulture	Red-tailed Hawk	Rock Dove
Red-shouldered Hawk	Northern Bobwhite	Mourning Dove

Eastern Screech Owl
Great Horned Owl
Barred Owl
Red-headed
  Woodpecker
Red-bellied
  Woodpecker
Downy Woodpecker
Northern Flicker
Pileated Woodpecker
Blue Jay
American Crow
Fish Crow

Carolina Chickadee
Tufted Titmouse
White-breasted
  Nuthatch
Brown-headed
  Nuthatch
Carolina Wren
Marsh Wren
Blue-gray Gnatcatcher
Eastern Bluebird
Northern Mockingbird
Brown Thrasher
Loggerhead Shrike

European Starling
White-eyed Vireo
Pine Warbler
Common Yellowthroat
Northern Cardinal
Rufous-sided Towhee
Red-winged Blackbird
Eastern Meadowlark
Boat-tailed Grackle
Common Grackle
Brown-headed Cowbird
House Sparrow

Transients, spring and fall

Broad-winged Hawk
Ruby-throated
  Hummingbird
Yellow-bellied
  Sapsucker
Eastern Wood Pewee
Tree Swallow

Bank Swallow
Gray-cheeked Thrush
Swainson's Thrush
Veery
Wood Thrush
Yellow Warbler
Cape May Warbler

Black-throated Blue
  Warbler
Prairie Warbler
Blackpoll Warbler
Hooded Warbler
Rose-breasted
  Grosbeak

Winter residents, fall to spring

Northern Harrier
Sharp-shinned Hawk
American Kestrel
"Empidonax"
  Flycatcher
Eastern Phoebe
House Wren
Ruby-crowned Kinglet
Hermit Thrush
American Robin

Gray Catbird
Water Pipit
Cedar Waxwing
Orange-crowned
  Warbler
Yellow-rumped
  Warbler
Black-and-white
  Warbler
American Redstart

Northern Waterthrush
Chipping Sparrow
Field Sparrow
Vesper Sparrow
Savannah Sparrow
Song Sparrow
Swamp Sparrow
White-throated Sparrow
Northern Oriole
American Goldfinch

Summer residents, spring to fall

Cattle Egret
Black Vulture
Mississippi Kite
Yellow-billed Cuckoo
Common Nighthawk
Chuck-will's-widow
Chimney Swift
Great Crested
  Flycatcher

Eastern Kingbird
Gray Kingbird
Purple Martin
Northern Roughwing
  Swallow
Barn Swallow
Yellow-throated
  Vireo
Northern Parula

Yellow-throated
  Warbler
Prothonotary Warbler
Summer Tanager
Blue Grosbeak
Indigo Bunting
Painted Bunting
Orchard Oriole

ALLEN MILL POND
Suwannee River Water Management District
461 acres.   Map 53, C-2.

From US 27 4½ miles northwest of Mayo, north 3¾ miles on SR 251B.

Open during daylight hours.

The District property boundaries are marked with red-banded trees or posts and District signs. The property has 1.6 miles of frontage on the Suwannee River (see entry). A central feature is Allen Mill Pond Spring, a second-magnitude spring with a half-mile run to the river. The run powered a mill in the mid-nineteenth century. Allen's Ferry was nearby.

The site has upland pine forest, upland hardwood forest, bottomland forest, and floodplain swamp. Much of the upland forest was logged years ago. Management policy is to promote and preserve the native species: longleaf pine, loblolly pine, turkey oak, live oak, and post oak. Many large live oaks, sweetgums, blackgums, and cypresses remain in the lowlands.

Wildlife often seen includes bobcat, otter, beaver, wild hog, fox, bob-white quail, wild turkey.

The site has about 2 miles of trails along river and run. Hunting is prohibited, making this a good place to hike in hunting season.

PUBLICATION: Leaflet with map.

HEADQUARTERS: Route 3, Box 64, Live Oak, FL 32060; (904) 362-1001.

ANASTASIA STATE RECREATION AREA
Division of Recreation and Parks
1,022 land acres.   Map 68, B-2.

Off SR A1A, on Anastasia Island, just north of St. Augustine Beach.

This park is often crowded. Out of season or when weather discourages picnicking and swimming, its natural qualities are worth a visit. The entrance, where A1A is turning inland, is easy to overlook.

A salt lagoon, tidal marsh, and coastal hammock with live oaks lie between the highway and the sea. Road and campground are on the landward side. Beyond the lagoon are sand dunes and 2 miles of fine sand beach.

Birding is often good here and at other marshes on the island, especially during spring and fall migrations.

Camping: 139 sites. All year. Telephone reservations accepted.

HEADQUARTERS: 1340 B A1A South, St. Augustine, FL 32084; (904) 461-2033.

ANDREWS WILDLIFE MANAGEMENT AREA
Florida Game and Fresh Water Fish Commission
3,877 acres.   Map 64, D-1.

From Fanning Springs, southeast 2 miles on US 19. Right on CR 211; see sign.

After hours of walking in young slash pine forests, we were delighted to enter the cool shade of this old-growth hardwood hammock on the banks of the Suwannee River (see entry). Most of the site was bought by the State in 1985 to protect one of the few large stands of mature hardwoods remaining in Florida.

River Landing Road, a dirt track in good condition, leads to a small parking area at the river's edge. Terrain is gently sloping, from about 40 feet elevation down to bluffs about 15 feet high along the river. Except for the road, the only development is an interpretive exhibit at the entrance.

About 800 acres are within the river's floodplain. Along the river are swamps and sloughs.

Prior to 1935 the area was used for logging, hunting, fishing, and grazing. Much of the virgin cypress was cut in the early 1900s. The Andrews family then purchased the land for weekend recreation and limited hunting, managing it to protect natural values and enhance wildlife habitat. The State's plan is to maintain a "high-quality resource-based natural area where wild plants and animals are the feature attraction."

Present visitor use is light. Planners have ruled out developments such as a boat ramp, which would increase traffic. They hope the State will acquire an adjoining 1,000-acre tract with similar qualities. This would secure a wildlife corridor to Manatee Springs State Park (see entry) two miles to the south.

Plants: Chief interest is a hardwood forest that grades from xeric (dry) through mesic (intermediate) to hydric (wet), with mature species characteristic of each type and little visible evidence of past cutting. Three Florida Champion trees (persimmon, Florida maple, and bluff oak) have been found.

Two National Champions, basswood and winged elm, have been recorded. All are in the mesic community, near trails.

Both overbrowsing by deer and feral hogs, and tree crown closure, have opened the understory. Managers hope to reduce the hogs and balance the deer population by controlled hunting.

Trees of interest include live and turkey oak, southern magnolia, black cherry, dogwood, American holly, and redbay. Understory includes sweetleaf, sparkleberry, blueberry, saw palmetto, greenbrier, and fox grape. Swamp species include bald cypress, red maple, blackgum, water and overcup oaks, water hickory, river birch.

Birds: 51 species have been recorded; the list will grow. In a short visit we saw several species not yet listed. Diverse habitats and ease of foot travel make for good birding.

Mammals: Observed mammals include gray and flying squirrels, beaver, raccoon, striped skunk, river otter, gray and red foxes, coyote, bobcat, whitetail deer.

ACTIVITIES

Hiking: Except in hunting season, quiet walking on roads and marked trails. ORVs are prohibited. Nature trails are planned.

Hunting: Rules available at check station. Camping is prohibited.

Fishing: Bank. Species include largemouth bass, catfish, black crappie, sunfish.

Canoeing: No prohibition of launching is posted, but with more convenient put-ins nearby why manhandle a canoe down and up the steep bank? Passing canoeists are permitted to camp overnight on the shore.

PUBLICATION: WMA regulations and area map.

HEADQUARTERS: Florida Game and Fresh Water Fish Commission, 620 South Meridian St., Tallahassee, FL 32399; (904) 488-1960.

BEVERLY BEACH

Seacoast. On SR A1A, N of SR 100.   MAP 68, D-3.

A narrow sand beach beside the highway. Parking and access are unrestricted. Across the road are private homes. When we passed on a mid-week July day, the beach was uncrowded.

BIG SHOALS TRACT
Suwannee River Water Management District

BIG SHOALS WILDLIFE MANAGEMENT AREA
Florida Game and Fresh Water Fish Commission

BIG SHOALS STATE FOREST
Division of Forestry
3,495 acres.   Map 54, B-3.

From White Springs on US 41, north on CR 135. WMA entrance is just north of town. Forest and Tract entrance is Old Goodwin Bridge Road, 3 miles north.

This block of land lies between CR 135 and the Suwannee River (see entry).

BIG SHOALS TRACT

The 815-acre Tract is on 3½ miles of the narrowest, least developed section of the river and includes Big Shoals, one of Florida's few whitewater rapids. The river flows between high bluffs. The principal upland communities are pine flatwoods and pine/oak, with areas of floodplain forest, cypress swamp, hammock, and scrub. Flowering plants are abundant on the rich bottomlands.

A canoe launch site is at the road's end. This is an alternate put-in and take-out at mile 18.6 on the Suwannee River (Upper) Canoe Trail (see entry). Here also are two nature trails. The longer, a 2½-mile round trip, passes between the river and Shoal Pond, about ⅓ mile long.

The site is owned by the Suwannee River Water Management District and managed in cooperation with the Division of Forestry and Florida Game and Fresh Water Fish Commission. Hunting is prohibited on all but 210 acres.

BIG SHOALS WILDLIFE MANAGEMENT AREA

The WMA includes all 3,500 acres and 6 miles of river frontage, but the three parcels are managed in different ways. Hunting is permitted everywhere except in part of the Tract and at entrances. The land along the lower 2½ miles of river may eventually become a State Park.

Terrain is generally flat away from the river bluffs except for a few sinkholes, springs, and the banks of Four-Mile Branch, the site's chief drainage. Pine flatwoods and pine/oak upland are the principal plant communities, with areas of floodplain forest, cypress swamp, hammock, and scrub. Beech/magnolia groves occur along Four-Mile Branch.

Wildlife includes wading and upland bird species, wild turkey, gray squirrel, wild hog, whitetail deer, gopher tortoise, various reptiles and amphibians.

BIG SHOALS STATE FOREST

The forest overlaps the other sites, the Division of Forestry having responsibility for forest management.

PUBLICATIONS

Big Shoals Tract. Suwannee River Water Management District.
WMA leaflet with map. Florida Game and Fresh Water Fish Commission.

HEADQUARTERS: *WMA:* Florida Game and Fresh Water Fish Commission, Northeast Region, RFD 7, Box 440, Lake City, FL 32055; (904) 758-0525. *Tract:* Suwannee River Water Management District, Route 3, Box 64, Live Oak, FL 32060; (904) 362-1001.

BULOW CREEK CANOE TRAIL
13 miles.   Map 74, A-3.

From Flagler Beach, west on SR 100 to Old Kings Road. Left about 3 miles to Bulow Plantation Ruins State Historical Site.

The 13 miles includes an optional 7-mile excursion upstream and back, worth it if you have enough time. Bulow Creek meanders quietly through coastal marshes to the Intracoastal Waterway at Tomoka Basin. The area is isolated, with lush vegetation and few signs of human activity.

The wetlands are cut by a network of tidal creeks. The landward boundary of tidewater is marked by marsh elder and saltmarsh mallow. Beyond the marshes is higher ground with dense stands of mature magnolia, oak, and slash pine. Plants of the lower tidewater area include saltgrasses, needlerush, and sand cordgrass.

At about the midpoint, the creek meets Walter Boardman Lane (see entry, Volusia County Scenic Highway), an optional take-out or put-in. The designated Canoe Trail ends at High Bridge Park, off Walter Boardman Lane, but canoeists can continue to Tomoka State Park (see entry).

Birding is excellent. Alligators are common.

Upstream portions may be shallow during dry seasons.

PUBLICATION: *Bulow Creek Canoe Trail.* Division of Recreation and Parks.

BULOW CREEK STATE PARK
Division of Recreation and Parks
2,577 land acres; 564 acres submerged.   Map 74, A-3.

Main entrance is north of Ormond Beach on Old Dixie Highway, via North Beach Street, between Tomoka State Park and Walter Boardman Lane.

On the Volusia County Scenic Highway (see entry) we happened to see an obscure park sign, backed up, and parked. Beyond the gate was a single-lane dirt track, rutted, grass growing in the center. Unsure of road conditions, we decided to explore on foot.

The track led first through an attractive forest of slash pine, oak, and magnolia. The understory is largely palmetto, with an abundance of dog fennel and passion flower. After crossing a clear-cut area now thick with high palmettos, we entered an oak hammock. Here we saw the familiar blaze of the Florida Trail. The trail turns west before the track ends at a marsh.

Later, on Old Dixie Highway, we came to the main entrance. Here is a feature that prompted the State to acquire this site: an old-growth live oak forest. Most distinguished is the Fairchild Oak, said to be 2,000 years old, with a circumference of 23½ feet and gigantic lower branches. Several nearby trees have trunk diameters larger than 5 feet. A picnic area is nearby.

There's no visitor center or office. A mobile home, the park officer's residence, has no sign. We started down Pumphouse Road and turned back; encroaching brush and branches were scratching the motor home's sides and roof. A car can make it. We were the only visitors.

Hiking: Hiking is the only way to see the diverse natural features of the park. Section 13E of the Florida Trail was planned to display them. Its west boundary lies along the east slope of the Atlantic Coastal Ridge, 20 to 25 feet above sea level. Lowlands at 5 to 10 feet elevation comprise most of the land acreage. They extend westward to the extensive tidal marshes along Bulow Creek. (See entry, Bulow Creek Canoe Trail.)

A low peninsular ridge lies between the creek and the Halifax River–Intracoastal Waterway.

Several shallow ponds are linked to the tidal creeks that drain to Bulow Creek.

The nearest authorized camping to the trail is at Tomoka State Park or Flagler Beach SRA (see entries).

HEADQUARTERS: 3351 Old Dixie Highway, Ormond Beach, FL 32074. No telephone.

CAMP BLANDING WILDLIFE MANAGEMENT AREA
Florida Armory Board and Florida Game
and Fresh Water Fish Commission
62,340 acres.   Map 66, A-3.

East of Starke. Entrances on SR 16 and SR 21.

Camp Blanding is an active military training base, used by the Army and Air National Guards and other entities. A permit is required to enter. We mention it here because it is crossed by the Florida Trail and because those who know the area say it has great ecological diversity and richness.

That diversity includes turkey oak sandhills, lowland pine and hardwood ravines, slash pine flatwoods, mixed hardwood hammocks, mature longleaf pine stands, cypress heads, cypress swamps, and sinkhole ponds. Kingsley Lake is the source of the Black Creek and Rice Creek drainage systems, which supply seven other lakes.

ACTIVITIES

Hiking, backpacking: The Florida Trail crosses the southern tip of the camp, just below Lowry Lake. Hikers should call (904) 533-2268 in advance; at times the trail is closed. The nearest campsite is at Mike Roess Gold Head Branch State Park (see entry).

Hunting: Managed hunts, by special permit, chiefly deer.

PUBLICATION: WMA folder with map.

HEADQUARTERS: Florida Game and Fresh Water Fish Commission, Northeast Region, RFD 7, Box 440, Lake City, FL 32055; (904) 758-0525.

CARY STATE FOREST
Division of Forestry
3,412 acres.   Map 56, A-3.

From I-10 west of Jacksonville, north 11 miles on US 301. Main entrance is on the right beyond SR 119, Motes Road.

In the mid-1930s, Florida received a federal grant to buy unproductive and tax-delinquent land. Much of the Cary State Forest was acquired for $4 an acre. Since then the Division of Forestry has had timber sales (currently two a year) and sponsored naval stores operations. Most forest renewal has been by natural regeneration.

An environmental education program was inaugurated in 1972 with the dedication of an outdoor teaching pavilion and a 150-acre demonstration area.

Two-thirds of the site is pine flatwoods. The several nature trails include boardwalks through one large cypress swamp and two smaller swamps. Graded roads crisscross the area.

Wildlife: Birding is best in and around the swamps. The red-cockaded woodpecker has been reported. Deer, feral hog, squirrel, raccoon, opossum, rabbit, and bobcat are common. Black bear are seen occasionally.

ACTIVITIES
Camping: A primitive campground with bathhouse is on the main entrance road.
Hiking: Nature trails and 18 miles of forest roads.
Hunting: The site is also the Cary Wildlife Management Area. The southeast corner, which includes the education area, is closed to hunting.

PUBLICATIONS
Leaflet with map.
Leaflet: *Pine Flatwoods Nature Study Trail.*
Wildlife Management Area leaflet.

HEADQUARTERS: District Office, Division of Forestry, 8719 West Beaver St., Jacksonville, FL 32220; (904) 693-5055.

CEDAR KEYS NATIONAL WILDLIFE REFUGE
U.S. Fish and Wildlife Service
780 acres.   Map 69, D-3.

Twelve small islands near Cedar Key. Boat access only. Restricted entry.

The Refuge is a satellite of the Lower Suwannee National Wildlife Refuge (see entry), though much older. They have similar bird populations and share a bird checklist. The islands are important nesting sites. Four of the islands are declared Wilderness Areas.

The refuge manager took us on a boat tour of the islands. As we cruised, three porpoises frolicked in our wake.

The islands are generally forested, fringed with salt marshes and mangroves, surrounded by shallow sand and mud flats that make them almost inaccessible at low tide.

The interiors of all 12 islands are off limits to visitors. Beaches can be visited all year, except on Seahorse Key, which is closed January 1 to June 30.

Hunting, camping, fires, pets, weapons, metal detectors, and collection of artifacts are prohibited.
The waters surrounding Seahorse Key are closed to boating January—June.

PUBLICATIONS
 Leaflet.
 Bird checklist.

HEADQUARTERS: c/o Lower Suwannee National Wildlife Refuge, Rt. 1,
 Box 1193C, Chiefland, FL 32626; (904) 493-0238.

CEDAR KEY SCRUB STATE RESERVE
Division of Recreation and Parks
4,988 acres.   Map 69, C-3.

From US 98 southeast of Chiefland, southwest 16 mi. on SR 24, the road
to Cedar Key. SR 24 is on the southeast boundary. SR 347, which inter-
sects, cuts across the Reserve.

The boundaries include offshore islands and surrounding waters. Except for
small parking areas on both highways, the site is undeveloped. The land
was acquired because of its unique natural qualities, which will be preserved.

Those qualities include sand pine scrub, an association of flora and fauna
becoming rare in Florida. Other habitats include scrubby flatwoods, slash
pine flatwoods, freshwater ponds, swamp, freshwater and saltwater marshes,
and brackish tidal creeks. Terrain is generally flat, but a few white sand
ridges rise to an elevation of 30 feet.

The site has no improved roads. Past logging and hunting left tracks that
serve as hiking routes; some are overgrown, some muddy after rain.

Sand pine scrub. This association occurs on ridges in the eastern sector.
There is a scattering of longleaf pine. The understory includes scrub, Chap-
man, and myrtle oaks, and Florida rosemary. The threatened Florida arrow-
root or coontie, a fernlike plant, occurs here.

Wildlife of the association includes the threatened Florida scrub jay and
Florida mouse, gopher tortoise, and Florida gopher frog.

Freshwater ponds and marshes. These wetlands occupy scattered low-
lying areas. Common plant species include sawgrass, Baker's cordgrass, cabbage palm, dahoon holly, loblolly bay, and redbay. Birds often seen include
little blue and Louisiana herons, snowy egret, and limpkin. Endangered or
threatened wildlife species present include the Florida mink, one-toed am-
phiuma (an eel-like salamander), striped newt, and spotted turtle.

Salt marshes. Penetrated by many tidal creeks, marshes border the Gulf.
They are a highly productive estuarine community. Marsh plants include
smooth, seashore, and salt meadow cordgrasses; black needlerush, glass-

wort, and saltwort. Birds often seen include the wood stork (endangered), brown pelican (threatened), roseate spoonbill; great blue, little blue, and Louisiana herons; snowy egret, black-crowned and yellow-crowned night-herons, glossy and white ibises, royal tern, black skimmer, and seaside sparrow.

ACTIVITIES

Hiking: The WMA map shows trails.

Hunting: Hunting is managed by the Florida Game and Fresh Water Fish Commission.

Canoeing: In shallow tidal waters. Launch at one of the nearby facilities.

Motorized land vehicles are prohibited.

PUBLICATION: WMA leaflet.

HEADQUARTERS: c/o Waccasassa Bay State Preserve, P.O. Box 187, Cedar Key, FL 32625; (904) 543-5567.

CHRISTIAN TRACT, SUWANNEE RIVER
Suwannee River Water Management District
327 acres.   Map 53, C-2.

From Dowling Park, 2 miles south on local roads to east bank of river.

Open daylight hours.

The tract is one of several on the Suwannee owned by the District and other public agencies. This one has over a mile of river frontage. Its canoe launch site is an alternate put-in and take-out on the Suwannee River (Lower) Canoe Trail (see entry).

The bottomland has live oak, hickory, American holly, redbay, and other hardwoods. Higher ground is a sandhill community with longleaf pine and scrub oak. A nature trail along the river passes a small spring. Other trails pass several large sinkholes.

The site is managed in cooperation with the Division of Forestry.

Camping, hunting, and off-road vehicles are prohibited.

PUBLICATION: Leaflet with map.

HEADQUARTERS: Suwannee River Water Management District, Route 3, Box 64, Live Oak, FL 32060; (904) 362-1001.

DE LEON SPRINGS STATE RECREATION AREA
Division of Recreation and Parks
401 land acres.   Map 74, C-2.

Off US 17 just north of De Leon Springs.

Open 8 A.M. to sunset.

We looked and almost turned away: an attractive site but developed for intensive use. The spring, described in 1832 by John James Audubon, is now a popular swimming pool hemmed in by walls, walks, and gardens. A second look persuaded us to mention it. There's a nature trail. Also, one can rent a canoe here and paddle directly into the Lake Woodruff National Wildlife Refuge (see entry).

PUBLICATION: Leaflet with map.

HEADQUARTERS: P.O. Box 1338, De Leon Springs, FL 32028; (904) 985-4212.

DEVIL'S MILLHOPPER STATE GEOLOGICAL SITE
Division of Recreation and Parks
63 acres.   Map 65, C-2.

2 miles northwest of Gainesville on CR 232. (No intersection on I-75.)

Open 9 A.M. to sundown.

Sinkholes, some old, some new and unexpected, are a feature of Florida's geology. They appear when underlying limestone gradually dissolves and layers above collapse. Devil's Millhopper is old and large, 500 feet across, 120 feet deep.

From the parking area, a walkway leads through a mature woodland past the interpretive center to the rim of the sinkhole. A half-mile nature trail circles the sinkhole. A boardwalk and 221-step stairway descend to the bottom.

On a hot summer day, it's cooler below. Large trees growing on the sinkhole's slopes are evidence of its age. The exposed layers display the area's geological history. Imbedded fossils of bones, teeth, and shells reveal what creatures once lived here: land animals in the upper layers, marine animals below, deposited on what was sea bottom. Water from springs and surface runoff flows into the sinkhole, vanishing into a natural drain.

Even this small park has a diversity of habitats: hardwood hammock, pine and turkey oak woodland, swamp, and the moist sinkhole. Common birds include black and turkey vultures, bobwhite, morning dove, barred owl, chuck-will's-widow, common flicker, red-bellied woodpecker, blue jay, tufted titmouse, Carolina wren, mockingbird, brown thrasher, blue-gray gnatcatcher, cardinal, rufous-sided towhee, summer tanager.

INTERPRETATION

The *interpretive center* has excellent exhibits showing how sinkholes are formed and explaining the fossil record. A ranger is usually on duty.

Guided walks are offered, usually at 10 A.M. Saturday.

PUBLICATIONS

Leaflet.

Fact sheet.

NEARBY: San Felasco Hammock State Preserve (see entry) is under the same management. Rangers offer occasional guided hikes.

HEADQUARTERS: 4732 Millhopper Road, Gainesville, FL 32606; (904) 336-2008.

FAVER-DYKES STATE PARK

Division of Recreation and Parks

752 acres.   Map 68, C-2.

South of St. Augustine. Proceed north on US 1 from I-95, immediately turning right on Faver-Dykes Road.

This delightful, informal park on Pellicer Creek is lightly used. When we visited on a sunny July afternoon, we were the only visitors. The campground had been unoccupied for several days.

The unpaved entrance road leads through a mature stand of longleaf pine and turkey oak. Picnic tables are among the trees. Nearby are pines with an understory of palmetto. The highest point in the park is 25 feet above sea level.

Boats can be launched on Pellicer Creek. (See entry, Pellicer Creek Canoe Trail.) The tidal creek, deep and 30 to 40 feet wide, meanders through attractive marshes. Swimming is prohibited, in part because of alligators.

Other inhabitants of the wetlands are wading birds, waterfowl, river otter, and raccoon. Bald eagles nest along the creek. Uplands fauna include wild turkey, owls, several hawk species, squirrel, bobcat, opossum, fox, and deer. Songbirds are abundant in spring and fall.

ACTIVITIES
   Hiking: One nature trail is near the picnic area, another at the campground. With so little traffic, the entrance road is also a pleasant route. One can find unmaintained woods, roads, and trails.
   Camping: 30 sites. All year. No reservations.
   Fishing: Speckled trout, redfish, sheepshead, flounder.

PUBLICATION: Leaflet with map.

HEADQUARTERS: 1000 Faver-Dykes Rd., St. Augustine, FL 32086; (904) 794-0997.

FLAGLER BEACH STATE RECREATION AREA
Division of Recreation and Parks
145 acres.   Map 75, A-1.

   Seacoast, on SR A1A at SR 100.

The SRA has 2,400 linear feet of sand beach, but one can beachcomb for several miles from here. A campground with 34 sites is on the dunes a few yards from the water, next to a day-use swimming area. Across the road, between the highway and the Intracoastal Waterway, are the office, picnic area, nature trail, and boat ramp.
   Flagler Beach is a small residential community with little commercial development on A1A. The only parking area is at the municipal beach and fishing pier. Since parking isn't permitted elsewhere along A1A, the beach is seldom crowded.

ACTIVITIES
   Camping: 34 sites. Don't expect to camp here without a reservation. Bring shade.
   Fishing: Pompano, whiting, drum, and bluefish in the surf. Speckled trout, redfish, and flounder in the Waterway.

PUBLICATION: Leaflet with map.

NEARBY: North Peninsula State Recreation Area (see entry); Volusia County Scenic Drive (see entry).

HEADQUARTERS: 3100 South A1A, Flagler Beach, FL 32136; (904) 439-2474.

FORT CLINCH STATE PARK
Division of Recreation and Parks
1,119 acres.   Map 41, C-3.

Off SR A1A north of Fernandina Beach.

Open 8 A.M. to sunset.

The park occupies the north tip of Amelia Island, just south of the Georgia boundary. It combines a living history program with preservation of an isolated island ecosystem.

The fort was built before the Civil War, during which it changed hands twice without hostilities. Its guns were intended to guard the mouth of St. Marys River and the port of Fernandina. Decommissioned in 1898, partially restored, it is again garrisoned, this time by Park employees in Union military dress.

Amelia Island, 13½ miles long, is bounded by the Atlantic Ocean on the east, a broad marsh system and the Intracoastal Waterway on the west, the St. Marys River entrance on the north, the Nassau River on the south. Back of the sand beach is a complex of dune ridges, most 10 to 15 feet high, a few rising to 55 feet. The adjacent waters are protected as an Aquatic Preserve.

The entrance road traverses the site to the fort on Cumberland Sound. A spur leads to a pier or jetty where the Sound meets the sea. About half of the park is maritime hammock, considered an outstanding example of this association. The park includes part of an extensive system of salt marshes.

Sites where migratory birds cross water are usually strategic observation posts, and this park is no exception. We copied a handwritten preliminary bird list of about 120 species compiled in 1978, a mix of waterfowl, wading birds, marsh and upland species.

ACTIVITIES
Camping: 62 sites. Reservations accepted.

Hiking: Except for the nature trail, no routes are marked on the map. However, the ocean, sound, and river frontages are accessible and largely suitable for beachcombing.

Fishing: Surf, pier, and bank. Speckled trout, redfish, drum, sheepshead, flounder, whiting, pompano.

INTERPRETATION
Fort and visitor center: Rangers in Union uniforms man and maintain the fort in the manner of 1864. Exhibits.

Nature trail passes through coastal hammock.
Campfire programs and *guided walks*. Seasonal.

PUBLICATIONS
  Leaflet with map.
  Interpretive booklet.

HEADQUARTERS: 2601 Atlantic Ave., Fernandina Beach, FL 32034; (904) 261-4212.

FORT MATANZAS NATIONAL MONUMENT
National Park Service
298 acres.   Map 68, C-3.

On SR A1A 15 miles south of St. Augustine.

The Spanish fort was built in 1740–1742 to protect one of the approaches to St. Augustine from the British fleet. A visitor center has exhibits. When we visited, men in uniforms of the period were presenting an interpretive program, but we were told this occurs rarely.

From here a ferry takes visitors across the Matanzas River to the fort. Across A1A is a ramp over the dunes to the beach. Near the parking lot is a 0.4-mile boardwalk nature trail. The dense undergrowth harbors many songbirds in spring and fall migrations.

What makes this site an entry is the inlet area to the south, at the north end of the Claude Varn bridge. Here the Monument includes ocean beach, dunes, frontage on the inlet, and a broad area of low dunes, tidal flats, and wetlands at the river. The last time we stopped, several hundred brown pelicans were sunning on sandbars and riding air currents just above the bridge. Many shorebirds could be seen.

It's one of the few ocean beaches where dogs are allowed, albeit on leash, which delighted our Labrador. Fishing is permitted on the bridge.

HEADQUARTERS: c/o Castillo de San Marcos National Monument, 1 Castillo Dr., St. Augustine, FL 32084; (904) 471-0116.

GUANA RIVER STATE PARK
Division of Recreation and Parks
2,398 acres.

GUANA RIVER WILDLIFE MANAGEMENT AREA
Florida Game and Fresh Water Fish Commission
8,700 acres.   Map 58, C-2, D-2.

On SR A1A 13 miles north of St. Augustine.

This undeveloped park on about 11 miles of Atlantic seacoast isn't yet shown on most maps or included in most park guides. The Wildlife Management Area is fine habitat for fish, waterfowl, and other wildlife.

Few such large undeveloped tracts remain on the Florida coast. These 12,000 acres have an exceptionally rich variety of natural features. They include miles of sand beach and stabilized dunes, an extensive undisturbed area of Atlantic coastal strand, an extensive maritime hammock with mature trees, estuarine wetlands, large areas of pine flatwoods, and open water.

Natural processes have been slowly erasing the marks of past land use. Spanish colonists were the first European settlers, raising cattle, hogs, and ponies. They were followed by British colonials who cultivated rice, indigo, and sugar cane. Their dikes, levees, and ditches remain, as do the vestiges of a sugar or rice mill, sawmill, houses, and graveyard. Later landowners tried unsuccessfully to promote a resort. Hunting rights were leased to private clubs.

A WMA was established in 1957 by arrangement with the property owner. The State then built a low dam across the Guana River, forming a shallow 2,200-acre lake sometimes called Lake Ponte Vedra, more often Guana Lake. State acquisition of the area began in 1984 and was concluded in 1987. The Guana River has been designated an Aquatic Preserve.

Birds: The area has long been popular for waterfowl hunting, and the Florida Game and Fresh Water Fish Commission has sought to increase game bird populations. The Duval Audubon Society has listed many species here. Some of special interest to birders include bald eagle, wood stork, roseate spoonbill, Florida scrub jay, American oystercatcher, common loon, horned grebe; white-winged, black, and surf scoters; snow goose; king, clapper, and Virginia rails; short-billed dowitcher, black skimmer, peregrine falcon, pileated woodpecker, brown-headed nuthatch, northern parula, bobolink.

Mammals: Species observed include opossum, shorttail shrew, gray squirrel, gray fox, raccoon, striped skunk, river otter, bobcat, whitetail deer.

STATE PARK
The State Park occupies most of the barrier beach, a narrow strip almost 5 miles long on both sides of A1A, and the southern tip of the peninsula between the Tolomato River and Lake Ponte Vedra (Guana Lake). High dunes rise between A1A and the beach. The highest, 35 to 40 feet, are at the north end of the Park. Across the highway are 1,100 acres of upland forest and 500 acres of salt marsh.

The dunes have suffered damage by uncontrolled traffic. In the absence of parking areas and ramps over the dunes, visitors parked anywhere. Pedestrians and vehicles wore pathways through the dunes. Trampling of dune vegetation was followed by sand blowouts (wind erosion). The county permitted vehicles to be driven on the beach, often crushing the eggs of nesting sea turtles and terns.

As we approached from the south, the first sign marked the Guana River State Park–Guana Dam Area. A sand road crosses the low dam. Fishermen were active above and below the dam. Several boat trailers were parked. About two miles farther north, a sign announced we were entering the State Park.

There's a dense growth of bay and palmetto on both sides. Several cars were parked along the roadside where informal (and unauthorized) trails lead to the beach. Posts had been erected to prevent driving over the dunes.

The beach is straight and wide. Less than a dozen visitors were in sight.

Farther north we came to the first of two formal parking areas with boardwalks crossing the dunes to the beach. Here the Division of Recreation and Parks is controlling damage and beginning restoration.

Visitors may be confused by highway signs reading "No Parking on the Right of Way." What is the right of way?

Dune systems can be restored. Barring vehicles from the beach, providing parking areas, and constructing boardwalks over the dunes are first steps in park management. We hope access points will be limited so visitors who choose to walk the beach for a half mile or more can escape from crowds.

WILDLIFE MANAGEMENT AREA

The WMA occupies all but the southern tip of the peninsula between the Tolomato and Guana rivers. The peninsula is 12½ miles long and ¼ to ½ mile wide. On the east side is a broad ridge 10 to 15 feet high. The west side is nearly flat, sloping gradually to the river marshes. The area has a number of small basins and ponds, some spring-fed, others ephemeral. Guana Lake, only a foot or two deep, attracts fishermen and crabbers. Between the upland peninsula and the Intracoastal Waterway (Tolomato River) are extensive intertidal wetlands cut by pristine estuarine creeks, where the canoeist can enjoy isolation.

A few unimproved roads cross the WMA, best suited to 4-wheel-drive vehicles. The one we saw was closed; perhaps it's open to vehicles only in hunting season.

The WMA is remarkable for its floral diversity. We can give only a sampling of the lengthy inventory.

Basin marsh: Along the edges, Carolina willow, wax myrtle, loblolly bay. The many emergent species include cattails, arrowhead, cordgrass, spikerush, spiderwort, bulrush, pickerel weed, white water lily. Submergent and floating species include water fern, sago pondweed, duckweed, bladderwort.

Brackish marsh: Plant species include widgeon grass, saltgrass, cordgrass, black needlerush, aster.

Cypress swamp: Species include pond cypress, maple, loblolly bay, swamp blackgum.

Hardwood swamp: In the overstory, water oak, red maple, swamp blackgum. Swamp dogwood and buttonbush below.

Pine flatwoods: Botanists believe the peninsula was a pine forest until it was logged about 1940. Stands of slash and pond pine are now scattered. A restorative management plan is being developed. Understory of the pine flatwoods includes ferns, saw palmetto, greenbrier, wax myrtle, blackberry, milkwort, yaupon, huckleberry, thistle.

Maritime forest hammock: Extensive stands are on uplands west of the lake. Overstory species include live and laurel oaks, slash pine, southern redcedar, cabbage palm, pignut hickory. In the understory: resurrection fern, saw palmetto, Spanish bayonet, orchid, red mulberry, Indian firecracker, wild grape, prickly pear, meadow beauty, yellow jessamine.

ACTIVITIES

Hiking: On miles of beach in the State Park. Unimproved roads in the park and WMA.

Hunting: Chiefly waterfowl, in the WMA.

Fishing: Surf in the park. Fresh- and saltwater species in Guana Lake.

Swimming: Ocean.

Boating, canoeing: On the lake and on Guana River above and below the dam. 10-hp limit on the lake. With 1-foot depths common, we'd prefer paddling.

PUBLICATIONS

Park leaflet with map.

WMA leaflet, from Florida Game and Fresh Water Fish Commission.

HEADQUARTERS: *Park:* South Ponte Vedra Blvd., Ponte Vedra Beach, FL 32082; (904) 825-5071. *WMA:* Florida Game and Fresh Water Fish Commission, Central Region, 1239 SW 10th St., Ocala, FL 32674; (904) 732-1225.

GULF HAMMOCK WILDLIFE MANAGEMENT AREA
Florida Game and Fresh Water Fish Commission
25,625 acres.   Map 70, D-3.

From Lebanon Station, south 2 miles on US 98. Entrance on the right.

Florida's oldest WMA is owned by Georgia-Pacific Corporation and used for production of pulpwood. The company's agreement with the Commission permits public use.

The site lies between the Waccasassa and Withlacoochee rivers but has no river frontage. The Waccasassa Preserve lies between the WMA and the Gulf of Mexico. The entire area is flat, drained by small ditches and creeks, and has a few small ponds. It is crisscrossed by unpaved roads in varying condition.

Communities include oak and mixed hardwood hammocks, loblolly and slash pine plantations, cypress ponds, and freshwater swamps.

We saw nothing exceptional here. However, if you're passing by on US 98 and it's not hunting season, the WMA offers a quiet place to walk. Birding should be good in winter and spring.

Camping is prohibited except hunter camping in season.

PUBLICATION: WMA leaflet.

HEADQUARTERS: Florida Game and Fresh Water Fish Commission, Northeast Region, RFD 7, Box 440, Lake City, FL 32055; (904) 758-0525.

HAGENS COVE
Florida Game and Fresh Water Fish Commission
Acreage indefinite.   Map 62, B-2.

From Perry, south on SR 361 to the Gulf. About 2 miles beyond Keaton Beach, turn right at sign.

This recreation area is at the northwest end of the Tide Swamp Unit, Big Bend Wildlife Management Area (see entry). The picnic area was well occupied when we visited. Children were playing on the beach and in the water. A hundred yards out the water was only shin deep. The beach was alive with sand crabs.

On the right of the entrance is what must have been a campground: wooded sites with tables and grills. A large sign says firmly "No Camping."

We mention this site because the tidal flats and marsh west of the "campground" are easy access to good birding. We saw tire tracks on the exposed flats but thought it prudent to walk.

ICHETUCKNEE SPRINGS STATE PARK
Division of Recreation and Parks
2,241 acres.   Map 64, A-2.

From Fort White on US 27, north on SR 47, left on SR 238.

Almost 200,000 people visited this park in 1988, about 50,000 fewer in 1989. Part of the decline may have been caused by stricter environmental protection. The features that make the park so uniquely attractive are at risk.

About 85 percent of visitors come in the five-month period May–September. The smallest number come in December. The assistant park manager told us, "Everyone who comes to Ichetucknee either tubes or canoes down the river, swims in the springs area, or picnics and enjoys the scenery."

Tubing: That's the big attraction, as it was before the State acquired the site in 1970. Ten named springs gush 230 million gallons of water daily to form the river, which flows 3½ miles to the park boundary and on to the Santa Fe River. Water emerges at about 72°F. The river flows past picturesque limestone formations, pine flatwoods and sandhills, hardwood forest, floodplain swamps, and a wild rice marsh.

As crowds increased on the river, so did damage to vegetation on the river banks. Swim fins stirred bottom sediments. Wild animals sought quieter haunts. Horseplay and conflicts between tubers and canoeists plagued management.

Tube launching is now restricted to two sites: upper and midpoint (Dampier's Landing). Environmental damage has been heaviest upstream, so a limit of 1,500 people per day, and 750 from June 1 through Labor Day, has been put on the upper put-in. Tubers are encouraged to use the midpoint launch; a park tram carries them back from the take-out. Whether these measures are enough to halt damage to the resource is an open question.

Our draft entry commented that opportunities to see the park on foot are limited. The response included a hand-drawn map of a new trail loop not shown on the park leaflet. Now two connecting loops totaling 1.9 miles pass overlooks, through hardwood hammock and sandhills, past a sinkhole and other features.

PUBLICATIONS
    Leaflet with map.
    Tubing information.

HEADQUARTERS: Route 2, Box 108, Fort White, FL 32038; (904) 497-2511.

JENA UNIT, BIG BEND
WILDLIFE MANAGEMENT AREA
Florida Game and Fresh Water Fish Commission
8,682 acres.   Map 63, D-1.

From Steinhatchee, south on CR 361. Take first right fork on Gentle Woods Road.

When purchased by the State, the Unit was part of a larger tract owned by a timber company. The State land is a relatively narrow strip between the paved road and coastal marshes of the Big Bend Aquatic Preserve. The strip continues beyond Rocky Creek almost to the dead end of SR 361.

The WMA map shows a number of unimproved roads leading from the paved road to the marshes, the longest little over a mile. Those we saw seemed more suitable for hiking than driving, with boots needed in wet weather.

The area is mostly flat and poorly drained. Associations include cypress, gum, and bay swamps; hardwood hammocks; and slash pine plantations. Wet habitats include cypress ponds, small creeks and drainage ditches, and tidal marshes.

Hunting has been the chief visitor activity. Under State management, the site is expected to attract more hikers and birders.

PUBLICATION: WMA leaflet with map.

HEADQUARTERS: Florida Game and Fresh Water Fish Commission, Northeast Region, RFD 7, Box 440, Lake City, FL 32055; (904) 758-0525.

LAKE WOODRUFF NATIONAL WILDLIFE REFUGE
U.S. Fish and Wildlife Service
19,145 acres.   Map 74, D-1.

Headquarters: On CR 4053, 4490 Grand Ave., ½ mile west of De Leon Springs.

Most of the Refuge is open water, freshwater marshes, streams, and timbered swamps. Only about 1,000 acres are uplands: pine flatwoods and scrub oak/pine. Just south of headquarters is a narrow dirt road to a public viewing area. Here visitors can walk on dikes around three pools; the longest circuit is 2½ miles. Two nature trails are nearby.

Most of the Refuge is accessible only by boat. Boats can be rented or launched at De Leon Springs State Park (see entry). We rented a pontoon boat at a marina on the St. Johns River across from Hontoon Island State

Park (see entry) and thought this the best way to spend a day exploring the Refuge. Birding was excellent.

Most of the Refuge is east of the river, downstream from the SR 44 bridge. We saw a few Refuge boundary signs on the west. A broad creek on the east between channel markers 36 and 38 is the access from the river to Lake Woodruff.

Most navigable waters within the Refuge belong to the State of Florida. The refuge manager said State ownership doesn't conflict with the Refuge's mission.

Birds: October through February are the best months to visit, the manager advised. However, the Refuge bird list surprised us. Of the more than 200 bird species recorded, most of the abundant or common species are residents. Of the waterfowl, only the wood duck, blue-winged teal, and ring-necked duck are rated seasonally abundant or common. Mottled duck, pintail, green-winged teal, American wigeon, ruddy duck, and hooded merganser are rated uncommon.

From the boat in July we saw dozens of osprey. Also many great blue, little blue, green-backed, and tricolored herons; snowy egret, white ibis, black vulture, limpkin, red-winged blackbird, fish crow. We saw two kingfishers, one swallow-tailed kite. Several of these species are rated "uncommon" in the Refuge's 1990 bird list.

Mammals: The Refuge checklist includes many moles, shrews, gophers, mice, voles, rats, bats, and pipistrels, which only the patient and observant visitor is likely to see and identify. More often seen are opossum, raccoon, river otter, striped skunk, bobcat, gray and fox squirrels, cottontail and marsh rabbits, armadillo, longtail weasel, gray fox, and whitetail deer. Manatee travel the St. Johns River going to and from Blue Spring State Park (see entry) and sometimes enter Refuge waters. Black bear are seen occasionally. Panther have been reported.

Other wildlife: The checklist includes many reptiles and amphibians. Turtles sun on logs at the river edge. Alligators are commonly seen on the banks. The many species of salamanders, toads, and frogs are less evident to the casual boater. The 33 reported reptiles include four venomous species: coral snake, cottonmouth moccasin, Florida ground rattlesnake, and eastern diamondback rattlesnake.

OTHER ACTIVITIES

Hunting: Limited. Special permit. Consult headquarters.

Fishing: Species common to Florida rivers.

Airboats are prohibited.

PUBLICATIONS
    Leaflet with map.
    Bird checklist.
    Checklist of mammals, amphibians, reptiles, fishes.
    Map of public viewing area near headquarters.
    Fishing regulations.

HEADQUARTERS: P.O. Box 488, De Leon Springs, FL 32130; (904) 985-4673.

LITTLE TALBOT ISLAND STATE PARK
AMELIA ISLAND STATE RECREATION AREA
BIG TALBOT ISLAND STATE PARK
FORT GEORGE ISLAND
Division of Recreation and Parks
4,687 acres.   Map 58, A-1.

    On SR A1A northeast of Jacksonville.

This cluster of Atlantic coastal sites is on six of Florida's most northern barrier islands. Little Talbot was the first to have State Park status, and all four are administered from here. The State Recreation Area occupies a minor part of Amelia Island. The State owns major portions of the three other islands.

    Easy of access and near a major city, the fine ocean beaches on Amelia and Little Talbot draw crowds in season. Larger crowds now, perhaps, since a survey ranked Little Talbot's beach twelfth among 650 in the United States. Fewer people walk the nature trails or explore the wetlands.

    Known as the "sea islands," the cluster is separated from the mainland by a complex of salt marshes, meandering creeks, tidal flats, and narrow estuaries. Like all barrier islands, their shapes are constantly changed by wind, storm, tides, and currents. Some changes are caused by bridge abutments, jetties, dredging, and other alterations of natural contours.

    The island's many habitats have a rich array of flora, including a number of rare species and three Florida Champion trees. Flowering plants occur in the wetlands, on dunes and shell mounds, at forest edges, and in forest understory.

    Birds: A checklist of 194 species notes seasonality and abundance. Park rangers told us the best birding seasons here are summer and winter. Many shorebirds, including least terns, nest here.

Mammals: The only large mammals are porpoises and whales seen offshore. Often seen are river otter, bobcat, raccoon, marsh rabbit.

Other wildlife: A ranger is assigned to find and protect sea turtle nests during their laying season. The islands have many species of reptiles and amphibians.

FORT GEORGE ISLAND

373 acres.

This is a recent State acquisition. Plans for development haven't been completed. Approaching from the south on SR A1A, we turned at a sign for the Kingsley Plantation. Although most of the island is State-owned, this State Historical Memorial is the only evidence of ownership we saw. (New signs are in preparation.) The golf course at the north end is State land but leased to the city.

The island road is a narrow blacktop between big trees, many of them live oaks, arching overhead. On the left are private homes. Salt marshes are on both sides beyond the trees. Where soil has been stripped from around trees they seem to be growing on shell mounds. Quarrying of shell mounds destroyed or damaged archeological sites.

We parked and took a rickety catwalk across a marsh, beyond which we saw the Fort George River and Little Talbot Island. ("This catwalk is private," we were told. "No one's real sure why, when, or who—but it's becoming even more rickety.")

Elevations range from sea level to about 60–65 feet on Mount Cornelia, said to be the highest coastal elevation south of Cape Hatteras. Construction of the golf course involved excavating four miles of drainage ditches and several borrow pits.

At one time much of the land was cleared for plantings of cotton and sugar. Today the predominant forest community is maritime hammock, including live oak, other hardwoods, redcedar, pines, and sabal palm. An understory of ferns, mosses, orchids, and various shrubs and ground covers adds to the natural beauty of the forest, which is further enhanced by the penetration of several sloughs from surrounding marshes.

With the return of the forest has come a revival of many wildlife species. Some have adapted to change: Otters are seen in golf course ponds.

As part of the planning process, the Division of Recreation and Parks is studying the special natural features of the island. The diverse flora includes a number of endangered species, such as rare orchids. Shell mounds have been colonized by specialized plants. A great blue heron rookery is at the north end.

Pending further development, the island offers opportunities for quiet walking in the woods and seasonal birding.

LITTLE TALBOT ISLAND STATE PARK
2,633 acres.

13 miles north of Jacksonville Beach on SR A1A.

Largest of the four units (yes, larger than Big Talbot!), this was the first to be designated a State Park and provided with facilities. It is still the most popular.

About six miles long, the island is less than a mile wide. SR A1A crosses the Fort George River to its southern end, runs north back of the dunes, then turns northwest across marshes to Big Talbot, leaving the northern third of Little Talbot roadless. Campground, bathhouse, and other facilities are near the entrance station. Another bathhouse and picnic area are to the south.

The park has 6 miles of wide beach on the Atlantic Ocean, backed by high dunes. Most other shoreline is salt marsh except for 1½ miles on the Fort George River.

About one-third of the island, chiefly in the north and back of the dunes, is mature forest featuring live oak, magnolia, and other hardwoods. Lower elevations have wet flatwoods, depression marsh, and tidal salt marsh. Vegetation in the south is mostly small pines, scrub palmetto, and depression marsh. The island has several small ponds.

ACTIVITIES

Camping: 40 sites. Telephone reservations accepted.

Hiking: Nature trail near campground. 4-mile hiking trail circles the roadless north end.

Fishing: Said to be excellent. Bass, trout, sheepshead, flounder, whiting.

Swimming: Ocean. Some surfing.

Boating, canoeing: A ramp near the campground was in poor condition in 1990. Canoe is the preferred craft for exploring the tidal creeks.

BIG TALBOT ISLAND STATE PARK
1,430 acres.

Crossed by SR A1A, northwest of Little Talbot Island.

Big Talbot has no ocean frontage. It is surrounded by Simpson Creek on the east, Fort George River on the west and south, Nassau Sound on the north. Most of this frontage is tidal marsh except 2,500 feet on Simpson Creek and 3,800 feet on the Fort George River.

Sheltered from storms by Little Talbot Island and with higher ground, Big Talbot was settled in the eighteenth century. SR A1A traverses the island, and there are inholdings. Almost the entire island is forested.

Unusual for such islands are bluffs 7 feet high at the north end. As these erode, trees are undermined and fall to the beach. On the west, the continuing death and decomposition of marsh vegetation has built solidifying layers, extending the land. The exposure of old marsh led to discovery in 1984 of an entire mammoth skeleton, estimated to be about 30,000 years old.

Sawpit Pond, on A1A at the north end of the island, is a freshwater habitat that attracts migrating waterfowl. Local Audubon groups make outings here. Rangers have seen otters.

Big Talbot has several hiking trails. Spur trails from A1A are worth exploring. The bluffs offer a view of the marshes. Also here: a day-use area and undeveloped, but usable boat ramp.

AMELIA ISLAND STATE RECREATION AREA
229 acres.

7 miles north of Little Talbot Island on SR A1A.

Florida's most northern barrier island is a popular resort. The island lies between the Atlantic Ocean and the South Amelia River. This site on its south tip was acquired by the State in 1983.

Before acquisition, and for a time thereafter, public use of the beach was unregulated. Visitors parked at random along A1A and crossed the dunes or drove 4-wheel-drive vehicles over dunes. Now protected, dune vegetation is recovering.

Approaching over a causeway from Big Talbot, we saw four cars parked on the beach, people swimming and fishing in the inlet.

The outer dunes are relatively low, from 3 feet at the south end of the site to 15 feet at the north. The older back dunes are higher, up to 25 feet. In the shelter of the dunes are pockets of cabbage palm, redcedar, and yaupon, with a few live oaks and slash pines. Salt marshes fringe the west side.

ACTIVITIES

Camping: On Little Talbot only.

Hiking: Trails on Big and Little Talbot. Beaches. Open woodlands.

Fishing: Saltwater species, notably redfish, drum, sheepshead, sea trout, mullet, flounder.

Swimming: Ocean beaches. Supervised in summer at Little Talbot.

Boating, canoeing: No good facilities for launching power boats, but many places where power boats can beach. Fine canoeing in tidal creeks and estuaries.

Horse riding: Amelia Island. From a concession. A 45-minute route.

PUBLICATIONS
Little Talbot leaflet.
Camping information.
Hiking trail guides.
Bird checklist.
Kingsley Plantation leaflet.

HEADQUARTERS: 12157 Heckscher Drive, Ft. George Island, FL 32226; (904) 251-3231.

LOWER SUWANNEE NATIONAL WILDLIFE REFUGE
U.S. Fish and Wildlife Service
51,365 acres.   Map 69, B-2.

From US 19/98 southeast of Chiefland, southwest on CR 347. See signs.

The Refuge has 25 miles of frontage on the Gulf of Mexico and is on both sides of the Suwannee River. CR 347 is its east boundary. North and south entrance gates, with information, are on this route. Farther south, CR 326 is access to a disjunct bit of the Refuge, a boat ramp, archeological site, and a county campground. CR 357 and CR 349 penetrate the Refuge on the north side of the Suwannee.

In 1979 The Nature Conservancy purchased 5,300 acres here, including Shired Island and nearby coastal marshes. Soon it was transferred to the Fish and Wildlife Service. Subsequent acquisitions have brought the acreage to its 1991 size. The goal is 65,000 acres.

The Refuge is a complex of floodplain hardwood forests, coastal plain flatwoods, and salt marshes, cut by 50 miles of navigable freshwater streams and 50 miles of tidal creeks. The highest point is 20 feet above sea level. It is one of the largest undeveloped delta/estuarine areas in the nation, part of a huge area along the Gulf that includes the Cedar Keys National Wildlife Refuge (see entry), State Wildlife Management Areas, timber company lands, and offshore Aquatic Preserves. No portion of the Refuge has yet been declared a Wilderness Area, but most of it is roadless.

About 10 miles of interior roads link the gates on CR 347. Several miles of foot trails are in this south portion of the Refuge. On the north side of the river, about 4 miles of road are off CR 357. The best way to explore the Refuge, in our view, is by canoe or small outboard craft. We recommend staying out of the Refuge in hunting season.

Plants: Nine forest types are found on the Refuge, including floodplain hardwoods, various hammocks, coastal plain flatwoods, and sand ridges. The many tree species include oaks, pines, hickories, cypress, elms. The 785-acre Cummer Tract is an isolated, almost undisturbed forest ecosystem. Some forest areas are parklike, easy to hike through; others have dense, almost impenetrable understories. Seasonal wildflowers are abundant.

Birds: A checklist of over 250 species is available. Spring is the season for migrating shorebirds, raptors, and songbirds. Numerous wading birds are on the Refuge in summer. Many waterfowl winter here. Waterfowl numbers have been in decline on the entire flyway for several years. The decline in numbers seen here has been partially offset by good habitat. Some 30,000 to 100,000 waterfowl are recorded here and at Cedar Key. Wild turkeys are often seen along Refuge roads.

Mammals: No checklist is available. Canoeing in the early morning or evening, one might spot otter or raccoon. Deer are often seen on Refuge roads, bear seldom. Manatee and dolphin frequent the coastal waters.

Reptiles and amphibians: Alligators are common. Snakes include cottonmouth, watersnakes, indigo snake, and three species of rattlesnake. Of several turtles, gopher tortoise is most often seen.

ACTIVITIES

Camping: None on the Refuge. A Dixie County campground is on CR 367 near Shired Island. A Levy County campground is on CR 326.

Hiking: 45 miles of Refuge roads and trails.

Hunting: Almost the entire Refuge is open to hunting, subject to Florida Game and Fresh Water Fish Commission regulations and Refuge rules.

Fishing: Fresh- and saltwater species, notably bass, bluegill, sunfish, redfish, sea trout.

Boating: All navigable waters are open to all pleasure craft. Ramps are at the ends of CRs 357, 349, and 326. Several marinas are nearby.

Dogs must be on leash.
Off-road vehicles and driving off roads are prohibited.

INTERPRETATION

Information kiosks are at the entrances and near the Refuge headquarters.

Three *nature trails* have interpretive panels: River Trail, 0.8 miles, features floodplain forest and the Suwannee River; Shell Mound Trail, 0.25 miles, marsh and archeological site; Dennis Creek Trail, 1.0 mile, coastal ridges and tidal creeks.

PUBLICATIONS
    Leaflet with map.
    Bird checklist.
    Hunting regulations.
    Fishing regulations.

HEADQUARTERS: Rt. 1, Box 1193C, Chiefland, FL 32626; (904) 493-0238.

LAKE OCKLAWAHA (RODMAN RESERVOIR)
U.S. Army Corps of Engineers
10,000 acres of lake; 1,327 acres of upland.   Map 67, D-1.

Rodman Dam is 12 miles south of Palatka on SR 19.

The Cross-Florida Barge Canal was proposed in 1818, studied and debated
for years, eventually authorized. Construction began in 1930; objections
halted it in 1936. Congress authorized it again in 1942 but provided no
money. That came in 1963, and work resumed in 1964. Widespread protests caused President Nixon to order construction halted in 1970, but a federal judge said he couldn't. By now Florida's government was in opposition
and appropriations stopped. In 1986 Congress finally deauthorized the canal.
Questions remained: What to do with the land purchased for the right-of-
way, and what to do with Lake Ocklawaha?
    The 10,000-acre lake (which somehow became "Ocklawaha") was formed
by damming the Oklawaha River, a major element of the project. Also completed was a canal linking the lake to the St. Johns River. Many environmentalists and politicians want the dam torn down, the river returned to its
former bed, and the inundated forests restored. It won't happen soon, although
the right-of-way will probably become a permanent greenway. The upland
adjoins the Ocala National Forest.
    The Corps maintains what it has built and operates four recreation areas
on the lake. The Rodman Recreation Area, near the dam, has a campground.
All four have picnic sites and boat ramps.
    Fishing and boating are the most popular visitor activities, involving 90
percent of those who come. Camping ranks third.

ACTIVITIES
    Camping: 38 sites at Rodman area. 15 primitive sites at the Kenwood
Recreation Area. Pets are permitted.
    Hiking, backpacking: Few come here to hike; the uplands around the lake
have no marked trails. The Rice Creek section of the Florida Trail begins

at the Rodman Dam spillway, follows the Barge Canal toward the St. Johns River.

Fishing: Ten game species include striped and largemouth bass, black crappie, bream, shellcracker, channel catfish.

Boating: Several launching ramps. No hp limit.

Canoeing: Excellent 28-mile canoe trail upstream. Below the dam, 9 miles by canal to St. Johns River.

Swimming is not recommended because of aquatic weeds and underwater obstructions.

PUBLICATION: Folder with map, recreation information.

HEADQUARTERS: U.S. Army Corps of Engineers, Range Headquarters, P.O. Box 1317, 602 N. Palm Ave., Palatka, FL 32177; (904) 328-2737.

MANATEE SPRINGS STATE PARK
Division of Recreation and Parks
2,075 acres.   Map 70, A-1.

West of Gainesville. From US 19/98 at Chiefland, west on SR 320, Manatee Springs Road.

The State acquired this site to protect the large artesian spring, the 1,250-foot run to the Suwannee River, a winter haven for the endangered manatee, and the unusual natural setting. The main spring, one of Florida's largest, gushes 117 million gallons a day at a standard 71°F. It rises in a bowl about 30 feet deep.

From the entrance the park drive passes through pine and hardwood forest to the camping, picnicking, and parking areas. The park has 3½ miles of Suwannee River frontage.

The Park's highest point is 20 feet above the river. In addition to springs, the terrain includes sinkholes and flooded sinks. A swamp of cypress, gum, ash, and maple is along the river. The original stand of longleaf pine was cut by the early 1900s; restoration is a management objective.

Fishing in the Suwannee River, camping, and swimming in the spring are the principal visitor activities. About half the visitors come from nearby.

ACTIVITIES
Camping: 100 sites. All year. Telephone reservations accepted.
Hiking: 8½-mile North-End Trail System.
Fishing: Bass, bream, catfish, speckled perch.

Canoeing: Put-in within the Park. The Suwannee River is a major canoe trail (see entry).

Boating: Launch sites on the river are available outside the park.

INTERPRETATION: *Evening programs* are scheduled in summer.

PUBLICATION: Leaflet with map.

HEADQUARTERS: Route 2, Box 362, Chiefland, FL 32626; (904) 493-6072.

MATTAIR SPRING TRACT
Suwannee River Water Management District
1,189 acres.   Map 54, B-1.

From Live Oak, northeast on US 129. 1.8 miles beyond I-10, turn east on CR 136A. North on Ramsden Road 1.25 miles, then east to site.

Open daylight hours.

This forested site has 4.6 miles of frontage on the Suwannee River (see entry, Suwannee River Canoe Trail), which partially surrounds the site. Mattair Spring emerges from a limestone bank and has a run of several hundred feet to the river.

The original ecosystem was largely grassland with a few longleaf pines and oaks. Most of the interior was planted in slash pines before State acquisition. Gradual restoration is a management objective. Along the river front are mixed pines and hardwoods.

Wildlife has not been cataloged, but species noted include many warblers, hawks, woodpeckers, and screech owls. Mammals include fox, deer, bobcat, squirrel, opossum, raccoon. Gopher tortoises are present, and habitat is being modified to promote the species.

The tract has several miles of nature trails, including one along the river. The site is managed in cooperation with the Division of Forestry.

Canoeing: The river banks are too high and steep for canoe launching. Overnight camping by canoeists on the Suwannee trail is permitted if they can find a site.

PUBLICATION: Leaflet with map.

HEADQUARTERS: Suwannee River Water Management District, Route 3, Box 64, Live Oak, FL 32060; (904) 362-1001.

MIKE ROESS GOLD HEAD BRANCH STATE PARK

("Gold Head Branch" on some maps and lists.)
Division of Recreation and Parks
1,561 acres.   Map 66, B-3.

From Palatka, 29 miles west on SR 100; then north 6 miles on SR 21.

The park is on the dry sand hills of the Florida peninsula's central ridge. The highest elevation is about 200 feet. A deep, humid ravine bisects the area. Runoff from springs at the head of the ravine gathers to form Gold Head Branch, a stream draining to Lake Johnson, largest of several small lakes. Water levels can fluctuate greatly. The site also has a marsh.

Something about the stonework at the entrance seemed familiar, so we asked. This is, indeed, one of several parks developed by the Civilian Conservation Corps in the 1930s. It was considered as the location for a CCC museum, but Highlands Hammock State Park had a suitable building.

Campgrounds, picnic area, cottages, and other development are clustered in less than one-quarter of the site. The undeveloped area is preserved in or being returned to its natural state.

The park is busiest in summer. Picnicking, camping, and swimming are the chief activities, half of the visitors coming from nearby. Trail use by park visitors is light.

Plants: Most of the area is high, dry pineland. Except for turkey oak, few deciduous species are common here. A hardwood hammock borders the ravine, and the ravine itself supports a diversity of trees, shrubs, ferns, and wildflowers. Many species are identified along the nature trails.

Birds: A checklist of 124 species indicates seasonality and relative abundance. As might be expected, upland passerines are the most common, but the list includes a number of waterfowl and wading birds attracted by the four small lakes.

Mammals: Observed mammals include cottontail and marsh rabbits, red and gray foxes, pocket gopher, fox squirrel, raccoon, opossum, pocket gopher, an occasional black bear.

ACTIVITIES

Camping: 74 sites. Telephone reservations accepted. Except on holidays and May to Labor Day weekends, sites are usually available. The park also has 14 vacation cabins.

Hiking, backpacking: On a 29-mile segment of the Florida Trail. A primitive campsite is limited to 12 backpackers, by reservation.

Fishing: In designated lakes. Bass, bream, speckled perch.
Canoeing: On Lake Johnson. Rentals.

INTERPRETATION
Nature trail follows and descends into the ravine.
Campfire programs and *guided walks* are scheduled seasonally.

PUBLICATIONS
Leaflet with map.
Tree checklist.
Bird checklist.
Ridge Trail and Loblolly Trail guides.
Cabin information.

HEADQUARTERS: 6239 State Road 21, Keystone Heights, FL 32656; (904)
473-4701.

NORTH PENINSULA STATE RECREATION AREA
Division of Recreation and Parks
442 acres.   Map 75, A-1.

From Flagler Beach, south on A1A.

Land acquisition began here in 1984. The first document in our files said
135 acres, the second 257. The State's objective is to acquire the adjacent
undeveloped land between the ocean and the Halifax River, the Intracoastal
Waterway. This is one of the rare sections of coastal barrier to have escaped development thus far.

The site is directly south of the Flagler Beach State Recreation Area (see
entry) and is under the SRA's management. No site improvements have been
made other than provision of a parking area for about 20 cars and a path
to the beach. Parking has been prohibited elsewhere along A1A to prevent
further damage to the dunes by random crossings.

The present site has 1.6 miles of fine ocean beach. Plans call for future
development of a campsite and other visitor facilities between A1A and
the Halifax River. The land beyond the river is Bulow Creek State Park
(see entry), and the river provides access to the Bulow Creek Canoe Trail (see
entry). To the south is the Tomoka Marsh Aquatic Preserve.

When we stopped here on a fall weekday, only four cars were in the parking area.

HEADQUARTERS: c/o Flagler Beach State Recreation Area, 3100 South A1A,
Flagler Beach, FL 32036; (904) 439-2474.

OCALA NATIONAL FOREST

U.S. Forest Service
382,664 acres; 430,446 acres within boundaries.   Maps 72, 73.

Between the Oklawaha and St. Johns rivers. Crossed by SRs 19 and 40.

Other Florida public forests were established in the 1930s. The Ocala was established in 1908, the first National Forest east of the Mississippi.

On the west, a visitor center is just inside the Forest on SR 40. Information includes campsite availability. On the south, on SR 19, information is available at the Pittman Work Center near Lake Dorr. Most of the many inholdings are on the west side, north and south of SR 40, and around Lake Kerr.

The higher central portion of the Forest has been called a "wet desert." Rainfall is ample, 55 inches per year, but the water seeps quickly through deep sand. The area supports the world's largest forest of sand pine, the only tree that grows to commercial size in this dry environment. On either side of the central highlands are several hundred lakes surrounded by grassy prairies and forests of longleaf and slash pines.

Four major springs are within the Forest: Alexander, Juniper, Silver Glen, and Salt springs, all intensively developed recreation areas. Creeks drain to the Oklawaha and St. Johns rivers and to lakes beyond the boundary. Cypress, palms, and other subtropical species grow along the waterways, often in dense stands.

National Forests offer a less restrictive environment than Florida's State lands. One has a choice of campgrounds, from developed to primitive, or one can camp in wilderness solitude. Backpackers can enjoy trailside camping. Dogs on leash are welcome in National Forests, in campgrounds, and on trails.

When we arrived late one afternoon, the ranger at the visitor center suggested camping at Fore Lake. It's on the west edge of the Forest and near inholdings, but it seemed quiet and isolated. The lake, one of a group, is small but attractive, with a swimming beach and fishing pier. The setting is a hardwood hammock with mature live and water oaks decorated with Spanish moss and resurrection fern.

Plants: We could find no comprehensive account of the Forest's plant communities. Even the inexperienced eye can see the difference a few feet of elevation makes. Open pinelands give way to dense thickets, hardwoods to palms, prairie grasses to riparian shrubs. Wildflowers change with the seasons.

Birds: Checklist of 219 species notes seasonality and abundance. The list indicates that variety is great but numbers relatively low. In spring, the peak season, only 8 species are called "abundant," only 47 "common."

Mammals: No checklist is available. Species reported include bobcat, raccoon, black bear, opossum, cottontail, armadillo, whitetail deer.

FEATURES

Alexander Springs Wilderness, 7,700 acres, is in the southeast corner of the Forest, on the St. Johns River. The Lake Woodruff National Wildlife Refuge is across the river. The area is best explored by canoe or by small motor craft entering from the St. Johns River. (Airboats and jet skis are prohibited.) Alexander Springs Creek flows into a complex of marsh, small lakes, and waterways, all draining to the St. Johns River. The 7-mile canoe run from Alexander Springs ends at the edge of the Wilderness.

Billies Bay Wilderness, 3,120 acres, is also largely wetlands. Alexander Springs is at the edge of the area.

Juniper Prairie Wilderness, 13,260 acres, is bounded on the south by SR 40, on the east by SR 19. The Florida Trail crosses the center, north to south. The area is a mix of forest and wet and dry prairies, with over a hundred small lakes, ponds, and sinkholes. Juniper Springs is at the southwest corner.

Little Lake George Wilderness, 2,500 acres, is at the northeast corner, on the shore of Little Lake George, at the confluence of the Oklawaha and St. Johns rivers. Most of it is wetland.

Alexander Springs Recreation Area. On warm-weather weekends, the campground here is full and it's difficult to find a parking place. One of the state's largest springs gushes 80 million gallons of water daily at a constant temperature of 72°F. Canoes are available for a 7-mile run. Swimming, snorkeling, and scuba diving are popular. A 1.1-mile nature trail traverses several habitats and identifies plants used by Indians. The subtropical setting includes hardwood swamp, palms, and sand pine ridge. The site is on the Florida Trail.

Juniper Springs Recreation Area is second only to Alexander Spring in popularity. Juniper and Fern Hammock springs together put out 20 million gallons of water daily, their runs joining as Juniper Creek. Canoeists depart from Juniper Spring. Here, too, the campground is usually full in season. The site is on the Florida Trail.

Salt Springs Recreation Area is on SR 19 east of Lake Kerr, at the edge of developed inholdings. The spring pours 52 million gallons of 72°F water daily into Salt Springs Run, which empties into Lake George. A 4.6-mile spur connects with the Florida Trail. Facilities include campground, boat launch, marina, swimming area. No camping reservations.

Lakes Big Bass, Big Scrub, Farles, Halfmoon, Clearwater, Island Ponds, Dorr, Fore, Grassy Pond, Delancy, and *Eaton* all have campgrounds. Facilities differ. The larger lakes have ramps. Few have swimming beaches. (Kerr, the largest lake, is surrounded by private land but has marinas.)

ACTIVITIES

Camping: 21 campgrounds and two hunt camps are widely scattered. Most are on lakes. Reservations are accepted at only two campgrounds. Camping opportunities range from sites with facilities to primitive areas, from sites accessible by car to open camping when access is on foot, horse, or off-road vehicle. Only developed campgrounds and hunter camps can be used in hunting season.

Hiking, backpacking: A 67-mile segment of the Florida Trail crosses north to south. 100 miles of horse trails are open to hikers. Short trails lead from several recreation areas. Many unpaved back roads are suitable for hiking.

Hunting: The Forest is also the Ocala Wildlife Management Area. The Florida Game and Fresh Water Fish Commission manages wildlife. Principal game species: deer, rabbit, squirrel, quail, dove. No hunting for bear or fox squirrel.

Fishing: Many lakes and streams. Bass, panfish.

Swimming: At eight recreation areas. Unsupervised. Snorkeling and scuba at Alexander Springs; scuba divers must have certification.

Boating, canoeing: Access to the two major rivers. Power boats are permitted on the larger lakes. Canoe runs below the major springs. Many canoeing opportunities on lakes and creeks.

Horse riding: Flatwoods Trail, 40 miles, red markers. Prairie Trail, 40 miles, white markers. Baptist Lake Trail, 20 miles, blue markers. Trailheads are off SR 19, about 2 miles north of Altoona.

Sand roads may have soft areas in dry weather.
Pets must be leashed in developed recreation areas. They are not permitted in picnic and swimming areas.
Many areas are closed to off-road vehicles.

PUBLICATIONS
Forest map. $2.
Hiking through the Ocala National Forest.
Wilderness Areas on the Ocala National Forest.
Leaflets:
    Alexander Springs Recreation Area.
    Juniper Springs Recreation Area.
    Salt Springs Recreation Area.
    Lake Eaton Sink.
Bird checklist.
Ocala Trail (Florida Trail) map and information.
Campground information.

Off-road Vehicle Use.
Horseback Riding.

HEADQUARTERS: National Forests in Florida, 227 N. Bronough St., Suite
4061, Tallahassee, FL, 32301; (904) 681-7265.

RANGER DISTRICTS: Seminole Road, U.S. Forest Service, 40929 State Road
19, Umatilla, FL 32784; (904) 669-3153. Lake George Road, U.S. Forest Service, 17147 E. Silver Springs, Silver Springs, FL 32688; (904)
625-2520.

O'LENO STATE PARK
RIVER RISE STATE PRESERVE
Division of Recreation and Parks
1,834 acres; 4,182 acres.   Map 65, A-1.

On US 41/441, 6 miles north of High Springs.

We first saw O'Leno on a hot summer day. The entrance road ends in open
hardwood forest at a bend in the Santa Fe River. The parking lot was almost
full. Many picnic shelters and tables were in use. Most visitors seemed to
be swimming, some jumping from platforms into the river. A suspension
bridge over the river was closed for repairs; it's open again and offers a
fine river view. The Park seemed at first to be just an attractive and popular
swimming hole.

In fact, most visitor activity is concentrated in less than 200 acres (of the
more than 6,000). The Park has an exceptional variety of natural features,
including one of the longest trails in any Florida State Park. Park and Preserve
are on both sides of the Santa Fe River for several miles.

"O'Leno" derives from "Old Leno," as local people referred to the once-
thriving town of Leno in its decline. It died soon after 1900. A dam once
provided power for a lumber mill. The town was the terminus of the first
telegraph line penetrating Florida. Its downfall began as the supply of standing timber dwindled and the first railroad bypassed the town. Rangers can
point out the remains of old roads. The suspension bridge and many of the
Park's buildings were constructed by the Civilian Conservation Corps in
the 1930s.

"River Rise" refers to a geological feature. The Santa Fe River disappears
underground a short distance below the swimming area. It reappears three
miles downstream. Related geological features include sinkholes, small lakes,
springs, and a natural bridge.

The River Rise State Preserve adjoins the Park. It is roadless and will remain undeveloped. Access is by trail from the Park or by canoe (see entry, Santa Fe River Canoe Trail).

The land slopes from flat and gently rolling uplands down to floodplain, from 95 feet of elevation to less than 35 feet.

Plants: A list of tree species is available. Sixteen native biological communities are within the two sites. The uplands are chiefly high pinelands and hardwood hammock. The developed area is upland mixed forest. Most of the original longleaf pine forest was cut years ago. Management plans call for restoring longleaf pines and associated species on portions of the sandhills, upland pine forest, scrubby flatwoods, and mesic flatwoods.

Some of the extensive wetlands are virtually inaccessible. The rich diversity of floodplain species is best seen by hiking the River Sink trail or the much longer River Rise trail, or by canoe.

Birds: A preliminary list of 135 bird species doesn't note seasonality or abundance. Most of those listed are upland species.

ACTIVITIES
Camping: Two campgrounds, 64 sites. Telephone reservations accepted. The campground is sometimes full on June–August weekends.

Hiking, backpacking: Four trails: Limestone, ½ mile; trailhead marked on the entrance road. River Sink, 1 mile; Pareners Branch Loop, 3½ miles; and River Rise, 13 miles; all begin at the suspension bridge.

Hikers on the River Rise trail are asked to sign in and out. Backpackers have a primitive site at Sweet Water Lake.

Fishing: River and in some of the small lakes.
Swimming: Designated area.
Canoeing: No put-in is in the Park. The 26-mile Santa Fe River Canoe Trail (see entry) begins at a US 41/441 bridge and skirts the Preserve.
Horse riding: Permitted on the River Rise trail.

INTERPRETATION Programs have been offered occasionally. Inquire.

PUBLICATIONS
Park leaflet with map.
Tree checklist.
Bird checklist.
Hiking trail information.

HEADQUARTERS: Route 1, Box 1010, High Springs, FL 32643; (904) 454-1853.

OSCEOLA NATIONAL FOREST
U.S. Forest Service
179,732 acres; 183,811 acres within boundaries.   Map 55, A–C.

The southwest corner is at Lake City. US 90 is the south boundary. Crossed by I-10, SR 250.

The area between the Forest and the Georgia boundary is largely undeveloped wetlands: Impassable Bay, Pinhook Swamp, and Little River Bay. Across the line in Georgia is the Okefenokee Swamp. The Forest Service recently acquired 22,000 acres of Pinhook Swamp, a step toward establishing a corridor of publicly owned land between the Swamp and the Forest.

The Forest is higher, between 120 and 215 feet of elevation, and drier, but it has extensive hardwood swamps, one large lake, and many small ponds. Four creeks drain to the Suwannee River, two to St. Marys River. Five are classified as Outstanding Florida Waters.

The federal government bought this land in 1931 after it had been logged, grazed, burned, and abandoned. Since then the primary management has been commercial timber production. Forest management has improved wildlife habitat. The range of elevations and soil types assures a diversity of flora and fauna. Wildlife is managed by the Florida Game and Fresh Water Fish Commission.

The chief recreation center is at 1,774-acre Ocean Pond, a shallow, circular lake just off US 90. The Forest's only developed campground is here. Otherwise, hunting seems to be the most popular visitor activity, about 9,000 visitor-days per year.

The best introduction to the Forest is to drive SR 250 from just north of Lake City to Taylor, at the northeast corner, turning off on any of several unpaved Forest roads. An interesting loop drive is to turn north on Forest Road 235, which skirts the Big Gum Swamp Wilderness, Buckhead Swamp, and the Osceola Natural Area. Return to SR 250 on Forest Road 232, which skirts the west side of the Wilderness. Take time to hike one or more of the unmaintained trails leading into the swamps.

Plants: About 60 percent of the Forest is in flatter uplands. About one-quarter of this is plantations of slash and longleaf pine, the rest in natural regenerations of slash and longleaf. The cypress/blackgum swamps, bay swamps, and creek swamps make up the other 40 percent. Wildflowers are in bloom at every season.

Birds: No checklist is available. Species reported include herons, egrets, osprey, broad-winged hawk, barred owl, red-cockaded woodpecker, bobwhite, turkey, great crested flycatcher, bluebird, meadowlark, white-breasted nuthatch, Carolina chickadee, white-eyed vireo, warblers.

FEATURES
Big Gum Swamp Wilderness, 13,600 acres, is a roadless wetland in the north central sector. The Forest map shows several trails leading from the perimeter, only one crossing the area.
Ocean Pond Recreation Area has camping, swimming, boating.
Olustee Recreation Area, also on Ocean Pond, has swimming and boating.

ACTIVITIES
Camping: 50 sites at Ocean Pond, often full. Eight scattered primitive hunt camps. Informal camping almost anywhere.
Backpacking: The Florida Trail, known here as the Osceola Trail, enters at the Olustee fire tower on US 90, passes the north shore of Ocean Pond, then continues northwest through pine/palmetto flatlands and hardwood swamps. Along the way are numerous small ponds. Leaving the Forest after 20.4 miles, the trail follows the Suwannee River for several miles to the Stephen Foster Cultural Center.
Hunting: Deer, hog, small game, a few waterfowl.
Fishing: Bass, bream, crappie.
Swimming: Ocean Pond.
Boating: Ocean Pond.

PUBLICATIONS
Forest map. $2.
National Forests in Florida Recreation Area Directory.
Red-cockaded Woodpeckers in the Osceola National Forest.
Motorized Vehicle Management Plan.
Osceola Wildlife Management Area. Florida Game and Fresh Water Fish Commission, Northeast Region, RFD 7, Box 440, Lake City, FL 32055; (904) 752-2577.

HEADQUARTERS: National Forests in Florida, 227 N. Bronough St., Suite 4061, Tallahassee, FL, 32301; (904) 681-7265.

OSCEOLA RANGER DISTRICT: U.S. Hwy. 90, P.O. Box 70, Olustee, FL 32072; (904) 752-0331.

PAYNES PRAIRIE STATE PRESERVE
Division of Recreation and Parks
18,036 acres.   Map 65, D-3.

On US 441, 10 miles south of Gainesville.

We first saw Paynes Prairie on a visit to Florida in 1971. The State had only recently acquired the property and no signs marked it as public land. The great expanse of flat grassland looked like a cattle ranch. That's what it was in the late 1600s, the largest cattle ranch in Spanish Florida. We stopped, walked along the road embankment, saw a dozen sandhill cranes, and met a large kingsnake.

A century earlier we might have seen, instead, a steamboat crossing a large lake from Gainesville to Micanopy. The lake, a natural phenomenon, lasted about 20 years. At other times a traveler could have seen a Seminole village, the now-lost town of Osceola, railroad trains, homesteads. Only traces of these remain.

Almost 16,000 acres of the site is a basin 8 miles long, a huge freshwater marsh as much as 35 feet below its rim. In some places the drop is steep, providing natural overlooks. The best overlook is the observation tower near the handsome visitor center. The visitor center is the place to begin any tour. Its staff, programs, and exhibits explain why Paynes Prairie has been designated a National Natural Landmark and what to look for at each season of the year.

In addition to the observation tower, there is an observation platform at a wayside on US 441.

The principal plant communities of the basin are wet prairie and basin marsh. Both are treeless. Trees and shrubs, where you see them, are indicators of land disturbances. The entire basin is frequently flooded. Dikes and abandoned railroad embankments provide extensive hiking routes across the basin.

A marsh can be dry at times. Hiking one day, we saw a line of fire being blown our way, not rapidly enough to be alarming. Looking back from higher ground, we saw it was a prescribed fire, part of management's plan to maintain the natural cycle.

Within the basin is Alachua Sink, a large sinkhole. When this sinkhole became plugged about 1870 a vast lake formed, deep enough for steamboats. About 20 years later, natural forces breached the plug and the lake drained, leaving the steamboats stranded. Alachua Lake fluctuates in size, averaging about 240 acres, draining into the Floridan Aquifer.

Water is supplied to the basin from several sources: Sweetwater Branch, Prairie Creek, and lesser creeks; springs along the rim; rainfall; and surface drainage from higher ground.

Lake Wauberg, near the highway, is larger than Alachua but only partly within the Preserve. The Preserve has 1½ miles of shoreline but thick vegetation prevents access except at the swimming area and boat ramp. Private homes and docks are visible across the lake.

Plants: The Prairie is a botanist's delight. We were given a list of 427 species and told more await discovery. We hope a seasonal list of flowering species will be published some day. Every season has its display.

The 5,000 acres of uplands have been greatly changed over more than a century by land clearing, ranching, cultivation, construction of roads and railroads, erosion, and introduction of exotic species. One of management's objectives is restoration of the original forest of longleaf pine, turkey oak, and southern red oak. Development has been planned so visitors can enjoy the upland areas that remain in relatively natural condition, walking under high, dense canopies of oaks and related hammock species. One survivor is a National Champion Florida soapberry, 70 feet tall, with a 7-foot, 1-inch, circumference.

Birds: A checklist of 219 species notes abundance and seasonality. Although spring and fall are the busiest times, winter populations are exceptionally large and diverse, including numerous hawks and waterfowl and the largest eastern population of sandhill crane.

Mammals: The checklist of 26 species includes opossum, shrews, bats, armadillo, cottontail, marsh rabbit; gray, fox, and flying squirrels; pocket gopher, mice, rats, red and gray foxes, raccoon, longtail weasel, striped skunk, river otter, bobcat, and whitetail deer. Bison, exterminated in the early nineteenth century, were reintroduced in 1975. The original 10 increased to 25, then declined to 7. The Preserve plans to restock.

Reptiles and amphibians: Thanks in part to faculty and students from nearby University of Florida, this checklist is unusually long: alligator, 10 species of turtles, 4 lizards, 26 snakes, 7 salamanders, 15 frogs and toads.

ACTIVITIES
Almost all visitors come for sightseeing. About 40 percent camp. Picnicking, hiking, and birdwatching are secondary activities. Few visitors come to boat or swim.
Camping: 57 sites. No reservations. Seldom full.
Hiking, backpacking: Overnight hikes are limited to those led by rangers, the last weekend of each month, October–March. Trails begin at the Visitor Center, North Rim Interpretive Center, and at a wayside on US 441. Length of trails is from ½ mile to 6 miles.
Fishing: Chiefly from boats on Lake Wauberg.
Swimming: Designated area on Lake Wauberg.
Boating: Ramp on Lake Wauberg. Gasoline power is prohibited. (The prohibition doesn't apply to boats of private property owners across the lake.)
Horse riding: Designated trails; special rules. Inquire.

INTERPRETATION
Visitor center, a prize-winning modern structure, has exhibits, audiovisual programs, publications, information.

North Rim Interpretive Center was an early 1900s bunkhouse. It's now a trailhead and meeting place for ranger-led north rim tours.

Ranger-led activities, offered October–March, include *Prairie Rim Walk,* 4 miles, every Sunday; *Wildlife Walk,* in the basin, 2 miles, every Saturday; *Overnight Backpacking Trip,* last weekend of each month (fee).

PUBLICATIONS
Park leaflet with map.
Checklists of birds, mammals, reptiles and amphibians, fishes.
Trails map and information.
Chacala Trail map.
Ranger-led activities information.

HEADQUARTERS: Route 2, Box 41, Micanopy, FL 32667; (904) 466-3397. Visitor center: (904) 466-4100.

PELLICER CREEK CANOE TRAIL
4 miles.   Map 68, C-2.

Put-in at Faver-Dykes State Park (see entry).

The alternate put-in and upstream beginning of the trail is the US 1 bridge, 1 mile south of the I-95 interchange, six miles west of Marineland. We prefer to put in at the Park. It's tidewater, so current is not significant.

The trail meanders through quiet coastal marshes. Wildlife is abundant. Boat traffic is light.

Although the State-designated trail ends at the park, the creek continues on to the Matanzas River and Intracoastal Waterway. In these wider waters, canoeists should beware of coastal winds.

PUBLICATION: *Pellicer Creek Canoe Trail.* Division of Recreation and Parks.

RUTH SPRINGS TRACT
Suwannee River Water Management District
638 acres.   Map 64, A-1.

From Branford, west and northwest on US 27. 3.5 miles beyond the intersection with SR 349, turn north 0.9 miles on CR 425, then right on New Troy Road.

The District is one of several agencies attempting to preserve the Suwannee River. This tract has 2.6 miles of river frontage. It surrounds a small county park that includes Ruth Springs and its short run to the river.

Management plans to restore the original upland ecosystem: open grassland with a scattering of large longleaf and loblolly pines; turkey, live, and post oaks.

The floodplain has large live oaks, sweet- and blackgums, and cypress. A large river birch has been named a Florida Champion Tree.

Common wildlife includes bobwhite, turkey, wild hog, bobcat, otter, beaver, fox.

ACTIVITIES

Hiking: 6.3 miles of unpaved roads.

Canoeing: On the Suwannee River Canoe Trail (see entry).

Dirt bikes and off-road vehicles are prohibited.

PUBLICATION: Leaflet with map.

HEADQUARTERS: Suwannee River Water Management District, Route 3, Box 64, Live Oak, FL 32060; (904) 362-1001.

ST. JOHNS RIVER
273 miles.   Maps 87 to 58.

It's the nation's longest north-flowing river and Florida's largest. Its sources and upper reaches are described in the Upper St. Johns River Marsh entry in Zone 3. This entry begins at Lake Poinsett in Zone 3. From here the river flows northward through a series of lakes to empty into the Atlantic Ocean at Jacksonville.

Lake Poinsett, 4,334 acres, a favorite of fishermen, is largely surrounded by marshes. Beyond the lake, the river passes through wetlands, including 19 miles bordering the Tosohatchee State Reserve (see entry in Zone 3). (Map 87.)

Passing under SR 50, the river trends northwest through a complex of marshes, backwaters, and small lakes to 6,058-acre Lake Harney, turns west through more wetlands, and enters 9,406-acre Lake Monroe. DeLorme *Atlas* maps 80 and 81 show a number of boat ramps along the way.

From here to the ocean, there are more shoreline developments, recreation sites, and river traffic. The city of Sanford is on Lake Monroe. Operators of pleasure craft should be wary of barges and other cargo carriers.

Where the river leaves Lake Monroe, near the intersection of I-4 and US17/92, is Lake Monroe Park (see entry), a popular boat launch site.

More public sites are along the river now. See entries for Blue Springs State Park and Hontoon Island State Park in Zone 3, and Lake Woodruff National Wildlife Refuge (map 74). Lake George, 46,000 acres, is the second largest in Florida (map 73).

More wetlands. At Palatka the river becomes wider than most of the lakes along its course (map 67). Sections of heavy shoreline development alternate with floodplains and marshes. Finally, at maps 57 and 58, the river becomes a busy commercial avenue, intersecting the Intracoastal Waterway, but tidal marshes on both sides offer miles of twisting channels for exploration by canoe or other shallow-draft boat. One can easily become lost or stranded by an ebbing tide.

ST. MARYS RIVER CANOE TRAIL

51 miles.   Map 56, A-1.

Put-in at SR 121 bridge north of Macclenny.

We haven't yet canoed the St. Marys. We have conflicting information on the river's length (123 or 127 miles) and whether it's "St. Marys" or "St. Mary's." The U.S. Geological Survey makes it "St. Marys." (USGS and Post Office agree on "Macclenny.")

It flows from Georgia's Okefenokee Swamp. For most of its length, the river is the Georgia–Florida border. The State-designated canoe trail is a middle segment where the river flows north from SR 121 to US 301.

It's a wilderness river ("10 bridges in 125 miles" says one outfitter's flyer), clean water stained with tannin from the swamp, winding through dense hardwood forests, white sandbars offering stopping places to picnic, swim, or camp. All easy paddling, according to the State's leaflet and the outfitters.

Not so, wrote Bill Bair, feature writer for the Lakeland (FL) *Ledger*. He and a companion had planned a leisurely three-day trip on a 28-mile segment of the State trail. They weren't warned the river was low (as were all north Florida rivers at the time), and what they thought was a 28-mile segment proved to be more like 40. "There were long stretches where the only thing to do was to get out and pull." In the first afternoon, they traveled 4 miles.

Wilderness rivers offer great delights, but convenient exits on the St. Marys River Canoe Trail are few and far between. Only one landing, one commercial ramp, and one local park are along the way. Only on the lower reaches is development beginning.

Low water is easy to see even if there's no handy rain gauge at a highway bridge. Some usually placid Florida rivers become too dangerous to run after heavy storms. Conscientious outfitters warn their customers.

We hope to run the river some time soon. We're interested in the miles beyond the State trail, where the river meanders through wetlands. The DeLorme *Atlas* map shows no put-ins, but one can often improvise at a highway bridge.

PUBLICATION: *St. Mary's River Canoe Trail.* Division of Recreation and Parks.

SAN FELASCO HAMMOCK STATE PRESERVE
Division of Recreation and Parks
6,500 acres.   Map 65, B-2.

4 miles northwest of Gainesville on CR 232. About 4 miles west of Devil's Millhopper State Geological Site (see entry).

Open 8 A.M. to sunset.

The Preserve, a satellite of Devil's Millhopper State Geological Site, was purchased in 1974 because of its exceptional botanical and geological features. Most of the site is north of SR 232. Until 1990 public access was limited to ranger-guided hikes and to a nature trail on the south side of the road. When we visited that fall, the main area had been opened. A gate 100 yards west of and across the road from the nature trail gives access to two trail loops, one of 6 miles, the other 5. The gate was not conspicuously marked. The Preserve leaflet had not yet been revised to announce the opening.

The principal feature of the Preserve is a climax hardwood hammock with steep slopes and limestone outcrops. Trees include southern magnolia, American holly, spruce pine, and Florida maple. Sanchez Prairie, in the north sector, is a large swamp basin forested with planer tree (water elm) and Carolina ash. Other communities of interest include sandhill and hydric hammock. The site has several Champion trees and numerous rare plants, but an inventory had not been published.

The limestone formation at Devil's Millhopper underlies this site also. There are many sinkholes, some dry, some forming ponds. Creeks flow from small springs in deep ravines, then disappear.

Birds: We obtained a 1979 list of 130 species that doesn't note season or abundance. It includes numerous herons, hawks, woodpeckers, flycatchers, thrushes, vireos, and wood warblers. A new list is in preparation.

Mammals: No list of observations was available. The 1979 leaflet mentioned only bobcat, gray fox, and whitetail deer.

INTERPRETATION
Guided hikes, horse rides, overnight hikes, and other programs are scheduled on Saturdays. Inquire at Devil's Millhopper.
Nature trail samples the several habitats: pine forest, hardwood hammock, sinkholes, brooks.

PUBLICATION: Leaflet with map.

HEADQUARTERS: Devil's Millhopper State Geological Site, 4732 Millhopper Road, Gainesville, FL 32606; (904) 336-2008.

SANTA FE RIVER CANOE TRAIL
26 miles.   Map 65, B-1.

Trail begins at River Rise State Preserve (see entry, O'Leno State Park). 2 miles northwest of High Springs on US 41/441, turn left to ramp.

The Santa Fe River flows from Santa Fe lakes, at first a small meandering stream. Along its course, it is fed by more than three dozen springs, some of them large. At O'Leno State Park, it disappears into a sinkhole and flows underground for 3 miles.

The canoe trail begins downstream from the place where the river reappears. It flows generally west and northwest to join the Suwannee River (see entry) 3 miles beyond the trail's end at the US 129 bridge. About 4 miles earlier, it is joined by the Ichetucknee River. One can paddle upstream 2½ miles to Ichetucknee Springs State Park (see entry). Several tracts of public land, campgrounds, and boat ramps are along the way.

The river is usually clear. It curves gently through hardwood forest and swamps, flowing at 2 to 3 miles per hour. It's easy paddling, with a few shoals, except after a heavy rain.

Alternate take-outs are at mile 3 (US 27 bridge) and mile 13 (SR 47 bridge). Wildlife viewing is best early and late in the day, but wading birds, alligators, and turtles can be seen at any hour.

PUBLICATION: *Santa Fe River Canoe Trail.* Division of Recreation and Parks.

SILVER RIVER STATE PARK
Division of Recreation and Parks
4,161 acres.   Map 72, C-2.

On SR 40 just east of Ocala.

The land was acquired in 1986 and 1987. Its principal feature is the Silver River, which bisects the site. The Park has more than 5 miles of river frontage.

The river rises just upstream at Silver Springs, a famous commercial attraction. It's one of our favorite canoe runs. Pending opening of the Park, an easy put-in is at the county ramp a short distance east on SR 40. A county campground and the Ocala National Forest are downstream.

The Park land is a lush subtropical floodplain. Development is planned for 200 acres in the northwest portion, where the higher ground slopes gradually to the river. Existing jeep trails offer hiking routes in the northern half of the site. The land across the river is higher, with rolling hills. At present there are no plans for a river crossing.

SPRING CREEK UNIT, BIG BEND WILDLIFE MANAGEMENT AREA

Florida Game and Fresh Water Fish Commission
14,899 acres.   Map 62, A-1.

From Perry, 14 miles south on SR 361A.

This is now State land except for 2,000 acres owned by Georgia-Pacific Corporation. It is similar to Tide Swamp (see entry) and other coastal areas along the Big Bend. The Big Bend Aquatic Preserve Marsh Buffer is a strip between this site and the Gulf.

When we visited, the entrance road was in good condition. Woods roads and old tram roads offer hiking routes. The site is managed for outdoor recreation and coastal access. Except in hunting season it offers quiet hiking, with good birding along the coastal marshes.

PUBLICATION: WMA leaflet with map.

HEADQUARTERS: Florida Game and Fresh Water Fish Commission, Northeast Region, RFD 7, Box 440, Lake City, FL 32055; (904) 758-0525.

SPRUCE CREEK CANOE TRAIL

14 miles.   Map 75, D-1.

From I-95, exit west on SR 421, Taylor Road, the first interchange south of I-4. In 600 feet turn south on Airport Road, 1 mile to Moody Bridge.

From Moody Bridge, one can paddle 2½ miles upstream or 4½ miles downstream, returning to Moody Bridge in either case. Tidal flow is more significant than stream current, and it is slow.

Spruce Creek, draining the narrow coastal area between the Halifax River lagoon and St. Johns River, is only 14 miles long. Bluffs line the upper section, unusual for peninsular Florida. The creek enters Strickland Bay, then narrows again, passing through a salt marsh before meeting the Halifax River. Manatees are sometimes seen.

This is not the most exciting tidewater canoe route, but it offers a quiet half-day paddle through dense hardwood forests and coastal salt marsh.

PUBLICATION: *Spruce Creek Canoe Trail.* Division of Recreation and Parks.

SUWANNEE RIVER
177 miles in Florida.   Maps 38, D-3, to 69, B-2.

It's possible to canoe the entire length of the Suwannee River, about 235 miles, beginning in Georgia's Okefenokee Swamp. A levee and canal system controls flow from the Swamp. From the Florida state line to the Gulf of Mexico the river flows freely, a week's journey for earnest paddlers, two weeks for those who want to enjoy fully the splendid scenery. The two State-recommended canoe trails total 120.4 miles.

The river is relatively fast-flowing, its deep channel underlain by karst topography. Numerous springs add to its flow, as do tributaries, the largest of them the Alapaha and Withlacoochee rivers. (Florida has two Withlacoochee rivers.)

The Suwannee drains an area of almost 10,000 square miles, half of it in Florida. Within this basin are many municipal, industrial, and agricultural sources of pollution, and the river is further threatened by developments along its banks and those of its many tributaries.

To plan protection for this scenic and historical river, The Nature Conservancy sponsored the Suwannee River Preserve Design Project, published in 1983. Since then State agencies and the Conservancy have been buying riparian land. Dredge-and-fill regulations have been tightened and some actions have been taken against polluters. Florida's Senator Bob Graham has proposed that the Suwannee be declared a National Wild and Scenic River, which would add further protection.

As of 1989, the Suwannee River Water Management District had acquired 21 tracts along the river. The Department of Natural Resources manages two State Parks and two smaller tracts. The Division of Forestry has two tracts. The Florida Game and Fresh Water Fish Commission has one and has Wildlife Management Areas on several tracts of timber company land. The U.S. Fish and Wildlife Service has a National Wildlife Refuge. The Nature Conservancy has been buying riparian land. Counties and municipalities have a number of small riverside parks.

As of 1989, there were 57 publicly owned recreation sites along the river. Most have ramps. Several of the small county sites, lacking staff, have experienced vandalism and littering; don't leave a car without getting local advice. A minority of the public sites permit camping but canoeists can always find informal sites for rest and overnight stops.

The river has an abundance of flora and fauna, including many rare or endangered species. It has rich archeological resources.

SUWANNEE RIVER (UPPER) CANOE TRAIL
69 miles.   Map 38, D-3.

From White Springs, 7 miles north on SR 135, then east less than a mile to the SR 6 bridge.

At the Florida line the upper river begins in a swamp and flows south through pristine swamps with cypress, oaks, pines, and palmettos. Limestone outcrops along the banks contain many marine fossils. White sand beaches are fine campsites. Clear springs are good swimming holes. Wildlife is abundant.

Approaching Big Shoals at mile 18.6 (see entry) look and listen for rapids. They are the only serious whitewater in Florida, and even experienced canoeists are advised to portage around them.

The trail has alternate put-in and take-out points at miles 8.9, 18.6, 24.6, 26.8, 46.4, and 61.4. This section ends at Suwannee River State Park (see entry). Although Big Shoals is the only public land along the way listed in the leaflet, more has been and is being acquired.

One recent addition is the Mattair Spring Tract (see entry), with 4.6 miles of river frontage about 1.7 miles upstream from the US 129 bridge. Boundaries are marked by red-banded trees or posts.

SUWANNEE RIVER (LOWER) CANOE TRAIL
51.4 miles.   Map 53, A-2.

Put-in at Suwannee River State Park (see entry) off US 90 west of Live Oak.

"Lower" is a relative term; this trail ends at Brandford, little more than halfway to the river's mouth. Below this point, however, there is more development and more motorcraft are operating.

Below the State Park the river is wide, quiet, flowing at two to three miles per hour. Less swampland is seen on this section. The banks are often limestone bluffs. Some shoals are encountered at low water.

Alternate put-in and take-out points are at miles 0.5, 14.9, 25, and 29.4. The State trail ends at the US 27 bridge in Branford. Expect increasing motorboat traffic nearing Branford.

No publicly owned tracts are listed by the State leaflet. Since it was printed, the Ruth Springs Tract at mile 25 has been acquired by the Suwannee River Water Management District. (See entry.) It's a possible rest stop and take-out; no camping.

Branford to the Gulf: From Branford to Manatee Springs State Park (see entry) are many public and private recreation sites with ramps. Below the State Park, most of the land is in Wildlife Management Areas owned by timber companies, all of it open to hunting, some to other recreation. The floodplain is wide, and river access points are limited. The town of Suwannee is near the mouth.

PUBLICATIONS: *Suwannee River (Upper) Canoe Trail* and *Suwannee River (Lower) Canoe Trail.* Division of Recreation and Parks.

SUWANNEE RIVER STATE PARK
Division of Recreation and Parks
1,858 acres.   Map 53, A-2.

On US 90, 13 miles west of Live Oak.

Open 8 A.M. to sunset.

This was a busy place in years gone by. Steamboats plied the Suwannee and Withlacoochee rivers, which meet here. Wagons and stagecoaches rumbled through on the road between Pensacola and Jacksonville. The town of Columbus, population about 500, was an important shipping point for cotton, hides, and lumber from the town sawmill. During the Civil War, the Confederates built an earthworks here to defend the bridge.

All that is gone now. One can stand on the higher river bank overlooking the confluence and forest. Swannacoochee Springs discharge near the Withlacoochee's mouth. When the water is low, as it was last summer, one can see smaller springs bubbling along the limestone river banks. A short distance up the Suwannee, Lime Sink Run was dry, but at times its springs fill deep pools and gather in a 3,000-foot run, tinkling over rocks into the river. A few miles upstream, beyond Park boundaries, the Alapaha River enters. Other evidences of the underlying limestone are several sinkhole ponds. One of the springs on the Withlacoochee has a large underwater cave.

The developed area occupies a small portion of the Park's land. The long entrance road passes the ranger station and campground and ends at a parking area near the boat ramp. Any other land travel is on foot. Elevations range from 40 feet at the river to 80 feet. Hardwood hammocks are along the river. The uplands are an open forest of pines.

The Park is on the Suwannee River Canoe Trail and is the terminus of the Withlacoochee River (North) Canoe Trail (see entries). It is also on the Florida Trail.

Attendance figures are interesting. Because the Park has no major seasonal attraction, such as an ocean beach, visitation is spread more evenly through the year. Weather makes great changes. Visitation drops sharply in a cold winter month or in an unusually hot summer. Only about one visitor in eight spends the night. Picnicking is the principal activity. Many visitors are from out of state, attracted by the name Suwannee.

ACTIVITIES

Camping: 32 sites. No reservations.

Hiking, backpacking: This is the only section of the Florida Trail that is almost entirely riverside. Huge cypress and oak trees are in swamps the trail crosses. Along the way are forests of spruce and pine, patches of tall bamboo. Hikers must ford a few small spring-fed streams.

A nature trail is beside Lime Sink Run.

Fishing: Catfish, panfish.

Boating, canoeing: Ramp. There are no restrictions on power boats, but the river is most suitable for light outboard craft. This is the beginning of the Suwannee River (Lower) Canoe Trail (see entry).

PUBLICATION: Leaflet with map.

HEADQUARTERS: Route 8, Box 297, Live Oak, FL 32060; (904) 362-2746.

TIDE SWAMP UNIT,
BIG BEND WILDLIFE MANAGEMENT AREA

Florida Game and Fresh Water Fish Commission

20,285 acres.   Map 62, C-3.

Between SR 361 and the Gulf of Mexico, northwest of Steinhatchee.

This is now State land except for a 747-acre parcel owned by Procter & Gamble Cellulose Company. A strip half a mile to a mile wide on the Gulf shore is protected as the Big Bend Aquatic Preserve Marsh Buffer.

The north half of the property is tide swamp, a mixture of wet hardwood hammock and cypress swamp. An old, unmaintained logging road and huge cypress stumps are evidence of logging in the early 1900s. The swamp has been largely undisturbed since.

Visitors should consider the condition of unpaved interior roads, especially after rain. We visited during a drought, and the roads we saw were passable. Usually it's advisable to park near the entrance and hike in. Hiking routes include old tram lines.

Woodland types include pine/oak uplands, scrub, pine/palmetto flatwoods, hardwood creek stands, and salt and brackish marshes.

Hagens Cove (see entry) is within the Unit.

Wildlife: The site is managed to promote wildlife species and native plant communities. Deer, turkey, and bear were stocked in the 1960s. Deer, squirrel, turkey, and wild hog are common. Waterfowl use the open marsh. The marshes offer excellent birding.

Boating: Ramp at the end of Dallus Creek Landing road.

PUBLICATION: WMA leaflet with map.

HEADQUARTERS: Florida Game and Fresh Water Fish Commission, Northeast Region, RFD 7, Box 440, Lake City, FL 32055; (904) 758-0525.

TIGER BAY STATE FOREST
Division of Forestry
TIGER BAY WILDLIFE MANAGEMENT AREA
Florida Game and Fresh Water Fish Commission
6,911 acres.   Map 74, C-3.

On US 92, about 4 miles west of I-95, turn north on Indian Lake Road. In 0.8 miles turn left and follow signs to Wildlife Drive.

The site is also known as the Tomoka Wildlife Management Area. First-time visitors may be startled to find themselves approaching a large county prison. Wildlife Drive, beyond the first watchtower, is a residential street for prison employees. The WMA gate is at the end of the street.

We found the gate open and drove in. Beyond is a woods road through pine forest. Indian Lake, 64 acres, is a short distance north, on the tract boundary. Farther north is 48-acre Scoggin Lake, also on the boundary. Both lakes are bordered by wetlands.

We did not explore the portion of the site south of US 92, which is crossed by Dukes Islands Road. The map shows the area to be wetlands.

Tiger Bay Swamp occupies more than 60 percent of the tract. Smaller swamps and marshes are scattered throughout.

The previous owners cut all merchantable timber. Natural regeneration has been impaired by a dense understory.

We saw nothing exceptional here. A few local hunters and fishermen use the site. If you're driving this way, except in hunting season, it offers a quiet woodland walk.

PUBLICATION: WMA map.

HEADQUARTERS: Florida Game and Fresh Water Fish Commission, Central Region, 1239 SW 10th St., Ocala, FL 32674; (904) 732-1225.

TOMOKA RIVER CANOE TRAIL
13 miles.   Map 74, B-3.

From Ormond Beach, 4 miles west on SR 40 to bridge.

This trail isn't as quiet and remote as nearby Bulow Creek Canoe Trail (see entry). It passes under SR 40 and I-95, crosses the Ormond Beach airport, and passes under US 1 before entering coastal marshes. Even so, much of it is pleasantly natural, sheltered from disturbing sights and sounds.

After launching at SR 40, canoeists can paddle upstream against slow current for about 2 miles, then return. An intermediate take-out downstream is at the US 1 bridge, mile 4. The river is wider here, with tidal influence. Beyond US 1, it meanders through salt marshes. Tomoka State Park (see entry) is at mile 8. The trail ends at the park boat ramp, mile 9. Beyond is the Tomoka Basin.

Some canoeists camp at the park and paddle upstream through the marshes at dawn. Good birding.

PUBLICATION: *Tomoka River Canoe Trail.* Division of Recreation and Parks.

TOMOKA STATE PARK
Division of Recreation and Parks
917 acres.   Map 75, B-1.

From SR A1A at Ormond Beach, west on SR 40. Cross the bridge over the Halifax River and turn north on North Beach Street (Old Dixie Highway on some maps).

The Park is on a narrow peninsula projecting into Tomoka Basin, where the Tomoka River meets the Halifax River. The Halifax is here the Intracoastal Waterway. The Tomoka River and Basin, fringed by salt marshes, have numerous small islands and tidal flats.

When we visited on a sunny September weekday, the parking lots were about half full. Chief activities seemed to be picnicking, fishing, boating, and relaxing. Swimming is not permitted. The park is fully developed, with campground, recreation hall, picnic sites, visitor center, store, museum, fishing docks, boat basins and ramps, and a short nature trail. Shade is provided by large oaks.

March has been the peak month for attendance; it has been the only month in which campers outnumbered day visitors.

This is a fine base for exploring coastal rivers, creeks, and marshes by boat. There is direct access to the Tomoka River and Bulow Creek Canoe Trails (see entries). A cruise boat offers daily one-hour excursions on the Tomoka River.

ACTIVITIES
   Camping: 100 sites. Telephone reservations accepted.
   Fishing: Brackish waters. Speckled trout, redfish, drum, flounder, snook.
   Canoeing: Rentals.
   Boating: Ramps.

PUBLICATIONS
   Leaflet with map.
   Cruise information.

HEADQUARTERS: 2099 North Beach St., Ormond Beach, FL 32074; (904) 677-3931.

VOLUSIA COUNTY SCENIC HIGHWAY
Volusia County
About 12 miles.   Map 75, A-1.

At the North Peninsula parking area on SR A1A turn inland. Turn left on Walter Boardman Lane, then left on Old Dixie Highway.

We found this route by chance and thought it delightful, a quiet, narrow, winding road through an old-Florida landscape of creeks, marshes, and hammocks. Tree canopies close over the road. On either side is dense subtropical vegetation. The road crosses the Inland Waterway on a narrow wooden drawbridge.

Walter Boardman Lane is wider. Just beyond the turn is a small parking area and unpaved boat ramp on Bulow Creek. (See entry, Bulow Creek Canoe trail.) In about 0.2 miles, we spotted an inconspicuous sign: "Bulow Creek State Park" (see entry).

At the end of Walter Boardman Lane, the route turns left on Old Dixie Highway, a somewhat busier county road leading to Ormond Beach. On this road are the main entrance to Bulow Creek State Park and Tomoka State Park (see entries), with good views of Tomoka Basin and the Halifax River.

WACCASASSA BAY STATE PRESERVE
Division of Recreation and Parks
30,784 acres, including 6,775 submerged.   Map 70, C-1 to D-3.

On the Gulf Coast from near Cedar Key to Yankeetown. Headquarters on SR 24 east of Cedar Key.

Once there was a vast watery wilderness known as the Gulf Hammock. Most of it is now owned and has been greatly altered by timber companies. State acquisition of the Waccasassa Bay area began in 1971. It now encompasses 27 miles of coastline. Here the ecosystems are almost intact and the few changes are reversible. The site has been designated a National Natural Landmark.

In the years following acquisition, the Preserve was closed to the public. Now the bay and creeks are open for boating and fishing. Backpacking and primitive camping may be permitted when there is staff to monitor them. If you'd like to hike the uplands, headquarters staff may suggest a route.

(In 1991 we heard the State budget might require cutting staff to one person.)

We can't improve on the rhapsodic description in the site's Unit Plan: "Emerging from the forested upland onto the marshy lowland, one is delighted by the sweep of a landscape free of human technology. Rather than a condominium-dominated skyline, one gazes upon a coastal marsh that extends far outward, dotted by wooded islands and interlaced with tidal creeks. Beyond the marsh stretches the shimmering Gulf of Mexico."

All true, but you won't find an overlook. The highest ground, along the north and east boundaries, is only five feet above sea level. The land is flat, sloping almost imperceptibly to the Gulf.

Even slight differences in elevation produce different life zones. Highest is the coastal hammock. Trees here include cabbage palm, redcedar, and live oak. Somewhat surprisingly, much of the hammock floor is carpeted with grasses. Unlike some coastal hammocks, this area is sometimes flooded when a strong southeasterly wind drives a flood tide. It is also surprising to see many rock outcrops; bedrock is close to the surface.

Bordering the hammock is a narrow strip of coastal savannah, where trees and shrubs are scarce and vegetation is chiefly glasswort, saltwort, saltgrass, and sea lavender.

About 70 percent of the Preserve is salt marsh, an area one to three miles wide along the Gulf. The marsh is cut by numerous tidal creeks and dotted with cabbage palm and redcedar islands. These creeks offer the visitor the best opportunity to explore the Preserve. Also within the Preserve are freshwater swamps and the most northern mangrove forest on Florida's west coast.

Wildlife: The Preserve, where sea and land merge, is an extraordinarily rich complex of flora and fauna. Potholes in the savannah attract ducks and wading birds, and many feed in the offshore shallows. The hammock is favorable habitat for opossum, cotton and golden mice, woodrat, black bear, and whitetail deer, as well as a nesting area for osprey, bald eagle, hawks, and herons. The freshwater swamps are home for many reptiles and amphibians, river otter, water rat, and marsh rabbit.

Tidal flats extend for many miles into the Gulf. They reduce the impact of wave action on the shore and are a nursery for countless marine organisms. Plovers, sandpipers, gulls, and ducks feed on the exposed flats at low tide.

ACTIVITIES

Camping: A primitive campsite is accessible by boat only. Inquire.
Hiking: Inquire at headquarters.
Fishing: Creeks and Gulf.
Boating, canoeing: Ramp on CR 326 off US 19. The area is so large and the waterways so complex we recommend asking advice.

All motorized land vehicles are prohibited.
Hunting is prohibited.

PUBLICATION: Leaflet with map.

NEARBY: Cedar Key Scrub State Reserve (see entry).

HEADQUARTERS: P.O. Box 187, Cedar Key, FL 32625; (904) 543-5567.

WITHLACOOCHEE RIVER (NORTH) CANOE TRAIL
32 miles.   Map 37, D-1.

SR 145 bridge, north of Pinetta, at the Georgia border.

Florida has two Withlacoochee rivers. This one has most of its course in Georgia, and the section above the border is canoeable. The Florida-designated trail runs from the border to the river's confluence with the Suwannee at Suwannee River State Park (see entry).

The river flows at two to three miles per hour, curving gently through swamps, hardwood forests, and pastures, past a few small settlements. There are no special hazards, but beginners should exercise caution at high water. One may have to pull over small shoals at low water.

Bridges at miles 5 and 15 are alternate put-ins or take-outs.

No public campground is along the way, but one can find a suitable place for overnighting.

PUBLICATION: *Withlacoochee River (North) Canoe Trail.* Division of Recreation and Parks.

WITHLACOOCHEE STATE FOREST

Most of the Forest is in Zone 3. See entry there.

ZONE 3
CENTRAL FLORIDA

ZONE 3
CENTRAL FLORIDA

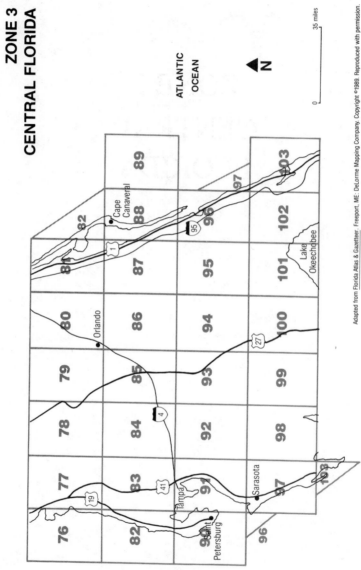

ATLANTIC
OCEAN

N

0 |——————| 35 miles

Adapted from Florida Atlas & Gazetteer. Freeport, ME: DeLorme Mapping Company. Copyright ©1989. Reproduced with permission.

ENTRIES IN ZONE 3

The number preceding the natural area entry refers to the map number in the DeLorme *Florida Atlas & Gazetteer.*

77 Fort Cooper State Park
77 Gum Slough Canoe Trail
77 Potts Preserve
77 Withlacoochee State Forest
77 Chassahowitzka National Wildlife Refuge
78 Flying Eagle
79 Lake County Waterways
80 Blue Spring State Park
80 Econlockhatchee River Canoe Trail
80 Hontoon Island State Park
80 Lake Monroe Park
80 Little Wekiva River Canoe Trail
80 Lower Wekiva River State Reserve
80 Rock Springs Run State Reserve
80 Soldiers Creek Park
80 Wekiva River–Rock Springs Run Canoe Trail
80 Wekiwa Springs State Park
81 Canaveral National Seashore
81 Seminole Ranch Wildlife Management Area
81 Tosohatchee State Reserve
82 Anclote Key State Preserve
82 Caladesi Island State Park
82 Honeymoon Island State Recreation Area
82 Merritt Island National Wildlife Refuge
83 Crews Lake Park
83 Hillsborough River State Park
83 J. B. Starkey Wilderness Park
83 Lettuce Lake County Park

83 Upper Tampa Bay County Park
83 Wilderness Park
84 Green Swamp
84 Green Swamp Wildlife Management Area
84 Polk County Rail Trail
84 Saddle Creek Park
84 Tenoroc State Reserve
84 Withlacoochee River Park
84 Withlacoochee River (South) and Canoe Trail
85 Lake Louisa State Park
86 Moss Park
87 Bull Creek Wildlife Management Area
87 St. Johns River
87 Upper St. Johns River Marsh
90 Egmont Key State Park
90 Fort De Soto County Park
90 Pinellas Trail
90 Sawgrass Lake Park
91 E. G. Simmons Regional Park
91 Little Manatee River State Recreation Area, Little Manatee River Canoe Trail
91 Weedon Island State Preserve
92 Alafia River Canoe Trail
92 Alderman's Ford County Park
93 Peace River Canoe Trail
94 Arbuckle Creek Canoe Trail
94 Arbuckle State Forest and Wildlife Management Area
94 Avon Park Air Force Range

Z ONE 3 IS CENTRAL FLORIDA. Cities near its north border are Inverness, Wildwood, Sanford, and New Smyrna Beach. Its southern border cuts across Lake Okeechobee. A glance at the state road map shows this part of Florida is heavily developed. Orlando and Tampa–St. Petersburg are fast-growing metropolises. Sections of the Gulf and Atlantic coasts have unbroken ranks of condominiums and subdivisions. Highways in this zone carry the state's greatest motor vehicle traffic.

A 16,000-acre wilderness in Tampa? A wilderness beach on the ocean? A 3,900-acre lake with a pristine shoreline? A birders' mecca in St. Petersburg? These and many more natural areas are in the zone. Indeed, we have more entries here than in any of the three other zones.

The zone has more lakes than any other part of Florida. Several of our favorite canoe runs are here. Segments of the Florida Trail run beside the Kissimmee River and through the Green Swamp and Withlacoochee State Forest. At Highlands Hammock State Park, Florida's first, one can see alligators, raccoons, large turtles, and wading birds at close range. The dikes at Merritt Island National Wildlife Refuge offer miles of hiking with outstanding birding.

Several countries in central Florida are developing outstanding park systems. The Upper Tampa Bay County Park, for example, has several nature trails with boardwalks, one of the best nature centers we've seen anywhere, and canoeing through a mangrove swamp.

Most coastal resorts are intolerably crowded from December into April, yet quiet, uncrowded places of exceptional beauty are only minutes away.

COMMON BIRDS OF ZONE 3
by Chuck Geanangel

Central Florida has a remarkable number of birding hotspots. Two of them, Fort de Soto and Saddle Creek, are county parks. Pelican Island, the first federal refuge, is now a satellite of the Merritt Island National Wildlife Refuge where great numbers of migratory waterfowl gather. Lake Kissimmee State Park is one of the best places to see Bald Eagle. The St. Johns and other rivers attract many Osprey and White Ibis.

Lists like these are at best a rough guide in trip planning. "Winter residents" will almost certainly be present in winter, but fall arrivals and spring departures vary from species to species and year to year. It was tempting to mention specialties and rarities that attract birders from afar, but one can't be sure of seeing them. When you visit a park or refuge, ask for a bird list. Then ask for the news: What special birds are present? When and where can they be seen?

WATER HABITATS, FRESH, BRACKISH, AND SALT

Permanent residents, here all year

Pied-billed Grebe
Double-crested
  Cormorant
Anhinga
Great Blue Heron
Great Egret
Snowy Egret
Little Blue Heron
Tricolored Heron
Green-backed Heron

Black-crowned Night-
  Heron
White Ibis
Glossy Ibis
Wood Stork
Wood Duck
Mottled Duck
Osprey
Purple Gallinule
Common Moorhen

Limpkin
Killdeer
Black-necked Stilt
American Avocet
Greater Yellowlegs
Lesser Yellowlegs
Spotted Sandpiper
Least Sandpiper
Laughing Gull
Black Skimmer

Permanent residents of the coastal region

Brown Pelican
Reddish Egret
Yellow-crowned
  Night-Heron
Clapper Rail
Black-bellied Plover
Wilson's Plover

Semipalmated Plover
Piping Plover
American
  Oystercatcher
Willet
Whimbrel

Ruddy Turnstone
Sanderling
Dunlin
Royal Tern
Sandwich Tern
Common Tern

Transients, spring and fall

Roseate Spoonbill

Semipalmated
  Sandpiper

Pectoral Sandpiper

Winter residents, fall to spring

Common Loon
Horned Grebe
American White
  Pelican
Green-winged Teal
Blue-winged Teal
Northern Shoveler
American Wigeon
Ring-necked Duck

Lesser Scaup
Hooded Merganser
Ruddy Duck
Sora
American Coot
Western Sandpiper
Stilt Sandpiper
Dowitcher
Common Snipe

Bonaparte's Gull
Ring-billed Gull
Herring Gull
Caspian Tern
Forster's Tern
Red-breasted
  Merganser
Belted Kingfisher

Summer residents, spring to fall

Least Tern

Black Tern

Gray Kingbird

LAND HABITATS

Permanent residents, here all year

Cattle Egret
Black Vulture
Turkey Vulture
Bald Eagle
Red-shouldered Hawk
Red-tailed Hawk
Crested Caracara
Northern Bobwhite
Sandhill Crane
Rock Dove
Mourning Dove
Ground Dove
Barn Owl
Eastern Screech Owl
Great Horned Owl
Barred Owl
Red-headed
  Woodpecker

Red-bellied
  Woodpecker
Downy Woodpecker
Northern Flicker
Pileated Woodpecker
Blue Jay
Scrub Jay
American Crow
Fish Crow
Carolina Chickadee
Tufted Titmouse
Brown-headed
  Nuthatch
Carolina Wren
Blue-gray Gnatcatcher
Eastern Bluebird
Northern Mockingbird
Brown Thrasher

Loggerhead Shrike
European Starling
White-eyed Vireo
Yellow-throated
  Warbler
Pine Warbler
Prairie Warbler
Common Yellowthroat
Northern Cardinal
Rufous-sided Towhee
Red-winged Blackbird
Eastern Meadowlark
Boat-tailed Grackle
Common Grackle
Brown-headed
  Cowbird
House Sparrow

Transients, spring and fall

Barn Swallow
Veery
Yellow Warbler
Magnolia Warbler

Cape May Warbler
Black-throated Blue
  Warbler
Blackpoll Warbler

Prothonotary Warbler
Hooded Warbler
Indigo Bunting

Winter residents, fall to spring

Northern Harrier
Sharp-shinned Hawk
American Kestrel
Yellow-bellied
  Sapsucker
"Empidonax"
  Flycatcher
Eastern Phoebe
Tree Swallow
House Wren
Ruby-crowned Kinglet

Hermit Thrush
American Robin
Gray Catbird
Water Pipit
Cedar Waxwing
Solitary Vireo
Orange-crowned
  Warbler
Yellow-rumped
  Warbler
Palm Warbler

Black-and-white
  Warbler
American Redstart
Ovenbird
Northern Waterthrush
Chipping Sparrow
Savannah Sparrow
Swamp Sparrow
Northern Oriole
American Goldfinch

Summer residents, spring to fall

Swallow-tailed Kite
Yellow-billed Cuckoo

Common Nighthawk
Chuck-will's-widow

Chimney Swift
Ruby-throated
  Hummingbird

Great Crested	Purple Martin	Black-whiskered Vireo
Flycatcher	Northern Roughwing	Red-eyed Vireo
Eastern Kingbird	Swallow	Northern Parula
Gray Kingbird	Yellow-throated Vireo	Summer Tanager

ALAFIA RIVER CANOE TRAIL
13 miles.   Map 92, B-1.

From SR 640 east of Lithia, north on CR 39 1 mile to Thompson Road, then left to Alderman's Ford County Park (see entry).

It's still a popular canoe trail despite concerns about water quality. A *Tampa Tribune* article was headed: "Scenic passage is a panorama of pollution." Both the north and south prongs of the river, which join here, have troublesome pollution, although the water looks clear. The State and Hillsborough County hope to improve matters. Plans include purchase of natural areas along the course.

Large oak, cypress, and cedar trees shade the winding stream. Minor shoals are encountered at low water. At high water the current is moderately swift.

An alternate take-out, at mile 10, is Lithia Springs County Park.

PUBLICATION: *Alafia River Canoe Trail.* Division of Recreation and Parks.

ALDERMAN'S FORD COUNTY PARK
Hillsborough County Parks and Recreation Department
1,141 acres.   Map 92, B-1.

From SR 640 east of Lithia, north 1.5 miles on SR 39.

Open 8 A.M. to sunset.

The park is at the confluence of the two prongs of the Alafia River and the beginning of the canoe trail (see entry). The river is too polluted for swimming but not for enjoyment of its natural setting.

The broad river floodplain has a dense hardwood forest. It is bordered by a forested slope with several springs and small creeks. The higher ground is an open forest of longleaf pine and scrub oak. The hillside forest has interesting plant species such as jack-in-the-pulpit, devil's walking stick, and swamp honeysuckle.

Hiking, backpacking: 2-mile trail leads to a wilderness preserve. A board-walk 1,875 feet long wanders through the floodplain. Nature trails and in-terpretive displays in the visitor center describe the native fauna and flora.

Two primitive camping areas. Reservations are required.

PUBLICATIONS
Park leaflet.
Boardwalk guide.

HEADQUARTERS: Parks and Recreation Department, 1101 E. River Cove Drive, Tampa, FL 33604; (813) 272-5840.

ANCLOTE KEY STATE PRESERVE
Division of Recreation and Parks
287 acres.   Map 82, C-2.

Boat access. 3 miles offshore, on the Pasco–Pinellas county line.

A 320-mile chain of barrier islands lies off the coast of peninsular Florida. Causeways and bridges have led to development of most of them. Anclote is one of the few still pristine. Its ecosystem is fragile, however, and abuse by visitors is a serious concern.

The chief attraction for visitors is 4 miles of sand beach on the Gulf side. Thousands of pleasure boats operate from nearby marinas and private docks, and Anclote is an easy run for them. Many pull up on the beach or anchor in the shallows, boaters coming ashore to swim and picnic.

Back of the beach and dunes is coastal strand dominated by cabbage palm with an understory of subtropical shrubs typical of the West Indies. On the south end of the island, this grades into slash pine flatwoods with wax myrtle prominent in the understory.

Two nuisance exotic plants, Australian pine and Brazilian pepper, both widespread in southern Florida, have a foothold on the island but are not yet displacing native species. Management hopes to eliminate or control them.

It's a fine habitat for birds. The southern bald eagle, red-cockaded woodpecker, piping plover, and least tern are among 43 species recorded. All-year observation would yield more.

ACTIVITIES
Camping: Primitive. No water.
Boating: Boats can be anchored off shore in calm weather.

Dogs are prohibited.

HEADQUARTERS: c/o Caladesi Island State Park, #1 Causeway Boulevard, Dunedin, FL 34698; (813) 443-5903.

ARBUCKLE CREEK CANOE TRAIL
37 miles.   Map 94, C-1.

From the public ramp at the south end of Lake Arbuckle on SR 64.

This is one of our favorite runs, partly because we live nearby. Undisturbed streams flowing through cypress swamps are rare in Florida. Several years ago we began urging that it be protected by land purchase or easement. Now it seems this may happen.

The stream just below the lake is sometimes choked by water hyacinth. When it is, we put in at a small county park off Horse Hammock Road, the first road south.

It's an easy half-day run to a public launch site on Arbuckle Creek Road, CR 700A. Parts of the creek beyond there are less attractive because of a high dike on the west side and a broad area of slow-moving water often thick with hyacinth, but it also has attractive swampland. A short rapids seldom has enough water to be run, but lining a canoe through isn't difficult. The creek ends at Lake Istokpoga.

The Avon Park Air Force Range borders the east side of the upper half of the creek. This is a quiet buffer zone, an undisturbed cypress swamp. On the west side are a few houses, ranch land, and cypress swamp. There's more cypress swamp below the Range. The chief intrusions are two road bridges and a rail trestle. We occasionally meet power boats coming from Lake Istokpoga or the Arbuckle Creek Road landing.

The creek and surrounding swamps are a valuable wildlife corridor between the two lakes. Botanists have identified a number of rare plant species here and called attention to a scrub and sand pine scrub community, a type becoming rare in Florida.

Birds recorded include the Florida scrub jay, limpkin, burrowing owl, tricolored heron, peregrine falcon, sandhill crane, wood stork, and caracara. The most numerous species we've seen is the white ibis.

ARBUCKLE STATE FOREST
AND WILDLIFE MANAGEMENT AREA
Division of Forestry,
Florida Game and Fresh Water Fish Commission
13,511 acres.   Map 94, C-1.

From Frostproof on Alt. US 27, east 0.6 miles on CR 630; right 4.5 miles
on Lake Reedy Boulevard. At Arbuckle Road left 1.5 miles to Rucks Dairy
Road.

Open daylight hours.

Lake Arbuckle, 3,900 acres, 4½ miles long, is the largest remaining lake
in Florida with a protected and undeveloped shoreline. On the east shore
is a buffer zone of the Avon Park Air Force Range (see entry). State acquisition of land on the western shore began in 1984 and was completed in
1986, in time to save the property from subdivision.

When the State acquires such a site, management responsibilities are often
shared by several agencies. Here the Division of Forestry is the lead agency,
with the Florida Game and Fresh Water Fish Commission providing wildlife management. The 2,816 acres between School Bus Road and the lake
will eventually be managed by the Division of Recreation and Parks for a
State Park.

Until a State Park is developed, public access to the site is by Rucks Dairy
Road on the north, which leads to a mile-square inholding, and School Bus
Road on the south; they connect. Hikers can use existing sand roads and
trails. The Division of Forestry has no plans to develop recreational facilities. Camping is prohibited except by hunters at a primitive site in hunting
season. Public camping and boat launching are available at the adjoining
Arbuckle County Park on the north end of the lake (see entry). A public
ramp is at the south end, near the Air Force Range gate.

The property is roughly rectangular, with the lake on the east. School
Bus Road was built as a shortcut for school buses transporting students from
the Air Force Range to Polk County schools. It has been improved for public use.

Commercial timber harvesting on the site began in 1906 and continued
until 1973. No old-growth stands then remained. Some flatwoods areas were
cleared and planted. Others have been in natural succession. Still others were
burned and used for cattle grazing. Although flatwoods are the most extensive community, the site has many stands of scrub and may be Florida's
most important remaining site for this natural association. Regenerating flatwoods also have a number of rare species, including the largest known system dominated by cutthroat grass.

Livingston and Reedy creeks, the latter flowing from Reedy Lake, join on the site and flow into Lake Arbuckle. Lake Godwin, 20 acres, is near the center of the site. Wetlands of less than an acre to several hundred acres are scattered throughout.

Wildlife: No checklists hae been published. A Florida Game and Fresh Water Fish Commission inventory lists over 200 bird species, 38 mammals, 71 reptiles and amphibians, and 43 fishes, including a number of threatened or endangered species. We have seen deer on each of our visits.

The natural qualities of the site are such that management emphasis will be on protection and enhancement of endangered species and natural communities.

ACTIVITIES

Camping: At adjacent county park until a state park is developed.

Hiking, backpacking: A 15-mile loop of the Florida Trail is across the lake in the Air Force Range. The Florida Trail Association is developing a trail in the Arbuckle State Forest. Hikers can now park along School Bus Road and follow old roads and trails or bushwhack.

Hunting: Regulated by the Florida Game and Fresh Water Fish Commission.

Fishing: Lake Arbuckle has been popular with fishermen. Bass and panfish are their chief interest.

Boating, canoeing: Pending development of a state park, launch at the county park or public ramp. The ramp at the south end of the lake is also a put-in for Arbuckle Creek (see entry).

PUBLICATIONS

Wildlife Management Area leaflet.

Division of Forestry pamphlet to be published in 1991.

HEADQUARTERS: Division of Forestry, Lakeland District, 5745 S. Florida Ave., Lakeland, FL 33803; (813) 648-3160. Florida Game and Fresh Water Fish Commission, South Region, 3900 Drane Field Road, Lakeland, FL 33803; (813) 644-9269.

ARCHIE CARR NATIONAL WILDLIFE REFUGE
U.S. Fish and Wildlife Service
Proposal: up to 20.5 miles.   Map 96, A-2.

Atlantic coast between Melbourne Beach and Sebastian Inlet.

This section of sand beach is one of the world's principal nesting sites for endangered sea turtles, with as many as 790 nests per mile. Recorded: 10,000 to 12,000 loggerhead nests, 300 green turtle nests, and occasional leatherback nests. The coast is still lightly developed but only scattered segments are publicly owned.

The U.S. Congress has approved establishment of a federal refuge. The State is acquiring portions. The Nature Conservancy is assisting. Officials of the two counties involved, Brevard and Indian River, have been more interested in seaside development than protection of endangered species.

Some decisions will have been made by the time this book appears, and at least part of the beach will have legal protection. As nesting season approaches each year, there is a call for volunteers to patrol the beaches, chiefly at night, reporting and protecting the nests.

The beach is named for the late beloved Archie Carr, who devoted his life to sea turtles. When a dinner honoring him on his seventy-fifth birthday was announced at Gainesville, Florida, a large tent had to be obtained to accommodate the horde of colleagues, former students, and friends who came from near and far.

HEADQUARTERS: c/o Merritt Island National Wildlife Refuge, P.O. Box 6504, Titusville, FL 32782; (407) 867-0667.

AVON PARK AIR FORCE RANGE
U.S. Air Force
106,110 acres.   Map 94, C-1.

From Avon Park on US 27/98, east on SR 64 to gate.

Open to visitors Thursday noon through Monday evening, by permit, subject to rules and restrictions. Weekly and annual permits are available from the Natural Resources Office. Hunters only in November and December. Telephone (813) 452-4223 for information on temporary closures.

The base is an active installation with bombing target ranges. Most of the base, which measures about 14 miles north–south, 12 miles west–east, is open to public use at specified times. The rules are strict but sensible and clearly stated.

Much of the public area is in relatively undisturbed natural condition, comparable to nearby Highlands Hammock, Florida's oldest State Park (see entry). Because the recreation opportunities have not been widely publicized,

99 percent of the visitors come from Florida, and 75 percent of them are hunters. Except in hunting season, public use is light. Campgrounds are seldom full except on holiday weekends.

The area is flat to rolling, elevations ranging from 40 to 125 feet. Lake Arbuckle and Arbuckle Creek are on the west, the Kissimmee River marshes and canal on the east. The public use area also includes a number of creeks and ponds. The principal natural community is pine flatwoods interspersed with sandhills and marshes. Included are old-growth pine flatwoods, cypress ponds, and sandhill plant communities. There are many flowering plants, including orchids and bromeliads.

Prospective visitors should obtain a copy of the Public Recreation Area Map. This shows the range areas, which are closed at all times, and restricted areas within which visitors must stay on designated roads. These include less than one-fourth of the base. The remainder is the public use area, divided into 14 management units. Any or all units may be closed temporarily. 'With the map is information on permits and access.

The map shows the extensive road network in the public recreation area. Paved and shell roads are normally suitable for 2-wheel-drive vehicles. Sand and grassroads, used chiefly by hunters, may require 4-wheel-drive.

Wildlife: The array of species is comparable to that found at Highlands Hammock State Park. Birding is exceptionally good, with frequent sightings of bald eagle, wild turkey, red-cockaded woodpecker, sandhill crane, swallow-tailed kite, limpkin, glossy ibis, wood stork, and Audubon's caracara.

ACTIVITIES

Camping: Three campgrounds, 100 sites. Campgrounds are primitive. Two have cold showers. Telephone (813) 452-4223 for information on weekend restrictions. (It's often busy.)

Hiking, backpacking: Four developed trails, ½ to 16 miles. Use of the Florida National Scenic Trail and the Lake Arbuckle National Recreation Trail requires picking up a free Hiking Trail Permit from the Natural Resources Office. Use of the Sandy Point Wildlife Refuge Trail and Lake Arbuckle Nature Trail requires the purchase of an Outdoor Recreation Permit.

Hunting: By special permit. Information and permits are obtained at the Natural Resources Office. Wildlife is managed in cooperation with the Florida Game and Fresh Water Fish Commission.

Fishing: Creek and river. Chiefly bass and bream.

Boating, canoeing: A ramp is on the C-38 Canal (Kissimmee River). Boaters should not land without permits.

PUBLICATIONS

Public Recreation Area Map.
Regulations.

HEADQUARTERS: Natural Resources Manager, 56 CSS / DEN, Avon Park Air
Force Range, Avon Park, FL 33825; (813) 452-4119.

BLUE SPRING STATE PARK
Division of Recreation and Parks
2,192 land acres.   Map 80, A-2.

From US 17/92 in Orange City, west on French Ave.

The park is best known for the manatees that take refuge in the 72°F spring
water from November through March, when the river is too cold for them.
Visitors come in any season to swim in the spring.

The St. Johns River (see entry) loops for about 2½ miles across the northwest corner of the Park. From the river, here less than 5 feet above sea
level, marine terraces rise to about 80 feet in the east and northeast. Water
from the spring flows about 2,200 feet to the river through Blue Spring Run,
from the banks of which visitors can see the manatees. Near the center of
the site is a floodplain lagoon extending about 2,500 feet south from the river.

The English botanist John Bartram provided the first written description
of this area and Blue Spring in 1766. In 1872 the Thursby family built a
large frame house on one of the several shell mounds left by the Timucuan
Indians. The house has been restored.

Park developments are concentrated in the northeast corner of the site.
The southern two-thirds is a protected natural area.

Plants: Ecologists have mapped more than a dozen distinct biological communities. The principal categories are swamp, marsh, flatwoods, hammock,
and sand pine scrub. A list of vascular plants is available, not yet classified
by season or abundance.

Wildlife: No bird or mammal lists were available when we visited.

FEATURES
Blue Spring's average flow is 55,000 gallons per minute. The opening,
an aquatic cave, covers less than an acre. Its vertical shaft angles into a "room"
at 80 to 90 feet, then constricts at 120 to 125 feet. The small opening here
and the torrent of water prevent further exploration.

Boardwalk beside Blue Spring Run is the best place from which to see
manatees.

INTERPRETATION
Slide programs, November 15–April 15.

Tour boat, the John Bartram, 2-hour cruises at 9:30 A.M. and 1 P.M., Monday–Friday. Fee.

ACTIVITIES

Camping: 51 sites; 6 cabins. Often full on weekends and holidays. Reservations.

Hiking, backpacking: A 4-mile hiking trail loops around the undeveloped portion of the site to a primitive camping area between the river and the lagoon. Campers must register.

Fishing: Largemouth bass, bluegill, shellcracker, speckled perch, blue and channel catfish.

Swimming: In the spring. Swimming with the manatees is prohibited.

Canoeing: Rentals. Canoes, no motors, are permitted in the run. Unlimited canoeing on the river and its tributaries. We have canoed from here to Hontoon Island (see entry) for a camping weekend. On our way back, a large manatee surfaced quietly beside us. On another occasion, we came down the Wekiva River and down the St. Johns to Blue Spring.

Boating: No ramp in the Park. Boaters on the river often pull up on the beach, stopping to see the manatees.

PUBLICATIONS

Leaflet with map.
List of vascular plants.
Springs.
Cabin information.
Tour boat information.

NEARBY: Hontoon Island State Park (see entry) is downstream.

HEADQUARTERS: 2100 West French Ave., Orange City, FL 32763; (904) 775-3663.

BULL CREEK WILDLIFE MANAGEMENT AREA
Florida Game and Fresh Water Fish Commission
22,206 acres.   Map 87, D-2.

From Holopaw on US 441, 5 miles east on US 192. Then 6 miles south on Crabgrass Road to hunter check station.

This is a delightful, secluded area with a 17-mile loop of the Florida Trail. The site was acquired by the St. Johns River Water Management District as a retention area for hurricane flood waters. It was heavily logged until the late 1920s and also used for turpentine production. Grazing continued until a few years ago. Since public acquisition in 1967, the tract has been returning to natural condition.

Crabgrass Creek flows east and south. Bull Creek, flowing north from Billy Lake, is joined by Little Creek, then joins Crabgrass Creek to become east-flowing Jane Green Creek, tributary of the St. Johns River. The area is dotted with marshes and seasonally wet ponds.

Plant associations are diverse: scattered stands of saw timber, cypress and swamp hardwoods, mature cabbage palms, pine flatwoods, prairie, and cypress domes. We have seen a lengthy inventory of understory shrubs and flowering plants. Birding is excellent, chiefly in spring.

ACTIVITIES
Hiking, backpacking: The Florida Trail circles the site, beginning and ending near the check station. Trailside camping is permitted at two places designated by white bands on trees.

Hunting: Various seasons, fixed annually by the Florida Game and Fresh Water Fish Commission.

Fishing: Billy Lake, several places in Bull Creek; canals.

PUBLICATION: Bull Creek WMA leaflet.

HEADQUARTERS: Florida Game and Fresh Water Fish Commission, Central Region, 1239 SW Tenth St., Ocala, FL 32674; (904) 732-1225.

CALADESI ISLAND STATE PARK
Division of Recreation and Parks
607 land acres; 1,170 acres submerged.   Map 82, D-2.

Boat access. Commercial ferry from Honeymoon Island (see entry) and Clearwater. (At last reports, Dunedin Pass, at the south end of the island, was filled in, making foot access from Clearwater Beach possible at times. A storm could reopen the pass.)

Open 8 A.M. to sunset.

Like Anclote Key (see entry), Caladesi Island is one of the chain of Gulf Coast barrier islands and one of the few still largely undeveloped. The State bought it in 1967, in time to prevent commercial development. Three cottages were in use in the 1940s, but the most evident past disturbance is a network of mosquito control ditches cut through the black and red mangrove communities.

Caladesi has more than 2 miles of white sand beach. Visitor use is concentrated here, where tide and storm soon erase the traces. The island's highest point is 11 feet above sea level. High tides driven by storm winds flood portions of the island every 10 to 20 years. Beach dunes extend the length of the island on the Gulf side. Sea oats, sea grape, and other dune vegetation are protected from trampling by cross-dune boardwalks. Back of the dunes is a strip of coastal strand, grading into maritime hammock characterized by live oak, cabbage palm, and redbay with a scattering of old-growth slash pine. The understory is largely saw palmetto.

Unlike Anclote, Caladesi has some provisions for visitors: a marina, concession, boardwalks, a nature trail, and exhibits. It has four times as many visitors as Anclote, and it is more heavily patrolled to prevent ecological damage.

The marina, where the ferry lands, has 100 slips for private boats. On busy days, about half of the visitors beach their boats or anchor in the shallows. Ferry passengers are limited to four hours on the island.

Swimming and picnicking are the chief visitor activities. Even on peak visitor days, people who cross the dunes or hike to the south and can enjoy a quiet natural setting.

Birds: A checklist of 162 species is available. Winter is the best birding season, but 44 of the species are permanent residents.

Mammals: A checklist is available but few occur: nine-banded armadillo, marsh rabbit, gray squirrel, raccoon, river otter. Atlantic bottlenose dolphin are often seen offshore.

Reptiles and amphibians: Loggerhead sea turtles nest on the Gulf beach. Young green sea turtles feed in marine grass beds. Gopher tortoises are common. Also present: several lizard species, mangrove water snake, southern black racer, eastern coachwhip, corn snake, yellow rat snake, eastern kingsnake, eastern diamondback rattlesnake. Amphibians include Florida cricket frog, green treefrog, eastern narrow-mouthed toad.

ACTIVITIES
Camping: Boat camping at the marina slips. No camping is permitted on shore.
Fishing: Mullet, trout, redfish, snook, tarpon, kingfish.
Swimming: Lifeguard in season.
Shelling: An extensive list of marine invertebrates and their habitats is available.

INTERPRETATION: Nature trail, 3 miles long, from the picnic area to the interior of the island, through the island's several natural communities. The trail returns along a pristine beach.

PUBLICATIONS
Leaflet with map.
Vertebrate checklists.
Guide to Coastal Vegetation.
Shelling guide.
Ferry information.

HEADQUARTERS: #1 Causeway Blvd., Dunedin, FL 34698; (813) 443-5903.

CANAVERAL NATIONAL SEASHORE
National Park Service
67,500 acres of land and water.   Maps 81, 82.

North: SR A1A south from New Smyrna Beach. *South:* SRs 406 and 402 east from Titusville.

On Florida's congested Atlantic Coast lie 24 miles of splendid sand beach. Almost half is roadless wilderness, accessible only on foot or by canoe.

In the 1960s the National Aeronautics and Space Administration acquired most of Merritt Island for the Kennedy Space Center. In 1963 part of the area became the Merritt Island National Wildlife Refuge (see entry). The Seashore was established in 1975. It's an unusual arrangement: Refuge and Seashore, administered by different agencies of the Department of the Interior, publish a joint leaflet that shows no boundary between them.

It's still NASA's property, a buffer zone for the Space Center. NASA maintains security. Playalinda Beach, the south end of the Seashore, has sometimes been closed prior to a space shuttle launch. Where SR 402 borders the Space Center, cars must not be parked or passengers discharged. At times cars are stopped at a roadblock to be checked for weapons. The North District of the Seashore is not affected by closures, but crowds gather to see each launch.

The 24 miles of white sand beach are backed by high, vegetated barrier dunes. Behind the dunes is Mosquito Lagoon, a long, tidal subtropical estuary fringed by marshes, hardwood hammocks, and mangroves. In the lagoon, chiefly in the north, are more than a hundred islands.

FEATURES

Apollo Beach, at the North District of the Seashore, is penetrated by about 6 miles by SR A1A, back of the dunes. Along the way are five parking areas with boardwalk dune crossings, a boat-launching site on the lagoon, nature trails, and an information center. At Eldora are a few private homes not yet acquired by the government.

Klondike Beach is the 12-mile midsection, reached only on foot or by canoe. The number of visitors declines rapidly with distance from parking areas. Few have hiked the 12½ miles, much less made a round trip. Beach camping is allowed, by permit, on the northern 5 miles of Klondike except during the turtle nesting season, May 15 to September 30, and on nights preceding a shuttle launch.

Here, as at the Cape Cod National Seashore, the National Park Service at first tolerated the long-established custom of nude swimming on remote sections of beach. Signs posted by local authorities now prohibit it.

Playalinda Beach. The 5-mile section at the South District of the Seashore is heavily visited. When we visited on a warm January weekday, all 12 parking lots were full, as they are most weekends and holidays. Eddy Creek is a boat-launching site on the lagoon.

Mosquito Lagoon is shallow and tidal. Its dense grass beds are feeding and breeding grounds for fish and other marine organisms. Skiers and other boaters wanting open water launch at Eddy Creek. The launch north of Turtle Mound, on the north end, is preferred by canoeists and birders who wish to explore the many islands. Haulover Canal, opposite Klondike Beach, provides access to the Indian River. The Intracoastal Waterway from the north hugs the west shore of the lagoon until it passes through the canal.

Birds: Over 250 species have been recorded at the Seashore and Refuge. Birding opportunities are greater at the Refuge because of its many impoundments and miles of dikes. The Canaveral beaches are patrolled by squadrons of pelicans and cormorants; gulls, willets, sanderlings, and turnstones feed in the waves' backwash; terns dive off shore. Many more species are seen on the islands, shores, and tidal flats of the lagoon.

Mammals: Dolphins are often seen off shore, whales occasionally. Manatees are sometimes seen in the lagoon, otters swimming near banks, raccoons and armadillos on shore.

Reptiles and amphibians: Loggerhead and green turtles nest on the sand beach between May and September, under strict protection. Alligators are common in the Refuge. Snakes, some venomous, keep to the thick underbrush.

Seashells are the only objects visitors are allowed to collect. Many varieties are found at low tides.

ACTIVITIES

Camping: Backcountry only, by permit, at primitive sites accessible on foot or by canoe. Most sites are on islands in the northern lagoon. Permits and maps can be obtained at the information center, North District.

Hiking: Beach and nature trails.

Fishing: Surf and lagoon.

Swimming: No lifeguards. Water is reasonably warm all year. Hazards are strong currents, jellyfish, Portuguese men-of-war.

Boating: Lagoon and Indian River. The nearest ocean access is at New Smyrna Beach.

Canoeing: Just north of Turtle Mound is the beginning of a self-guided 2-mile canoe trail. Two backcountry campsites are on the trail.

Thunderstorms with lightning are common in summer. Get under a shelter. Mosquito Lagoon was aptly named. Bring repellent.

INTERPRETATION
Visitor center, North District, has exhibits, slide show, literature, information.

Guided walks, turtle watches, children's programs are announced in the Activity Schedule.

Nature trails are at Turtle Mound, Eldora Hammock, and Castle Windy.

PUBLICATIONS
Folder with map and information.
Activity Schedule.
Backcountry camping information.
Castle Windy nature trail guide.
Common Birds of Canaveral National Seashore.
Guide to Seashells.
Hills of Sand.
Guide to Coastal Vegetation.
Turtle Mound.

HEADQUARTERS: 2532 Garden St., Titusville, FL 32796. For information: (407) 267-1110.

CHASSAHOWITZKA NATIONAL WILDLIFE REFUGE
U.S. Fish and Wildlife Service
30,436 acres, mostly marsh and water.   Map 77, C-1.

HQ is on US 19, 4 miles south of Homosassa Springs. Most of the Refuge is accessible only by boat.

The lower reaches of the Homosassa and Chassahowitzka rivers are a maze of islands, hardwood swamps, brackish marshes, salt bays, estuaries, and channels. This is a protected estuarine habitat, maintained chiefly as a wintering ground for ducks and coots, but fine habitat for many other wildlife species, breeding and feeding ground for fish and shellfish.

Unlike refuges where cultivation of crops, maintenance of impoundments, and other measures are needed to enhance carrying capacity, this one requires little habitat manipulation other than occasional burning of marshes. It's not the easiest place for wildlife viewing. There is a half-mile nature trail at headquarters, and roads west from here lead to sandhills on the east edge of the site. Boat access is from landings on either river or Mason Creek. Most Refuge visitors come to fish, only a few for birding or hunting. Most visitors come from nearby.

If you have a shallow-draft boat and like exploring, winter and spring are the times for good birding.

Birds: 250 species have been recorded. Seasonally abundant species include herons, egrets, pelicans, blue-winged teal, lesser scaup, wigeon, ring-necked duck, gadwall, red-breasted and hooded mergansers.

ACTIVITIES

Hunting: Chiefly waterfowl, but minimal in recent years. A WMA is adjacent.

Fishing: Redfish, speckled trout, bass, bream.

Boating: Airboat operators must have a Refuge permit; use is restricted to designated areas. Some areas are closed to all boats.

PUBLICATIONS
Leaflet with map.
Bird checklist.
WMA leaflet.

HEADQUARTERS: 7798 S. Suncoast Blvd., Homosassa, FL 32646; (904) 382-2201.

CREWS LAKE PARK
Pasco County Parks and Recreation Department
113 acres.   Map 83, B-1.

From US 41 north of Land o' Lakes, west 2½ miles, then north on Shady Hills Road.

Open dawn to dusk.

A 113-acre wilderness? The minimum under the Wilderness Act is 5,000 acres. But "wilderness" can also be a management philosophy, a commitment to minimum development, preservation, and restoration of natural ecosystems. That, we were told, is the plan here.

The Park is on a 700-acre lake about 3 miles long. One of its natural features is a live oak hammock by the lake with more than 300 old-growth trees. Another is a longleaf pine forest with trees 50 to 60 years old.

Developments include an information kiosk, half-mile bicycle and hiking trail, 2 miles of nature trails, 60-foot observation tower, fishing pier, boat ramp, and picnic shelters.

Birds: 162 species have been recorded.

Dogs must be leashed.

HEADQUARTERS: 16735 Crews Lake Drive, P.O. Box 11327, Spring Hill, FL 34610; (813) 847-8118, Ext. 8828.

ECONLOCKHATCHEE RIVER CANOE TRAIL

19 miles.   Map 80, C-3.

Northeast of Orlando. From Oviedo at the intersection of SRs 426 and 434, east 2 miles on SR 419 to bridge.

An intermediate put-in or take-out is at mile 8, the Snow Hill Road bridge. The trail ends at a bridge on SR 46 east of Geneva, but one can continue 1½ miles to the St. Johns River.

The Division of Recreation and Parks leaflet calls this a "scenic wilderness river." One does pass under a few bridges including an old railroad trestle that carries the Florida Trail, but most of the route is indeed wild, meandering through hardwood and cypress swamps and forests and past high sandhills. The current usually flows two to three miles per hour. Sandbars offer the only campsites; no public or private recreation sites are on the river, although State purchase of some land is proposed.

Water quality is good until the river is joined by the Little Econlockhatchee, which carries pollutants.

Check the depth gauge at the Snow Hill Road bridge, 2 miles northwest of Chuluota on SR 419; if it's below 3 feet, you'll be dragging. Water hyacinths are also a problem at low flows.

Orange and Seminole counties and the St. Johns Water Management District are considering rules to prohibit construction within 550 feet of the river and limit construction within 1,100 feet. They may be in force by the time this book is published.

PUBLICATION: Leaflet. Division of Recreation and Parks.

EGMONT KEY STATE PARK
Division of Recreation and Parks
440 land acres; 110 acres submerged.   Map 90, D-2.

Boat access only. At the mouth of Tampa Bay.

It was almost a State Park in January 1991, with headquarters, resident staff, and budget. The temporary snag: no lease.

Most of the island was a National Wildlife Refuge, but the Fish and Wildlife Service couldn't protect it. More than a hundred private boats may be beached on weekends; tour boats discharge passengers; visitors wander everywhere. The Service leased its 328 acres to the State. The Coast Guard owns the north tip of the island, but the lighthouse has been automated and Coast Guard personnel moved off. The Coast Guard buildings became State Park offices and residence, but a year later lawyers hadn't agreed on terms of lease. Perhaps they have by now.

It's a barrier island about 1½ miles long, the highest point five feet above mean high tide. About two-thirds of the land area is cabbage palm hammock, the rest prairie and beach. Wildlife inventories haven't been completed, but the island is within sight of Fort De Soto County Park (see entry), a birding hot-spot. It is still, legally, a National Wildlife Refuge, and a State Park staff of four provides better protection than occasional federal patrols.

If boat landings are restricted to designated places, visitors limited to the beach and established paths, and nest sites safeguarded, Egmont Key will again be an important resource for migratory birds.

HEADQUARTERS: Slip 656, 4801 37th St. South, St. Petersburg, FL 33711; (813) 894-6577.

E. G. SIMMONS REGIONAL PARK
Hillsborough County
458 acres.   Map 91, C-2.

From US 41 north of Ruskin, turn west on 19th Ave. NW.

On Tampa Bay. The 258 acres visitors see is open land cut by many mangrove-fringed lagoons. Except for the mangroves, it's not a natural area, but it is spacious, the developed facilities are widely spaced, and the birding is good. Manatees are sometimes seen in the lagoons.

The other 200 acres are mangrove swamp set aside as a bird and wildlife sanctuary. We walked along the edge and saw no way in.

ACTIVITIES

Camping: Two campgrounds; 60 sites. On an October Sunday, we found less than a dozen sites occupied.

Fishing: In the shallow bay and from stub piers in lagoons.

Swimming: Supervised area.

Boating: Ramp, boat basin.

HEADQUARTERS: P.O. Box 1416, Ruskin, FL 33570; (813) 645-3836.

FLYING EAGLE
Southwest Florida Water Management District
10,000 acres.   Map 78, B-1.

From SR 44 at Inverness, 1½ miles south on US 41, then 4 miles east on Eden Drive and Moccasin Slough Road.

When this entry was written in March 1991, the District owned the tract and had adopted a management plan. The site has four miles of frontage on the Withlacoochee River (see entry) and is within the river's floodplain. More than half is freshwater marsh and riverine swamp. Hardwood hammocks are scattered throughout the site. Large areas are inundated by heavy storms. The tract was acquired to maintain and restore the wetlands for flood storage, for aquifer recharge, and for cleansing the surface water entering the river. Public recreation consistent with these purposes is encouraged.

Prior to District acquisition, Flying Eagle had been a cattle ranch and used by a hunting club. Primitive roads and trails had altered surface water flow. Airboats had beaten trails through swamps and marshes. Airboats are now prohibited. Culverts or other means will be used to normalize surface flow.

Some existing roads will be improved to provide access to two primitive camping areas and the Apopka lakes.

ACTIVITIES

Camping: Primitive sites. May not be accessible by automobile, especially in wet weather.

Hiking, backpacking: Unmaintained primitive roads and trails.

Fishing: River and lakes.

Canoeing: No ramp is planned, but hand launching may be possible when there's road access to the river. Put-ins are available upstream and down. Canoe camping is permitted at designated locations.

Hunting is prohibited.
Airboats and off-road vehicles are prohibited.

HEADQUARTERS: Southwest Florida Water Management District, 2379 Broad Street, Brooksville, FL 34609; (904) 796-7211.

FORT COOPER STATE PARK
Division of Recreation and Parks
545 land acres.   Map 77, B-3.

From Inverness, southeast 2 miles on SR 39.

The Park is based on 121-acre Lake Holathlikaha, one of many large and small lakes in this region west of the Withlacoochee River. Although the lake has been designated an Outstanding Florida Water, it has been degraded in recent years. Emergent vegetation is encroaching; about 50 acres of former lake are becoming marsh. The lake water becomes oxygen depleted in summer.

Dry hardwood hammock is the principal natural community, occupying 311 acres. This association, considered rare, is here in excellent condition with few exotic plants. About 43 acres were cleared and planted in slash pine in the 1960s. Restoration has been proposed.

Almost 200 acres are sandhill community, an association also diminishing in Florida. The original longleaf pines were used for turpentine production. The community is relatively pristine except for numerous fire lanes.

The Division of Recreation and Parks intends to maintain the Park as a natural area with no further development.

HEADQUARTERS: 3100 Old Floral City Rd., Inverness, FL 32650; (904) 726-0315.

FORT DE SOTO COUNTY PARK
Pinellas County
900 acres.   Map 90, C-2.

On I-275, southbound through St. Petersburg, exit 4 westbound on SR 682, then south on SR 679, signed for Park.

This well-tended urban Park attracts 2 ¼ million visitors per year. Because of its shape and widely spaced developments, one can always find places for quiet walking. The Park is nationally famous among birders.

SR 679 crosses four small keys by bridge and causeway to arrive at Mullet Key, the main portion of the Park. To the right is the larger part of the key, shaped like a bent arm, with North Beach near its tip. Along this portion are swimming beaches, fishing piers, picnic areas, restaurant, and the old fort. To the left is the east swimming area and picnic ground.

The base and arms of Mullet Key are relatively narrow. On either side of the road are broad areas of grass. Most of the inner side, along the bayous, has a fringe of mangroves, oaks, and pines. The outer side of the base faces Tampa Bay. The long "forearm" faces the Gulf of Mexico. The park has 6 miles of beach front, half on the Bay, half on the Gulf.

Vehicles can drive on sand tracks paralleling the road on both sides. Here visitors can park for fishing or tailgate picnicking. Away from the swimming beaches, one can walk for a mile or two close to Gulf or Bay. On the other side of the road and at the north end of the Key, one can walk in sun or shade.

Many palms have been planted, in rows at the large parking areas, around buildings, and elsewhere. Especially at the north end we saw many casuarinas, not unattractive but usually regarded as an exotic pest.

The park supervisor gave us these estimates of annual visitor activities:

Picnicking	1,750,000
Swimming	700,000
Boating	200,000
Camping	165,000
Fishing	50,000
Sightseeing	25,000
Jogging, cycling	10,000
Birding	10,000
Hiking	10,000

The fort, built in 1898, has unusual weaponry. Tours are given frequently, aided by a living-history volunteer in uniform.

Birds: 283 species have been recorded, 247 of them at least three times. The checklist is unusually helpful in that it provides a map identifying 12 birding hot-spots, and the checklist notes where each species is most likely to be seen.

Because of the Park's location, at the southern tip of the peninsula that encloses Tampa Bay, migrating birds funnel through in large numbers. Early March through mid-May is the best period for spring migrants, the peak usually occurring around the second week of April. Of the many species of eastern wood warblers, only three have not been recorded here.

Fall is a good season for shorebirds, thrushes, warblers, and others. Shorebirds and ducks are the most numerous winter species. Summer is slow, but birders can always find something of interest.

ACTIVITIES

Camping: The 235 sites are in demand, 100 percent occupied January through April, fully occupied on weekends from May 1 through Labor Day. Sites can be reserved, not more than 30 days in advance, only in person, not by mail or telephone. Reservations are for a minimum of two nights, maximum of 14.

Hiking: One can wander freely for several miles.

Fishing: Two fishing piers. Supervisor says fishing in the grass flats is fair to good.

Boating: As large a launching ramp as we've ever seen.

PUBLICATIONS

Park information page with map.

Camping information; reservations procedure.

Bird checklist.

Common shells leaflet.

HEADQUARTERS: Box 3, Tierra Verde, FL 33715; (813) 866-2484. Camping information: (813) 866-2662.

FORT PIERCE INLET STATE RECREATION AREA
Division of Recreation and Parks

1,298 acres.   Map 103, A-1.

On SR A1A near Fort Pierce.

The SRA has two units: Fort Pierce Inlet, 340 acres, a picknicking and swimming site on the ocean; and 958-acre Jack Island, a fine natural area open to foot travel only.

The Fort Pierce Inlet site is on the north side of the inlet, with about 2,000 feet of sand ocean beach backed by dunes. Behind the dunes is coastal hardwood hammock circled by a nature trail and an area of spoil from dredging.

Jack Island, north of Pepper Beach and across the highway, is over a mile long, a coastal hammock mostly surrounded by mangrove swamp. Its vegetation has been characterized as West Indian. Plant species include gumbo limbo, strangler fig; red, black, and white mangroves; blolly, saltbush, white stopper, randia. A footbridge crosses to the island from the parking area. When we first visited, a yellow-crowned night-heron was at the water's edge.

A kiosk at the end of the bridge has exhibits describing the island's ecology, especially the mangroves. ("Jack Island is a special example of the mangrove forests that form vast areas of watery wilderness in the tropics and subtropics. These trees are extremely valuable as nursery sites for young marine animals and as food material in the form of leaves which are fed upon by countless numbers of small animals. The area also provides an important feeding ground for birds, raccoons, otters, and other animals.")

A 4.2-mile dike trail circles the island. Another, 1 mile long, cuts across it. An observation tower at the far end was condemned and torn down in 1989. Once, when the osprey was recovering from the DDT-caused population crash, we stood on the tower and saw thirty osprey aloft.

A nature trail is on the cross-route. Labels identify the principal plant species. We saw no footprints on the trail.

On each visit to Jack Island, we've seen many butterflies. Overhead are webs of golden-silk and crab spiders.

About 99 percent of the Recreation Area visitors come to swim; many of them also picnic and fish. The beach is often crowded on summer weekends and holidays. Jack Island has relatively few visitors, many of them birders.

Birds: A checklist of 190 species is available. It includes many waterfowl, wading birds, and shorebirds, among them the common loon, magnificent frigatebird, reddish egret, and roseate spoonbill. Also listed are many upland species, including 26 wood warblers.

NEARBY: About three miles north of Jack Island, we found an unnamed, undeveloped ocean beach. Along A1A are several unmarked pull-off parking areas and informal trails through the dunes. Signs that warn against swimming because of underwater objects suggest the beach is publicly owned, but the signs are anonymous. No sign prohibits dogs, so our young Labrador had his introduction to surf. On a mile or more of excellent beach, we saw three fishermen. The beach begins just north of the Ocean Resorts mobile home park. Don't tell anyone about it.

PUBLICATIONS
Leaflet with map.
Bird checklist.

HEADQUARTERS: 905 Shorewinds Drive (A1A), Fort Pierce, FL 34949; (407) 468-3985.

GREEN SWAMP WILDLIFE MANAGEMENT AREA
Southwest Florida Water Management District/
Florida Game and Fresh Water Fish Commission
54,000 acres.   Map 84, 2-3.

Access from Rockridge Road, off US 98 north of Lakeland; and SR 471, also north of Lakeland.

Gates are open only in hunting season. At other times, foot access from Rockridge Road only.

The Southwest Florida Water Management District has purchased about 54,000 acres in the Green Swamp (see entry). More purchases by the District and county governments are pending. The District's primary objectives are flood control, protecting the headwaters of five major rivers, and safeguarding the Floridan Aquifer. Wildlife is managed by the Florida Game and Fresh Water Fish Commission.

Hunting is the principal activity, but walk-in visits by hikers, birders, and sightseers are increasing. The Polk County Rail Trail (see entry), just east of the District land, is on an abandoned railroad embankment purchased by the State.

Wildlife: With an abundance of food, water, and shelter, the Swamp sustains a large and diversified population of wildlife. It's a wintering ground and stopover for migratory birds, a nesting area for dozens of resident species. Mammals include otter, raccoon, fox, squirrels, rabbits, armadillo, bobcat, wild hog, deer. Panthers have been reported on rare occasions, but there is no resident population.

ACTIVITIES

Hiking, backpacking: The access from Rockridge Road is also the trailhead for 19 miles of the Florida Trail. The trail crosses pine flatwoods, hardwood forest, cypress heads, swamp, and river floodplain. Part of the trail is on an old logging railroad grade. Expect some wading in wet weather. Camp at designated sites. The trail is closed to hikers for the first nine days of the general hunting season and on Thanksgiving, Christmas, and New Year's holidays.

Hunting: Managed by the Florida Game and Fresh Water Fish Commission.

Fishing: Withlacoochee River and small lakes. (The river here is too small for canoeing.)

PUBLICATION: *Green Swamp Wildlife Management Area.* Map and hunting regulations.

HEADQUARTERS: Florida Game and Fresh Water Fish Commission, South Region, 3900 Drane Field Road, Lakeland, FL 33803; (813) 644-9269. Southwest Florida Water Management District, 2379 Broad Street, Brooksville, FL 34609; (904) 796-7211.

GUM SLOUGH CANOE TRAIL
About 5 miles.   Maps 77, A-3; 78, A-1.

From US 41 at Inverness, northeast on SR 581 to the Withlacoochee River. See sign for fish camp. When launching, ask directions.

It has been several years since we canoed this trail, so we advise asking about present conditions. About ½ mile north of the put-in on the Withlacoochee River, turn northeast into Gum Slough. Paddling upstream wasn't difficult; we estimated the current to be about two miles per hour. The slough is a braided stream winding through delightful wetlands, passing only a few houses. We saw many wildflowers, among them the brilliant cardinal flower, and many birds.

The stream rises at Gum Spring, a splendid deep blue pool, the stream's source. One or two houses were on the bank. We met no other canoeists that day.

Much of this land, including that around the spring, is under consideration for State acquisition. We hope it happens.

Coming downstream is tricky. It's advisable to memorize or even sketch the places where braids separate and join. Make the wrong choice and you may have to turn back.

Camping: The Potts Preserve (see entry) occupies the west bank of the river across from the entrance to Gum Slough. Camping is permitted. A canoe launch is planned.

HIGHLANDS HAMMOCK STATE PARK
Division of Recreation and Parks
3,030 upland acres; 770 submerged.   Map 99, A-3.

From US 27 at Sebring, west on SR 634.

Open 8 A.M. to sunset.

Local residents saved this pristine cypress swamp and hardwood forest in 1931, before the State Park system was established. The Civilian Conservation Corps had an encampment here and built what are now the museum and concession buildings, as well as bridges and trails. It was a memorable experience. Even today, almost 60 years later, there's a CCC festival each November attended by former CCC members and their families.

The Park has served as model for the hundred-plus parks that followed, exemplifying their mandate: "State park lands are managed to appear as they did when the first Europeans arrived." In many parks this requires restoration; at Highlands Hammock, it just means keeping things as they are.

The Park has a picnic area and campground but no lake or river for swimming, fishing, or boating. Visitors come to enjoy nature. Along the loop road are eight nature trails through virgin hardwood hammock, pine flatwoods, sand pine scrub, scrubby flatwoods, bayheads, and marsh. Almost everyone takes the Cypress Swamp Trail, a boardwalk through wetlands and across the Little Charley Bowlegs Creek. Often an alligator swims quietly under the boardwalk, a foot below the visitor's feet.

One of the park features is a ranger-conducted tram tour through the backcountry. There's always a good assortment of wildlife to see.

We live only 50 miles away and take almost all our visitors here. The Park is never the same twice, changing from season to season, wet years to dry. Indeed, as one can see along the Young Hammock Trail, hardwoods are encroaching on marshes.

The Park has many exceptionally large trees, some as old as 1,500 years. A record sabal palm is near the road. A plant list is in preparation.

The State is negotiating for major additions to the Park.

Birds: A checklist of 177 species is available. One of the last sightings of the ivory-billed woodpecker was made here.

Mammals: A checklist is in preparation. Deer are often seen. Raccoons used to frequent the picnic ground; lately we've seen them only along streams.

ACTIVITIES
Camping: 154 sites. Campground is often full December–April. Telephone reservations accepted.
Hiking: Nature trails and woods roads.
Horse riding: 11-mile trail.

INTERPRETATION
Museum is near the concession and picnic area.
Tram tours are weekends only June 1 to September 30, daily except Monday October 1 to May 30. Afternoons. Inquire at entrance station.
Guided walks and *campfire programs* are offered occasionally. Inquire.

PUBLICATIONS
Leaflet with map.
Trail guide.
Bird checklist.
In preparation:
  Plant list.
  Mammal list.

Butterfly list.
Park history.

HEADQUARTERS: 5931 Hammock Rd., Sebring, FL 33872; (813) 385-0011.

HILLSBOROUGH RIVER STATE PARK
Division of Recreation and Parks
2,994 acres.   Map 83, D-3.

On US 301 12 miles north of Tampa.

Our first sight of this Park was welcome. We had joined a canoe outing at Crystal Springs, upstream. The leader hadn't scouted the route. Around the first bend, a downed tree blocked the river. We dragged the canoes up and over, clawed our way through the branches of the next windfall, and soon lost count of the obstacles. Twice, unable to go under or over, we portaged through cypress swamp. We finally arrived, muddy and weary.

It's a delightful stream, as long as the private land upstream from the Park remains undeveloped. We were warned not to trespass.

This is one of the oldest Florida parks. Many of its facilities were built by the Civilian Conservation Corps in the 1930s. The hammocks of live oak, sabal palm, magnolia, and hickory have the serenity of age.

A loop road circles the Park on the south side of the river. All facilities are here: campgrounds, picnic area, bathhouse, concession, and boat dock. A footbridge crosses the river to one of the several nature trails.

Located on a main highway near Tampa, the Park is popular. Because of swimming and canoeing, day use is highest in summer; campsites are most in demand winter and spring.

Fort Foster, built here during the Second Seminole War, has been reconstructed. Living-history demonstrations are offered on weekends.

Birds: A publication offers two checklists: one of species observed prior to 1942, and a supplement listing 152 species observed between 1965 and 1972. Both were prepared by competent observers. Changes include disappearance of the red-cockaded woodpecker and addition of the magnificent frigatebird.

Mammals: Armadillo and wild hog, unwelcome exotics, have been added to the earlier checklist. Mammals present include red and gray foxes, raccoon, striped skunk, river otter, bobcat, and deer.

Reptiles and amphibians: Checklist includes alligator; numerous species of turtles, lizards, and snakes; many frogs.

ACTIVITIES

Camping: 118 sites. Telephone reservations accepted.

Swimming: Artificial pond. Prohibited in the river.

Canoeing: Rentals available. A small rapids blocks access to the upper river.

Boating: Hand launch only; no ramp. 5 hp limit.

PUBLICATIONS

Leaflet with map.

Wildlife checklist.

HEADQUARTERS: 15402 US 301 North, Thonotosassa, FL 33592; (813) 986-1020.

HOBE SOUND NATIONAL WILDLIFE REFUGE
U.S. Fish and Wildlife Service

977 acres in 2 parcels.   Map 103, D-2.

Unit 1: From US 1 or SR A1A at Hobe Sound, east on SR 707 to end, then north on dead-end road. *Unit 2:* On US 1 south of SR 707.

The Refuge was established in 1969 when local residents contributed 229 acres to preserve the north end of Jupiter Island from development. (The north tip is St. Lucie Island State Park—see entry—accessible only by boat or by walking the beach about 3½ miles.) More gifts expanded the Refuge to its present size.

Unit 1: The local road from SR 707 to the Refuge is paved but narrow. Two cars can pass, taking care not to hit mailboxes. The parking area accommodates about 80 cars. Here visitors have access to 3½ miles of sand beach. The dunes and the area behind them are off limits. Some day there may be a nature trail back of the dunes.

Once beyond the few fishermen and sunbathers, we beachcombers were alone with the sandpipers, sand fleas, and cruising pelicans. Shelling was fair that day. In season, many sea turtles nest here. The Refuge is managed to protect the nests.

Unit 2: On the east side of US 1, this is Refuge headquarters, overlooking Hobe Sound. The small nature center in the headquarters building has some fine exhibits, usually including live snakes and other animals. The Hobe Sound Nature Center, Inc., a volunteer association, operates the museum and a program of interpretive activities. The museum closes at 3 P.M.

Sand pine scrub is a vanishing Florida habitat—the Sand Pine Scrub Nature Trail explains why it's worth saving. The scrub flourishes on the high dry land developers most want. Visitors who walk the trail find the habitat more appealing than its name. Be sure to have the trail guide with you.

PUBLICATIONS
Leaflet with map.
Sand Pine Scrub Nature Trail.

HEADQUARTERS: P.O. Box 645, Hobe Sound, FL 33475; (407) 546-6141.

HONEYMOON ISLAND STATE RECREATION AREA
Division of Recreation and Parks
408 land acres; 2,400 acres submerged.   Map 82, D-2.

From Alt. US 19 north of Dunedin, west on SR 586 (Causeway Boulevard).

Open 8 A.M. to sunset.

This island park with 3½ miles of Gulf beach is linked by causeway to one of Florida's most heavily populated areas. In the peak months, June–August, over 350,000 visitors arrive. Yet the manager told us the park is not too heavily used.

In the light of its history, it was also surprising to see that the park has relatively undisturbed natural areas. One reason is that man-made structures on low-lying barrier islands are periodically swept away by hurricanes. The hurricane of 1848 drove water 5 feet deep over the island's highest elevation. Caladesi Island (see entry) was part of Honeymoon Island (then named Hog Island) until the hurricane of 1921 cut them apart. Storms and beach erosion have destroyed the honeymoon bungalows for which the island was named.

The park occupies the outer half of the island, which is irregular in shape. As is typical of barrier islands, its shape is constantly changing as sand, shell, and other materials are moved by wind and tide. The highest point is about 7 feet above sea level.

The causeway was completed in 1964. Developers then began a huge dredge-and-fill project, adding 1½ million cubic yards of sand and limestone to the southwest corner of the island. Roads and condominiums were built. In 1974 the State acquired the north end of the island to save it from similar development.

Parking areas, bathhouses, and picnic area are in the south and central portions of the park. The northern sand spit is accessible only on foot. It has two long arms, the larger on St. Joseph Sound, the smaller on the Gulf, with a sheltered lagoon between. Natural communities include hammock, flatwoods with a rare stand of virgin slash pine, mangrove swamps, salt marshes, and sand dunes. Coastal strand species include palmetto, wax myrtle, Hercules club, seagrape, sea oats, Spanish bayonet, golden creeper, lantana, prickly pear. Black, white, and red mangroves are present.

Birds: No checklist. 104 species have been recorded, surprisingly few for a Gulf barrier island. The sand spit is a nesting area for least tern, American oystercatcher, black skimmer, sandpipers. In 1991 there were 14 osprey nests in the pine flatwoods.

Mammals: The island habitats are not favorable for many mammals. Species present include opossum, marsh rabbit, gray squirrel, raccoon.

Reptiles and amphibians: Species observed include green treefrog, Florida box turtle, gopher tortoise, eastern diamondback and pygmy rattlesnakes, southern black racer. The sand spit is a nesting area for sea turtles.

ACTIVITIES
Fishing: Surf.
Swimming: Lifeguards on duty in summer.

Dogs must be leashed but are permitted in the picnic area and on the south beach.

INTERPRETATION
Nature trail through 70 acres of pine flatwoods, mangroves, coastal strand, near tidal flats, sea grass. It passes osprey nests.
Guided hikes are scheduled occasionally.
Birding programs, second and fourth Saturdays, 10 A.M.
Castnet program, first Saturday, 10 A.M.
Exhibits, literature at entrance. Other exhibits throughout the Park.

PUBLICATIONS
Leaflet with map.
Shelling on Honeymoon Island and Caladesi Island.
Osprey Trail guide.

NEARBY: Dock for ferry serving Caladesi Island is at the park entrance. (See entry.)
HEADQUARTERS: #1 Causeway Blvd., Dunedin, FL 34698; (813) 734-4255.

HONTOON ISLAND STATE PARK
Division of Recreation and Parks
1,650 acres.   Map 80, A-2.

From DeLand (map 74, D-2), west on SR 44, left on Hontoon Road to ferry.

Open 8 A.M. to sunset. Ferry operates from 9 A.M. to one hour before sunset.

A State-operated passenger ferry makes the short St. Johns River crossing to the Hontoon Island dock. Many visitors come by private boat. On our first visit we canoed with camping gear from Blue Spring State Park (see entry).

About 3 miles long, the island is surrounded by the St. Johns River on the north and east, Hontoon Dead River on the west, Snake Creek on the south, with extensive marshes. Shell mounds mark early habitation by the Timucuan Indians. Later it was a pioneer homestead, boat yard site, fishing center, and cattle ranch. Since the State bought the island in 1967, management policy has been to assist restoration of the original ecosystem.

The higher areas are occupied by pine flatwoods. Bordering the river and its tributaries are palm/oak hammocks, cypress swamps, and marshes.

Few day visitors stray far from the dock, picnic area, and observation tower. By late afternoon only campers, cabin occupants, and boat campers remain. Campsites are usually available.

The leaflet map shows only a nature trail. We found other hiking routes through open forest. For us the chief pleasure of this area is canoeing the many winding channels through the marshes. Depending on the season, one can see dozens of osprey, flocks of white ibis, and many great blue, little blue, and green herons; moorhen, limpkin, great and snowy egrets, anhinga, black vulture. Alligators and turtles sun on the banks. Often we see kingfisher, swallow-tailed kite, red-tailed hawk, raccoon. In the river, a large manatee surfaced beside us. Deer, black bear, and river otter are occasionally seen.

FEATURES
An 80-foot *observation tower* offers sweeping views.

Nature trail leads to Indian shell mound, 1½ miles from the ranger station.

ACTIVITIES
Camping: 12 tent sites. Reservations can be made 60 days in advance. Gear must be carried from dock to campsite, about ⅛ mile. Six cabins are available by reservation one year in advance. Slips can be used by houseboats and other live-aboard craft.

Fishing: Largemouth bass, shellcracker, speckled perch, channel catfish.

Boating: 50 slips. No reservations.

PUBLICATIONS
Leaflet with map.

Cabin information.

HEADQUARTERS: 2309 River Ridge Road, DeLand, FL 32720; (904) 736-5309.

J. B. STARKEY WILDERNESS PARK
Southwest Florida Water Management District
8,000 acres.

Map 83, C-1.

From Port Richey, 3 miles east on SR 587. South on Tanglewood Road; left on DeCubelis Road.

The District began purchases of this tract in 1972, primarily to establish and protect a wellfield. The site also protects wetlands along the Pithlachascotee and Anclote rivers, which serve as water storage areas, detaining floodwaters. The District has given approval to Pasco County to use the property as a wilderness park. Facilities such as tent campgrounds and an equestrian center will be confined to the northwest corner. Activities beyond this area will be limited to hiking, bicycling, and horse riding. Pasco County has purchased a 64-acre adjoining tract for facilities with more intensive use, such as a boardwalk and observation tower.

The site is relatively flat, elevations ranging from 20 to 50 feet. The Pithlachascotee River crosses the northwest corner. The Anclote River approximates the south boundary. Both rivers are too shallow for canoeing, and neither offers good fishing.

Most virgin pine and cypress had been cut by the 1920s. Some second-growth timber was cut in the 1950s. The site was used as native range for cattle, but not cleared for pasture. Otherwise most of the site has remained in its natural state. Indeed, the owners who sold it to the District required that it remain natural and made available as a wilderness park.

The vegetative map of the site looks like a calico quilt. The pine flatwoods background is heavily overlaid with large and small patches of turkey oak, sandhill, hardwood hammock, sand pine scrub, riverine swamp, mixed wetland hardwoods, cypress swamp, and freshwater marsh and wet prairie. No inventories have yet been made, but the site is certainly rich in wildlife and in varieties of flowering plants.

Nonessential existing roads will be closed and naturalized. Separate loop trails will be developed for hikers and horse riders. Cyclists will be able to use an existing paved road, which will otherwise by limited to service vehicles.

ACTIVITIES

As of April 1991, the only activity permitted is walk-in daylight hiking. Future activities will include:

Camping: Pasco County plans two improved campgrounds on its land.

Hiking, backpacking: Primitive campsites will be available to hikers. The Florida Trail Association has been asked to assist in trail planning and development.

Horse riding awaits development of suitable trails and Pasco County's readiness to provide supervision.

HEADQUARTERS: Southwest Florida Water Management District, 2379 Broad Street, Brooksville, FL 34609; (904) 796-7211.

JONATHAN DICKINSON STATE PARK
Division of Recreation and Parks
11,500 acres.   Map 103, D-2.

On US 1, 13 miles south of Stuart.

Florida's second-largest State Park, Jonathan Dickinson was established in 1947. Located on the congested Atlantic Coast, one might expect it to be crowded. The campground is often full from November through April, and picnic tables are popular on any pleasant weekend. However, few visitors venture far from the developed area, a small part of the site.

The long entrance road leads to parking and picnic areas near the meandering Loxahatchee River. Several trailheads, a boat ramp, camping area, and concession are clustered here. The map in the Park leaflet doesn't show the boundaries. We understand they extend across the river.

Pine flatwoods and sand pine scrub are the most extensive plant communities. Cypress swamps are along Kitching Creek, mangroves beside the river. Near the entrance and the north boundary are rolling white sand dunes left in past ages by the receding ocean.

Swimming, once permitted, is now prohibited, which is one reason attendance declines in summer. The river and creek are attractions nonetheless, hikers enjoying their scenery, birders seeking some of the many species present, canoeists exploring quiet reaches beyond the foot trails.

The area was logged twice before the Park was established. Management is now using prescribed burns and other techniques to restore the original ecosystem. We paused at one recently burned area to see the quick greening.

On the way in, turn right on the dead-end road to the trailhead for Hobe Mountain. It's an easy 20-minute walk through sand pine scrub to an observation tower overlooking Jupiter Island, the Intracoastal Waterway, and the Park.

Back on the entrance road, we intersected a trail marked with the familiar blazes of the Florida Trail. No signs identified it, and the leaflet map didn't show it, so we asked. It was under construction, we were told. Another segment of the Florida Trail, beginning at the entrance station, was in use.

South of SR 706 the Loxahatchee River has become a ditch linked to a network of drainage canals and dikes. Flowing north beyond this disruption, it remains pristine. The lower Loxahatchee River was Florida's first to be named a National Wild and Scenic River. The South Florida Water Management District has bought a 4-mile strip of land along the river and its headwaters, adjoining the southwest corner of the Park.

Birds: Checklist of 147 species notes seasonality and relative abundance. The bald eagle is termed "uncommon," but we spotted an active nest and assume there are others.

ACTIVITIES

Camping: 135 sites. Telephone reservations accepted.

Hiking, backpacking: 9.3-mile segment of the Florida Trail begins near the entrance station. An overnight campground is limited to 8 people per site, 3 sites total. Reservations are required.

Boating, canoeing: Docks, ramps. Canoe rentals. Ask about an 8-mile run that begins outside the Park, ends here.

Horse riding: Open-air stalls. Horse trail. No rentals.

INTERPRETATION

Tour boat travels the river.

Trapper Nelson Interpretive Site is reached by tour boat or canoe.

Guided tours are offered at the Interpretive Site.

Campfire programs, all year.

Guided walks are scheduled in winter.

Four *nature trails* visit the several natural areas.

PUBLICATIONS

Leaflet with map.

Bird checklist.

Kitching Creek Trail guide.

Hiking trail guide.

HEADQUARTERS: 16450 SE Federal Highway, Hobe Sound, FL 33455; (407) 546-2771.

KICCO WILDLIFE MANAGEMENT AREA
Florida Game and Fresh Water Fish Commission
7,426 acres.   Map 94, B-3.

South from SR 60 at the Kissimmee River. Enter at lock.

Also see entry: Kissimmee River Trail, Zone 3.

The area is a strip more than 10 miles long on the floodplain of the Kissimmee River. It was purchased by the South Florida Water Management District because of the planned restoration of the Kissimmee River, which now flows through a canal. The site contains former river meanders that would be re-watered.

Canalizing the river exposed the floodplain for grazing. Prior to acquisition by the District, the land had been overgrazed. The new management has restricted grazing.

Approximately 2 miles south of SR 60, the River Ranch Resort land-holding divides the WMA into two parts. The south portion of the WMA can be entered at the resort or at Lock 65 of the canal. The Florida Trail runs the length of the WMA.

The original river floodplain was a mix of pine flatwoods, oak/cabbage palm hammocks, oak/palmetto scrub, and wetland sloughs. When the canal was dug, spoil was dumped along the floodplain. Spoil banks are now over-grown with willow, wax myrtle, dog fennel, saltbush, and grasses.

Portions of the natural communities remain. A cypress slough and wet-land marsh are at the south end of the tract.

Wildlife species observed in the WMA depend largely on the surround-ing lands. These include buffer zones of the Avon Park Air Force Range and cattle ranches, habitats ranging from wetlands to upland forest. Birding is good.

This entire area will be greatly altered when the river is restored to its old channel. Riparian land will revert rather quickly to its natural state. Resto-ration seems probable, but no schedule has been fixed.

ACTIVITIES

Hiking, backpacking: On the Florida Trail. Three designated campsites are in the south portion of the tract.

Hunting: Spring turkey.

Fishing: Canal and sloughs.

Boating, canoeing: Public ramp at SR 60.

PUBLICATION: WMA leaflet with map.

HEADQUARTERS: Florida Game and Fresh Water Fish Commission, South Region, 3900 Drane Field Road, Lakeland, FL 33811; (813) 648-3203.

KISSIMMEE RIVER

South Florida Water Management District,
U.S. Army Corps of Engineers
97½ miles.   Maps 94, B-3, to 101, C-3.

From Lake Kissimmee to Lake Okeechobee.

The Kissimmee story is too long to tell here, and a vital chapter is not yet written. It will record the first time a major river is restored after channelization, perhaps the first time the Army Corps of Engineers dismantles one of its major projects. What is now a ditch named C-38 will again be a meandering river.

The river originates in a 1,400-square-mile drainage basin north of Lake Kissimmee. Most of this land is flat. Before drainage projects were built, it flooded periodically. Gathered by creeks and ditches, water flows through several lakes to Lake Kissimmee.

Below Lake Kissimmee, the river meandered through a wide floodplain, dropping only 7 inches per mile, emptying into Lake Okeechobee, the chief water source for southern Florida.

Frequent flooding hampered development of central Florida. Ditch-and-drain had been State policy for generations. At the State's request and with federal funds, the Corps of Engineers dug a ditch 200 feet wide between the lakes. The 52-mile-long ditch dried the river bed and 35,000 acres of wetlands and floodplain.

It became an environmental disaster, polluting Lake Okeechobee and contributing to declines in its level during droughts. Wildlife species vanished with their habitat. After years of arguing and negotiating, almost everyone agreed the river had to be restored. By 1989 the method was approved. Engineering is well along. Action depends on money.

A 12-mile experiment is a dramatic demonstration of restoration and recovery. To see it by boat, drive about a mile east from Lorida on US 98, then north on Bluff Hammock Road, following signs to a public ramp. Cruise or paddle north on C-38 to the old river channel on the west side.

The experiment placed notched steel weirs across the ditch to divert part of the flow into the old channel. We canoed the restored river and camped on one of the several islands. It looked as if the river had never left. Native plants had regenerated rapidly, fish and wildlife returned. The test was successful, the method not. In periods of low flow, little or no water is diverted by the weirs, so water in the oxbows stagnates. Restoration requires elimination of the ditch, and this is now the plan.

Legally, it could be argued, the land below the historical high-water mark still belongs to the State. Ranchers and other owners of riparian land had been using the dried floodplain as if they owned it, had indeed paid taxes on it. If it were to be reflooded, they wanted compensation. State authorities concluded it would be less costly to buy the land rather than endure years of litigation. The South Florida Water Management District has begun acquisitions.

Congress, although approving restoration, has appropriated only a first installment of funds to do the job.

ACTIVITIES

Hiking, backpacking: Eventually the Florida Trail will extend along the Kissimmee River from Lake Kissimmee to Lake Okeechobee. A 27-mile north section and 9-mile south section are open. Ongoing land acquisitions by the Water Management District are expected to close the gap. The restored section of the Kissimmee River causes the gap. As other sections are restored, portions of the trail will be rerouted.

Hunting: See entry for Prairie Lakes.

Boating, canoeing: Ramps at SR 60, Bluff Hammock Road, and fish resorts. The ditch has been popular with fishermen and operators of high-speed power boats. When the river is full, water flowing through a weir notch is a cascade that a power boat at full throttle can ascend—with some risk.

Seven locks are on C-38. The *Guide* explains rules and operating hours.

PUBLICATION: *Guide to the Kissimmee Waterway.*

HEADQUARTERS: South Florida Water Management District, P.O. Box 24680, 3301 Gun Club Road, West Palm Beach, FL 33416; (407) 686-8800. For Waterway information: (800) 432-2045.

KISSIMMEE RIVER TRAIL
South Florida Water Management District
36 miles.   Maps 94, B-3; 101, B-1.

North end is at the SR 60 crossing of the Kissimmee River.
Also see entry for KICCO Wildlife Management Area.

Eventually this trail will extend along the Kissimmee River from Lake Kissimmee to Lake Okeechobee. A 27-mile north section and 9-mile south section are open. Ongoing land acquisitions by the District will close the gap.

The District recommends the River Ranch Resort, just south of SR 60, as the north trailhead. Beyond the KICCO WMA, it enters a section of the Avon Park Air Force Range (see entry). A permit isn't required to hike through but is required to begin the hike here or to camp. The north trailhead for the 9-mile south section is off US 98.

The gap was caused by restoring a section of the Kissimmee River (see entry). As other sections are restored, other portions of the trail will also have to be rerouted.

The trail passes through oak hammocks, scrub oak groves, sand pine forest, and open prairie, at times on the river bank. Wetland sections may require wading after rain. The FTA guide-book, *Walking the Florida Trail,* mentions places of historic interest along the way.

HEADQUARTERS: Box 24680, 3301 Gun Club Road, West Palm Beach, FL 33416; (407) 686-8800.

LAKE ARBUCKLE PARK
Polk County Parks and Recreation Department
7 acres.   Map 94, C-1.

From Frostproof, east on SR 630; right 4 miles on Lake Reedy Blvd.; at sign, turn left for 8 miles.

Lake Arbuckle is the last large Florida lake with a fully protected shoreline (see entry, Arbuckle State Forest). Until a State Park is developed on the lake, this County Park is the most convenient access to the lake and is the only campground.

The Park is popular with fishermen. Many bass tournaments begin here. Campsites are informal, used mostly by local residents.

ACTIVITIES
Camping: 40 sites.
Boating, canoeing: Ramp. Campers often pull their boats up on shore for the night.

HEADQUARTERS: Polk County Parks and Recreation Department, County Administration Building, Bartow, FL 33930; (813) 534-6074.

LAKE COUNTY WATERWAYS
Private   Map 79.

Lakes at or near Leesburg, Tavares, Eustis, Mt. Dora.

Florida has about 7,800 lakes, one-third of them in four of the 67 counties. Lake County has several hundred. Seven of the largest are linked by creeks or canals. No large public lands are on these lakes. Their shorelines are heavily developed. Some bordering wetlands and forests have thus far been spared.

We make this an entry because boater friends said we should and because an unusual four-color pictorial map depicts the lakes and waterways. We bought it in a marina and assume it has general distribution.

PUBLICATION: *Lake County Waterways.* Creative Graphics International, 611 Druid Rd. E, Clearwater, FL 33516. $1.95.

LAKE KISSIMMEE STATE PARK
Division of Recreation and Parks
5,030 acres.   Map 94, A-2.

Off SR 60, 15 miles east of Lake Wales.

Our day with the late Sam Keene should have been recorded as oral history. He came here with his family before there were roads or railroads. They raised cattle and drove them to the coast for shipment to Cuba, their chief market. The region is still cattle country. The Park includes a nineteenth-century cow camp where ranger-cowhands demonstrate life in 1876 and won't answer questions about anything that's happened since.

Lake Kissimmee, 34,948 acres, is Florida's third largest. The Park has about 3 miles of lake frontage. The rest of the 40-mile shoreline was mostly undeveloped until the early 1980s when ranches began selling waterfront property. A few homes were built, but action by State and County stopped dredge-and-fill operations and keeps construction back from the shore.

The Park is the principal public access to the lake. Fishermen still seek 12-pound bass, but flood control management of the lake level has impaired the habitat, and fishing is rated only "fair." The Park also has frontage on Lakes Tiger and Rosalie.

A long entrance road leads through pine flatwoods to the shore. Here are picnic areas, a boat ramp, concession, and observation tower. The Cow Camp is nearby.

Pine flatwoods are the largest of the several natural communities. The flatwoods at times are tinder-dry; in wet weather, hikers need boots. Other natural communities are floodplain prairies, live oak hammocks, swamps, and marshes. Many large live oaks are in the picnic area, their low branches an invitation to young climbers. Buster Island, in the flatwoods, is a dry, sandy mound bordered by hardwood hammock.

Birds: A team from the Lakes Region Audubon Society headed by Chuck Geanangel made a bird inventory several years ago, but the checklist had not yet been published in 1991.

"It's probably the best place in Florida to see eagles," Chuck said. Surveyors found as many as 26 in a day. From the observation tower, we once saw 10 aloft. The rare snail kite is becoming more common. Caracara, sandhill crane, and scrub jay are often seen. The list includes more than a hundred species.

Mammals: No checklist is available. Species observed include bobcat, gray and fox squirrels, deer. Feral hogs are considered a nuisance.

ACTIVITIES
Camping: 60 sites. No reservations.
Hiking, backpacking: 13 miles of the Florida Trail in two 6½-mile loops. Dogs, once permitted on trails, are now prohibited.
Boating, canoeing: Rentals by concessioner.

PUBLICATIONS
Leaflet with map.
Cow Camp leaflet.

HEADQUARTERS: 14248 Camp Mack Road, Lake Wales, FL 33853; (813) 969-1112.

LAKE LOUISA STATE PARK
Division of Recreation and Parks
1,790 acres.   Map 85, A-1.

From Clermont, south about 10 miles on SR 561, then east on Lake Nellie Road.

Open 8 A.M. to sundown.

The Park has 2½ miles of frontage on 3,634-acre Lake Louisa, one of 13 in the Clermont Chain of Lakes. It includes all of Bear Lake, portions of Lakes Hook and Dudes. The site is in the northwest corner of the Green Swamp (see entry). It is flood-prone and crossed by several creeks and drainage ditches.

The park is lightly used. At present it has no campground or boat ramp. Canoes and car-toppers can be launched.

By the time the site was acquired in 1973, most of its natural features had been destroyed. Most of the sandhills in and around the site had been converted to citrus plantations. Following recent freezes, many groves were sold to developers. In 1973 the Park site included 167 acres of citrus groves. About 538 acres of flatwoods had been cleared and converted to pasture;

only a few oaks remained. Bear Lake is surrounded by cypress trees. The site includes swamps and cypress domes.

The Division of Recreation and Parks has begun a long-term process of restoring the natural communities. Citrus trees have been removed. Management plans call for planting native species here and on pastures. Controlled burning will remove hardwoods from fire-adapted communities. Ditches will be backfilled. This will take years, but wildlife species are already moving back into the reverting areas. Marsh rabbit, gray squirrel, pocket gopher, red fox, bobcat, and deer are often seen.

Boating: Ramps, not on site, on the canal between Lake Louisa and Lake Susan, and at Lake Susan Lodge.

HEADQUARTERS: 12549 State Park Drive, Clermont, FL 34711; (904) 394-3969.

LAKE MANATEE STATE RECREATION AREA
Division of Recreation and Parks
556 acres.   Map 97, A-3.

From Bradenton, 14 miles east on SR 64.

Open 8 A.M. to sunset.

Land for this park was acquired by the State in 1970. Development has been modest: campground, picnic area, boat ramp and dock, parking areas, and a trail. The park has 3½ miles of frontage on Lake Manatee, a 2,400-acre reservoir formed by damming the upper Manatee River. Although private landholdings are on the lake, there has been little lakeside development.

We visited on a sunny Saturday morning in September. Parking at the swimming-picnicking area is sufficient for a hundred cars; only three were parked. No boat trailers were parked near the launching ramp. One fisherman was on the pier. Of the 60 campsites, 12 were occupied. Rangers told us January–March is their busiest season, but it's seldom crowded then.

The land is relatively flat, with only 25 feet difference between the highest and lowest points. Communities include mesic flatwoods, sand pine scrub, sandhills, and hammocks. We saw no old-growth timber but some tall longleaf pines. Scrub oak, wax myrtle, and palmetto are the chief understory species.

Looking out from the dock, we saw a forested shoreline, trees generally about 20 to 25 feet tall. Much emergent vegetation was in the nearby shallows, including water hyacinth in bloom.

Beach, ramp, and docks were designed for the water level reservoir managers would like to maintain. Florida's uncertain rainfall causes the docks to be flooded or stranded occasionally.

Birds: No inventory has been made. Park personnel report observations of bald eagle, osprey, swallow-tailed kite, roseate spoonbill, wood stork, and many more common species.

Mammals: Observed: raccoon, gray and fox squirrels, marsh and cottontail rabbits, cotton rat, bobcat, whitetail deer, red fox, opossum.

ACTIVITIES
Camping: 60 sites.
Hiking: No designated trails, but the horse trail seemed suitable.
Fishing: Largemouth bass, catfish, sunshine bass, bluegill, crappie.
Boating: On the reservoir and upper river. 20-hp limit. Rentals available.
Horse riding: 5-mile trail. Rangers request prior notice.

PUBLICATION: Leaflet with map.

HEADQUARTERS: 20007 State Road 64, Bradenton, FL 34202; (813) 741-3028.

LAKE MONROE PARK
Volusia County
42 acres.   Map 80, B-2.

On US 17/92 at the junction with I-4.

This small park is on the St. Johns River just below Lake Monroe. Most patrons are boaters. Some also camp.

ACTIVITIES
Camping: 44 sites.
Boating: Ramps in the Park and across the river.

Dogs are prohibited.

HEADQUARTERS: Volusia County Parks, Recreation and Facilities Department, 123 West Indiana Ave., DeLand, FL 32721; (904) 736-5953.

LETTUCE LAKE COUNTY PARK
Hillsborough County Parks and Recreation Department
240 acres.   Map 83, D-3.

In Tampa, from the I-75 bypass exit west on Fletcher Avenue. Entrance is on the right.

Open 8 A.M. to sundown.

This small park on a bend in the Hillsborough River has a wilderness preserve, a hardwood swamp forest on the floodplain. A 3,500-foot board-walk traverses the swamp, while an observation tower overlooks swamp, lake, and river. A 5,000-foot nature trail circles through the pine uplands.

A nature center provides information on the Park's habitats and the 300 plant species found.

The Park is in a major city and popular with both school and family groups. The best time for a quiet visit is just after the gate opens in the morning.

Pets must be leashed. They are not permitted in buildings or on boardwalks.

PUBLICATION: Leaflet with map.

HEADQUARTERS: 6920 E. Fletcher Avenue, Tampa, FL 33637; (813) 985-7845.

LITTLE MANATEE RIVER STATE RECREATION AREA
LITTLE MANATEE RIVER CANOE TRAIL
Division of Recreation and Parks
Park, 1,638 acres; canoe trail, 28 miles.   Map 91, C-3.

From Ruskin, east on SR 674, south on US 301. Cross the Little Manatee River, see sign, turn right on Lightfoot Road.

Open 8 A.M. to sunset.

On a fine Sunday morning in September, few people were here. No cars were parked at the picnic area or canoe launch. Six horse trailers were at the horse trailhead. The shaded camping area, recently opened, wasn't yet listed in directories. Six sites were occupied. We met no one on the trails.

The principal feature is Little Manatee River, which meanders through the park for about 5 miles. Dark with tannin, heavily shaded, the stream is about 20 feet wide, sand-bottomed, with steep banks. Influenced by tides, the flow rate averages about two miles per hour.

The entrance road first passes through a typical Florida scrub area, oaks and a few pines scattered at intervals of about 50 feet, the sparse understory chiefly palmetto with areas of bare white sand. Here the elevation is about 20 feet. Approaching the river and the developed area, the road enters a maturing pine forest. Along the river is a moist subtropical environment, a floodplain forest bordered by cattails, sedges, and many flowering plants. Here vegetation is so dense that most of the river bank is inaccessible. A nature trail with short sections of boardwalk provides a good sampling.

Future site developments include hiking trails, picnic shelters, swimming area, more campsites, cabins, a concession, playground.

ACTIVITIES
Camping: 30 sites, 3 designated for horse campers.

Hiking, backpacking: A 6.5-mile loop trail developed in cooperation with the Florida Trail Association is in the north area of the park. It's not accessible from the developed area and isn't shown on the park leaflet. Stop at the ranger station for directions and map. A backpackers' campsite is 0.2 miles off the trail 2.4 miles from the trailhead. Water is not available. Pets are prohibited. Six miles of horse trails are on the south side.

Fishing: Bass, bream, catfish.

Canoeing: The State-designated canoe trail includes only the 5 miles within the park. An outfitter provides equipment and services for runs up to 28 miles, including overnights. According to the outfitter, only 1 mile of the 28 is "inhabited." The river flows into the Cockroach Bay Aquatic Preserve.

Canoeing friends called the outfitter after a period of heavy rains. They were told the river was too dangerous to run at high water; the careful outfitter wouldn't rent canoes.

Horse riding: Six miles of trails in two large loops.

PUBLICATIONS
Leaflet with map.
Hiking trail map.
Little Manatee River Canoe Trail. Division of Recreation and Parks.

HEADQUARTERS: 215 Lightfoot Rd., Wimauma, FL 33598; (813) 634-4781.

LITTLE WEKIVA RIVER CANOE TRAIL
See entry, Wekiva River Canoe Trail   Map 80, B-2.

LOWER WEKIVA RIVER STATE RESERVE
Division of Recreation and Parks
4,636 acres.   Map 80, A-1, B-1.

From I-4, exit at Sanford onto SR 46 west. Entrance is on north side, about 5 miles west.

Open 8 A.M. to sunset.

Roughly V-shaped, the Reserve extends along the Wekiva River for about 5 miles above its junction with the St. Johns River. The larger eastern leg of the V is drained by the Wekiva River, the shorter western leg by its tributary, Black Water Creek. The Reserve has 1 mile of frontage on the St. Johns River.

The Wekiva River (see entry) has long been one of our favorite canoe trails. From the St. Johns upstream to SR 46 and beyond it is navigable by outboard craft, but there are snags and shallows.

Upstream from the Reserve are homes, weekend cottages, and boat liveries. The 4½ miles of the Wekiva River within the Reserve are undeveloped and pristine.

From the entrance, a sand road parallels the river on the east for about 4 miles. It is closed to vehicles and is the only road shown on the site map. Old maps show a network of logging roads between the river and Blackwater Creek. These are now abandoned and overgrown. Despite past disturbances caused by logging, land clearing for pasture, fire plow scars, and ditching, the general appearance of the Reserve is natural.

There is no legal land access to the area west of the Wekiva River, which includes the Black Water Creek drainage. This is about two-thirds of the acreage. While canoeing, we have seen few places to go ashore.

Most of the Reserve is designated Wilderness. The waters of the Reserve have been designated an Aquatic Preserve. The Wekiva River has been designated an Outstanding Florida Water and the portion within the Reserve is a "wild segment" in the State Scenic and Wild River program.

The terrain includes low, rolling sandhills, flatwoods, and swamp floodplain. Elevations range from 65 feet to 5 feet. Annual rainfall is about 50 inches, June–September usually the wet season.

Plants: Communities include sandhill, sand pine scrub, scrubby flatwoods, floodplain hardwood hammock, river swamp, freshwater marsh, bayhead, seasonal pond, and riverine. Especially along the watercourses, vegetation is dense. Within these diverse habitats are a great variety of plant species, many of them rare. Logging prior to State ownership removed much of the original pine, cypress, and other hardwoods. Management practices seek gradual restoration of these species.

Flowering species include aster, pawpaw, greeneyes, blue flag iris, lobelia, deer tongue, candyweed, bachelor-button, blazing star, blueberry, huckleberry, fetterbush, cardinal flower, many more.

Birds: Good birding all year. 135 species have been recorded. Many upland species are present during migrations. Seen along the river: tricolored and great blue herons, limpkin, great egret, wood stork, white ibis, bald eagle, osprey, kingfisher, swallow-tailed kite. Nearby: scrub jay, sandhill crane.

Mammals: We've seen few along the river: several gray squirrels, a river otter. The Wilderness is a refuge for black bear and other wildlife, including whitetail deer and fox squirrel.

Reptiles and amphibians: Alligator and cooter often seen. Snakes include black racer, eastern hognose, and indigo.

ACTIVITIES
Camping: Primitive. Two river sites and a hiking trail with campsite should be available by our publication time. A permit is required.
Hiking, backpacking: On old roads and trails. Trail development was planned when we visited.
Fishing: We've seldom seen anyone fishing the river.
Canoeing, boating: No ramp or put-in on site. Commercial sites are upstream and on the St. Johns River. (See Wekiva River entry.) We're told Black Water Creek is beautiful, canoeable but extremely tricky, with many obstacles. *Airboats are prohibited.*
Horse riding: Permitted; no special facilities.

Dogs are permitted on leash; not in campgrounds.

INTERPRETATION: A self-guided *nature trail* explores the sandhill community.

PUBLICATIONS
Leaflet with map.
Sandhill Nature Trail.

HEADQUARTERS: 8300 West Highway 46; Sanford, FL 32711; (407) 330-6728.

MERRITT ISLAND NATIONAL WILDLIFE REFUGE
U.S. Fish and Wildlife Service
139,305 acres.   Map 82, D-1.

From Titusville, east on SR 402.

If the site map confuses, don't worry; the situation is plain on the ground. This is a refuge not to be missed. One visit isn't enough to enjoy it all.

In the 1960s the National Aeronautics and Space Administration acquired most of Merritt Island for the Kennedy Space Center. In 1963 naturalists persuaded NASA to let part of the area become the Merritt Island National Wildlife Refuge. The Canaveral National Seashore was established in 1975 (see entry). It's an unusual arrangement: Refuge and Seashore, administered by different agencies of the Department of the Interior, publish a joint leaflet that shows no boundary between them. The Refuge boundaries include the Seashore.

In general, the National Seashore is a narrow barrier beach between the Atlantic Ocean and Mosquito Lagoon. The Refuge, much broader, is between the lagoon and the Indian River.

It's still all NASA's property, a buffer for the Space Center. NASA maintains security. Prior to a space shuttle launch, Playalinda Beach, the south end of the Seashore, is closed. Call (904) 428-3384 for information about closures. Most of the Refugue is unaffected.

Bring binoculars! Go first to the excellent visitor center, on the south side of SR 402 four miles east of Titusville. En route, from the bridge and causeway you'll see pelicans and, if you're lucky, porpoises. Impoundments on both sides of the road often have hundreds or thousands of waterfowl. In season tree swallows adorn the overhead electric lines. Look for osprey and kingfisher on the poles.

Wildlife populations at the Refuge change from season to season. The *Calendar of Events* is a monthly summary. For example,

January . . . Waterfowl concentrations peak . . .
March . . . Most waterfowl have returned to their northern breeding grounds except . . .
July . . . Many resident bird species are abundant . . .

In general, spring, fall, and winter offer the best birding, but a summer hike can be rewarding, especially if you bring repellent. Mosquito Lagoon earned its name. The displays and literature at the visitor center have good advice on planning your day, but ask the staff, too; they know where the birds are congregating.

The saltwater lagoons are fringed by red mangroves, with stands of shoalgrass and manatee grass. The Refuge has about 34,000 acres of fresh and salt marshes and swamps, with black and white mangroves, cordgrass, willow, and maple; 46,000 acres of uplands with scrubby flatwoods, pine flatwoods, oak hammocks, sweetgum associations.

For most visitors, the principal attractions are the 22,000 acres of impoundments. From the visitor center, go to Black Point Wildlife Drive, taking a leaflet at the entrance. This is a 7-mile auto tour on dikes. We wish there were more parking pull-offs on the first portion of the drive, but there are plenty later. The best strategy is to drive until you see some interesting birds in an impoundment, then stop and walk.

One can hike for miles on the dikes. The Refuge leaflet shows them as strings of small black dots. Like a maze, they make unexpected turns. Wanting to go south, you can find yourself headed north. Walk quietly, and you may see otters. A hundred coots may take off noisily as you approach. Tricolored herons squawk protest at your invasion.

The dikes on Black Point Wildlife Drive are not the only ones open to vehicles. Some others have dirt tracks to be driven cautiously, alert for signs prohibiting further vehicle travel.

The Merritt Island National Wildlife Refuge shelters 22 threatened and endangered species, more than any other single refuge in the United States.

Birds: An annotated checklist is available. On the Refuge, 315 bird species have been identified. Breeding populations include bald eagle, brown pelican, wood stork, and mottled duck. Spectacular migrations of passerines, especially warblers, occur in spring and fall. Eight species of herons and egrets are common all year; we have never failed to see the dance of the reddish egret. One fall we saw an incredible massing of tree swallows; the official estimate was half a million.

The leaflet says winter peak concentrations of waterfowl often reach 100,000. That varies sharply from year to year, depending on the severity of temperature, rainfall, and general conditions on the flyway. We think we've seen that many coots.

Storms can bring a species far from its native haunts. Appended to the checklist is a list of 41 "accidentals," some last reported 30 and more years ago. The list can't be kept current. For example, it says the cinnamon teal was last observed in 1970; we and others saw one in 1989.

Mammals: Species observed include bobcat, otter, Florida water rat, raccoon, armadillo, spotted skunk, marsh rabbit. Manatee are often seen in the lagoon, porpoise in the Indian River.

Reptiles and amphibians: Many species. Alligators are abundant. Leopardfrog, treefrog, diamondback terrapin, gopher tortoise, green anole, eastern glass lizard, diamondback rattlesnake, pine snake, indigo snake, cottonmouth.

FEATURES AND INTERPRETATION

Visitor center is open 8 A.M. to 4:30 P.M. weekdays; 9 A.M. to 5 P.M. weekends—except closed on Sundays May–October and all federal holidays.

Programs on snakes, birds, alligators, turtles, etc., are offered November–April.

Turtle watches, including night beach visits to see nesting sea turtles, in summer. By reservation one month ahead.

Black Point Wildlife Drive.

Cruikshank Trail, 5 miles, is on Black Point drive. Observation tower, exhibits, photo blind.

Oak Hammock Trail, ½ mile, and *Palm Hammock Trail,* 2 miles, are on SR 402 beyond the visitor center.

ACTIVITIES
Hunting: Designated areas; special rules. Inquire.
Fishing: Daylight hours. Obtain regulations.
Boating, canoeing: The Refuge leaflet shows two ramps off SR 3. See Canaveral National Seashore leaflet for others.

PUBLICATIONS
Leaflet with map.
Current activities.
A Place to See Wildlife.
Bird checklist.
Calendar of Wildlife Events.
Black Point Wildlife Drive guide.
Sport fishing regulations.
Hunting information.

HEADQUARTERS: P.O. Box 6504, Titusville, FL 32782; (407) 867-0667.

MOSS PARK
Orange County
1,551 acres.   Map 86, B-3.

From SR 528 east of Orlando International Airport, south about 3 miles on SR 15, then east and southeast 4 miles on Moss Park Road.

Open 8 A.M. Closed 8 P.M. in summer, 6 P.M. in winter.

Described as a peninsula or two islands, the park lies between Lake Hart and Lake Mary Jane. Recreation facilities occupy about 350 acres. About 1,200 acres are roadless, maintained in natural condition, accessible only on foot.

About half of the site is forested with slash and longleaf pines, live oak, and turkey oak. Its ecosystems include freshwater marshes, swamps, bogs, cypress domes, bayheads, old-growth oak hammocks, and pine flatwoods. The terrain is flat, only 6 feet between highest and lowest elevations.

No wildlife lists have been compiled. Reported sightings include sandhill crane, wood stork, bald eagle, pileated woodpecker, red-shouldered hawk, opossum, raccoon, squirrels, whitetail deer. Three sightings of panther were reported 1986–1990.   .

ACTIVITIES

Camping: Three campgrounds. No reservations for informal sites. Sites with hookups can be reserved in person.

Hiking: No trails have been marked, no trail map issued.

Fishing: Bass, speckled perch, catfish, bream.

Swimming: Designated beach only.

Boating, canoeing: Ramps. No hp limit. Occasional low water.

Pets are prohibited.

PUBLICATION: Leaflet with map.

HEADQUARTERS: Orange County Parks and Recreation Department, 118 West Kaley Street, Orlando, FL 32806; (407) 836-4290.

MYAKKA RIVER STATE PARK
Division of Recreation and Parks
28,876 acres.   Map 97, B-3, C-3.

From Sarasota, 17 miles east on SR 72.

Open 8 A.M. to sunset.

This is one of Florida's largest State Parks and one that remains in largely natural condition. It has a diversity of habitats and an abundance of wildlife. Most developed facilities are north of SR 72. A 7,500-acre wilderness preserve south of the highway is accessible on foot or by canoe.

The Myakka River, entering at the northeast corner, traverses the park for 12 miles, flowing through Upper Myakka Lake in the north portion, Lower Myakka Lake in the wilderness preserve. Canoeing the river and lakes is an admirable way to enjoy the Park's flora and fauna.

Much of the park is low-lying and subject to flooding during the June–September rainy seasons – if it rains. Annual rainfall ranges from 37 to 94 inches, and there have been successive dry years. Every year or two flooding has been extensive enough to require closing the park briefly.

The terrain is karst topography, features shaped by dissolving limestone: many ponds and sloughs, sinkholes, deep blind gullies, and the lakes.

The highest ground, occupying more than half of the Park, is dry prairie, a naturally treeless plain with a dense ground cover of wiregrass and other grasses, saw palmetto, herbs, and low shrubs. Years of suppression of natural fires has permitted an increased density of palmetto and invasion of oaks and other trees. Management plans call for prescribed burning to restore the natural condition. Burning also promotes the habitat's many species of flowering plants.

Somewhat lower in elevation are 4,500 acres of pine flatwoods, most of which are in the wilderness preserve. Although above flood level, the flatwoods are poorly drained and often have standing water in the wet season. Here is a great diversity of plant species, including wiregrass, palmetto, gallberry, fetterbush, blueberries, tarflower, and many more, with a corresponding diversity of wildlife.

Hundreds of marshes and small ponds are scattered throughout the park, supporting such plant species as pickerel weed, St. John's-wort, arrowhead, sawgrass, maidencane, and sedges. The largest marshes are along the river. Bordering the marshes in some areas are red maple, coastal willow, pop ash, water locust, and buttonbush wetlands.

Hydric hammocks, although totalling only 800 acres, are conspicuous because of their large live oaks and cabbage palms draped with Spanish moss and supporting many epiphytes. This is also favorable habitat for resurrection fern, shoestring fern, butterfly orchid, and mosses.

Basin swamps total only 900 acres, but they have produced large blackgum, red maple, and other trees.

Birds: A checklist of over 220 species notes abundance, seasonality, and habitats. Populations peak in winter; a recent Christmas bird count found 21,110 individuals of 106 species. Birding is usually good from the boardwalk and observation tower on Upper Myakka Lake.

Mammals: The available checklist includes whitetail deer, bobcat, river otter, gray squirrel, marsh rabbit, eastern mole, longtail weasel, cotton and rice rats, gray fox, striped and spotted skunks, raccoon. Feral hog and armadillo are unwanted exotics.

Reptiles and amphibians: Alligators are common. Often seen are turtles, gopher tortoise, green anole, ground skink, eastern glass lizard. Snakes: Many species, including green water, striped swamp, black swamp, peninsula ribbon, eastern indigo, Florida cottonmouth, dusky pygmy and diamondback rattlesnakes.

FEATURES
Wilderness Preserve has restricted access, by permit: 30 people, 12 boats, 20 fishermen. Day use only.
Scenic drive extending 7 miles from the main entrance to the north entrance offers good views of several habitats. (The north entrance is open only on weekends and State holidays.)
Boardwalk on Upper Myakka Lake.

ACTIVITIES
Camping: Two campgrounds, 76 sites. Telephone reservations are accepted.

Hiking, backpacking: 39 miles of the Florida Trail have several loops and cross-trails. Along the routes are five primitve camping areas where permits are required, limited to 12 people per site. Hiking in the Wilderness Preserve is by permit, 30 people per day; no camping.

Fishing: Invasion of hydrilla, an exotic waterweed, has somewhat reduced the quality of fishing: fewer big bass but plenty of panfish.

Canoeing on lakes and river. Rentals available.

Boating: A basin and ramp are on Upper Myakka Lake. Hydrilla limits the usefulness of motors during low water.

Horse riding: 15 miles of horse trails are available. No rentals. Registration and proof of Coggins test required.

INTERPRETATION

Interpretive center has plant and animal exhibits.

Boat tour, concessioner operated, on Upper Myakka Lake, when water levels permit. (Closed in September.)

Tram tour of hardwood hammock and river floodplain operates in winter.

Campfire programs and *guided walks* are offered at times; see announcements.

PUBLICATIONS

Leaflet with map.
Wildlife checklists.
Backpacking.
Wilderness Preserve.
Horse Trails.
Boat and tram tours.
Information leaflets on campgrounds, boat rentals, etc.

HEADQUARTERS: 13207 SR 72, Sarasota, FL 34241; (813) 361-6511.

OSCAR SCHERER STATE RECREATION AREA
Division of Recreation and Parks
462 acres.   Map 97, C-2.

Off US 41 between Sarasota and Venice.

Open 8 A.M. to sundown.

Should this SRA be an entry? It's small. Much of the land area has been disturbed. Urban development is gradually surrounding it. Visitation is heavy in winter.

We were persuaded to include it because of management's commitment to preserve and restore natural conditions and because 1,000 acres may be added. The SRA is bisected by a mile of brackish tidal creek. The bordering swamp and marsh are relatively undisturbed. The native scrubby and pine flatwoods, predominant communities here, have been disturbed but have a natural appearance. They can be restored and provide habitat for the endangered scrub jay.

We sent this entry to the park manager for checking and got this reply:

I'm sure you won't be disappointed. As we continue to return fire to the normal regime here, more and more of our communities are being restored. Thanks for the opportunity to share this gem with folks who appreciate "the real Florida."

The campground and play areas are west of the creek. On the east side, a nature trail follows it.

Wildlife: An annotated checklist has an impressive array of bird, reptile, and mammal species.

ACTIVITIES
Camping: 104 sites. Telephone reservations are accepted; recommended December–May and holidays.
Canoeing: Rentals available.

INTERPRETATION
Campfire programs, Saturdays, Thanksgiving to Easter.
Guided hikes, Sundays, 9 A.M., Thanksgiving to Easter.
Guided canoe programs, Wednesdays, all year.

PUBLICATIONS
Leaflet with map.
Wildlife checklists.

HEADQUARTERS: 1843 South Tamiami Trail, Osprey, FL 34229; (813) 966-3154.

PEACE RIVER CANOE TRAIL
110 miles.   Map 93, B-1.

From Fort Meade to Charlotte Harbor.

The river rises in the Green Swamp. When the water level is high we have put in at the US 98 bridge in Fort Meade. More canoeists begin at the city park in Zolfo Springs, which has a campground. Outfitters offer day trips and camping trips of up to eight days.

Another popular put-in is at the highway bridge in Arcadia. Paddling upstream from there one morning we came upon two men in scuba gear. Diving in less than four feet of water? They were paleontologists, panning stream bottom sediments to gather fossils. They showed us a fine collection, from eohippus leg bones to mako shark teeth.

We've been lucky. Even on weekends we have seldom seen more than a few canoeists on the river and only occasionally met a power boat. State agencies have received complaints of overuse, vandalism, and littering. One complainant said he'd seen a hundred canoes launched in one day. Some riparian landowners have posted "No Trespassing" signs.

Much of the upstream riparian land is owned by phosphate mining companies. Downstream, agriculture and ranching are the principal land uses. Outfitter offers of "wilderness" canoe trips exaggerate, but much of the canoe trail is through swamp and forest, with an abundance of wildlife, including threatened species. Mangrove communities are near the river's mouth.

Water quality is generally fair, better downstream than up. Pollutants still enter the river, but some former sources have been stopped and clean-up efforts continue.

A number of fish camps, boat ramps, commercial campgrounds, and public parks are along the river. Outfitters have their established campsites. Other canoeists should avoid even picnicking on private property without permission.

PUBLICATION: The Division of Recreation and Parks may have a Peace River Canoe Trail leaflet. It wasn't available when we asked.

PELICAN ISLAND NATIONAL WILDLIFE REFUGE
U.S. Fish and Wildlife Service
4,396 acres.   Map 96, B-3.

In the Indian River, south of Sebastian Inlet.

Pelican Island itself is only 3½ acres, less at high tide, but here the National Wildlife Refuge system began. Until the turn of the century, America's birds had little protection. In Florida, egrets were slaughtered for their plumes, waterfowl and many upland species for the market, pelicans for sport. In 1901 Florida's legislature prohibited killing birds other than game species. The National Audubon Society hired a game warden. Plume hunters murdered him.

Suddenly the young conservation movement had many vigorous supporters, including President Theodore Roosevelt. Just why the Audubon

Society and American Ornithological Union chose tiny Pelican Island as the prototype is unclear, but in 1903 they persuaded the President to sign an executive order setting aside the island as a wildlife sanctuary. The island had a lively colony of brown pelican, white ibis, snowy and great egrets, and herons: little blue, great blue, and tricolored herons, and black-crowned night-heron. From time to time since then hurricanes and other events caused the birds to nest elsewhere, but they returned.

The Refuge boundaries now include surrounding waters and other mangrove islands. The Fish and Wildlife Service has asked that 26,000 acres of State-owned wetlands be put under its management. That would provide accessible land for a visitor center and observation platform.

Until that happens, the Refuge can be visited only by boat. Boaters are asked to keep a respectful distance away from Pelican Island. We did, but that was close enough to see several dozen brown pelicans adorning the mangroves.

The Refuge is a satellite of the Merritt Island National Wildlife Refuge (see entry).

PUBLICATIONS
Leaflet.
Map.

HEADQUARTERS: c/o Merritt Island National Wildlife Refuge, P.O. Box 6504, Titusville, FL 32780; (407) 867-0667.

PINELLAS TRAIL
Pinellas County
5 miles.   Map 90, A-2, B-2.

Abandoned rail line between Largo and Seminole.

As of spring 1991, 280 abandoned rail lines in 35 states had been converted to 3,200 miles of hiking-biking trails. The first section of the Pinellas Trail opened in 1991. If plans become reality, by 1994 the trail will extend from St. Petersburg to Tarpon Springs, with an extension through East Lake and Oldsmar, a total of 47 miles.

POLK COUNTY RAIL TRAIL
Polk County Rails to Trails
28.5 miles.   Maps 84, D-3, to 78, C-3.

Abandoned Seaboard Coast Line route, Lakeland to Mabel, on SR 50 south of Center Hill.

The Polk County route was acquired by the State in 1991, but funds for construction must be raised locally. The route passes through the Green Swamp.

The Polk County group has recruited members and donors, hired a director, opened an office, and sponsored hikes over part of the route. We expect trail improvement will extend over several years.

HEADQUARTERS: P.O. Box 45, Winter Haven, FL 33882.

POTTS PRESERVE
Southwest Florida Water Management District
8,500 acres.   Map 77, A-3.

From Inverness, 5 miles northeast on SR 581. Left on Hooty Point Road or Dee Ranch Road.

When this entry was written in March 1991 the District owned the tract and had adopted a management plan. Entrances were closed to vehicles. Hikers could walk in, canoeists carry in, horse riders ride in. The additional activities noted later will be permitted when a ranger is in residence.

The Preserve is on the west side of the Withlacoochee River (see entry), across from the entrance to Gum Slough (see entry). Its western half is freshwater marsh and wet prairie with scattered small islands. These wetlands were part of the Tsala Apopka lakes complex until they were cut off by a dike road built to provide access to several islands. The wetlands are essentially pristine, in part because the previous owner banned airboats.

The District acquired the tract to protect and improve its several functions: flood control, water quality enhancement, and replenishment of the Floridan Aquifer. It also protects the several endangered and threatened species of plants and animals found here.

Hardwoods covering most of the eastern half were heavily logged before 1950. Where regeneration was allowed to occur, the forest is again in natural condition. A few old-growth trees remain. Intermixed with the hardwoods are stands of loblolly pine on ridges, cypress and hardwood swamps in depressions.

About 1,500 acres of scrub were converted to improved pasture. Another 500 acres of mixed hardwood hammock were modified for grazing, with a canopy of live oaks remaining.

PLANNED ACTIVITIES
The Hooty Point Road will be the chief vehicle entrance. Parking lot, ranger residence, and other facilities will be near the gate. An improved road beyond will end at a river camping area. Otherwise the tract will remain closed to motorized travel.

Camping: Primitive camping. Automobile, canoe, and foot access.

Hiking: On existing unimproved roads.

Canoeing: A dock and canoe launch will be near the entrance. This will be a fine put-in for the Gum Slough canoe trail.

Horse riding: On existing unimproved roads.

Hunting is prohibited.

Airboats and off-road vehicles are prohibited.

HEADQUARTERS: Southwest Florida Water Management District, 2379 Broad Street, Brooksville, FL 34609; (904) 796-7211.

ROCK SPRINGS RUN STATE RESERVE
Division of Recreation and Parks
8,736 acres.   Map 80, B-1.

From I-4, west about 8 miles on SR 46, then south on CR 433.

The site is roughly an inverted triangle. Rock Springs Run, its west side, is a common boundary with Wekiwa Springs State Park (see entry). The east side is the Wekiva River and Orange-Seminole county line. The apex, in the south, is at the junction of Rock Springs Run and the headwaters of the Wekiva River.

The site was acquired in 1983. Prior to acquisition, it had been extensively altered by logging, farming, and grazing. A network of logging roads and ditches had altered the drainage pattern. Even so, its appearance is natural. The original plant communities are still evident, and restoration is a prime management objective. Ditches will be filled, unneeded roads naturalized.

Limited recreation facilities have been provided. Hunting is the principal visitor activity in the fall. At other times hikers, birders, and canoeists can enjoy quiet isolation.

Elevations range from 15 feet at the streams to 57 feet. About two-thirds of the site is river swamp, freshwater marsh, and hardwood hammock. At higher elevations are pine flatwoods, scrubby flatwoods, and sand pine scrub.

Birds: 118 species have been recorded. Those often seen include Florida scrub jay, limpkin, and red-shouldered hawk.

Mammals: 35 species have been recorded. Black bears use the site in fall and winter, but it's easier to see tracks or scat than bear. The deer herd, once unbalanced by poor hunting practices, is now managed.

Reptiles and amphibians: The 47 species recorded include gopher tortoise and indigo snake. Alligators are common.

ACTIVITIES
Camping: Primitive canoe access sites on Run and River.
Hiking: Existing roads and trails in varying condition.
Hunting: Chiefly for deer.
Canoeing: Rock Springs Run and the Wekiva River are both popular with canoeists. (See entry, Wekiva River Canoe Trail.) Canoeists have access to the Reserve but there is no put-in.

Vehicles are prohibited except during special hunts. From the entrance visitors must hike 4 to 5 miles through uplands to the cool shade of river swamps. That can be hot in summer.

PUBLICATIONS
Leaflet with map.
The Wekiva River, Scenic and Wild. (Booklet, 36 pages, illustrated.) Written, edited, and published by The Wekiva River Writers. Available locally.
Wildlife Management Area leaflet. Florida Game and Fresh Water Fish Commission, Central Region, 1239 SW 10th St., Ocala, FL 32674; (904) 732-1225.

HEADQUARTERS: Route 1, Box 3650, Sorrento, FL 32776; (904) 383-3311.

SADDLE CREEK PARK
Polk County
740 acres.   Map 84, D-3.

On US 92 just east of Lakeland.

Open 5 A.M. to 9 P.M.

We include this popular urban park for two principal reasons. First, it's a hot-spot favored by birders; the Lake Region Audubon Society sponsors occasional bird walks. Second, it's an interesting demonstration of what can be done with an old phosphate mine.

Mining drastically alters the land, leaving a "moonscape" with large pits and spoil banks. Reclamation can take many forms. One is to approximate the original terrain and vegetation. Another is to encourage naturalization of the disturbed site, pits and all. The result can be a site with greater ecological diversity than the original.

The Park was donated to the county by American Cyanamid. The pits have become 500 acres of lakes and ponds, some interconnected, with dozens of heavily vegetated islands that are fine roosting and nesting sites for birds. Spoil banks are covered with trees and brush.

Most visitor activity is along the central road. Here fishermen launch their boats or fish from the bank, and families picnic. Birders know the trails that lead back into the brush.

ACTIVITIES

Camping: 40 sites. No reservations. The campground is often full January–April.

Hiking: About 1½ miles of trails.

Boating, canoeing: Three launching ramps. No horsepower limit is posted, but only light motors are appropriate.

Swimming: Supervised. We found the beach closed in April.

Dogs must be leashed.

HEADQUARTERS: Polk County Parks and Recreation Division, P.O. Box 60, Bartow, FL 33830; (813) 534-4340.

ST. JOHNS RIVER
273 miles.   Maps 87 to 58.

The sources and upper reaches of Florida's longest river are described in the entry for Upper St. Johns River Marsh. The entry for the river from Lake Poinsett to its mouth is in Zone 2.

ST. LUCIE INLET STATE PARK
Division of Recreation and Parks
808 land acres; 3,821 acres submerged.   Map 103, C-2.

Water access only. North end of Jupiter Island, on south side of St. Lucie Inlet.

In 1967 we cruised the Intracoastal Waterway, came ashore here, crossed the dunes, and explored what seemed to be a wilderness beach, no structures or people in sight. A severe storm had lashed the beach fairly recently. Trees and shrubs had been killed or uprooted.

Shortly we met a warden who told us the State had acquired several miles of the barrier island two years before. This is the north end of Jupiter Island. On the south it adjoins the Hobe Sound National Wildlife Refuge (see entry). One could walk here from the Refuge, a 5-mile hike, but visitors generally arrive by private boat.

Now there is a dock on the Intracoastal Waterway. A 3,300-foot boardwalk passes through two coastal hammocks of live oak, cabbage palm, paradise-tree, wild lime, and cocoa-plum to a long sand beach. Like other beaches in this region, it's an important nesting area for leatherback, green, and loggerhead sea turtles.

The Division of Recreation and Parks estimates annual visitation to be 14,000 people, January–March the peak months. On many mornings no boats are at the dock.

HEADQUARTERS: c/o Jonathan Dickinson State Park, 16450 SE Federal Highway, Hobe Sound, FL 33455; (407) 546-2771.

SAWGRASS LAKE PARK
Pinellas County
390 acres.   Map 90, B-3.

In St. Petersburg. From US 19, east on 62nd Avenue North; north on 25th Street.

Open 7 A.M. to sunset.

Pinellas County has an impressive array of parks. At Sawgrass Lake the theme is environmental education. An observation tower overlooks the 20-acre lake. Over a mile of elevated boardwalk traverses one of the largest maple swamps in central Florida. Boardwalk and 2,900 feet of trail through hardwood hammock are interpreted by an excellent self-guide pamphlet. 200 species of birds have been recorded.

The Environmental Center has displays with fossils and living specimens, a 300-gallon aquarium, film presentations, tape recordings, an arboretum, and literature. The center is staffed by naturalists.

Guided tours and other special programs are available to student and special-interest groups. The center is open to all.

PUBLICATIONS
Leaflet with map.
Self guide.
Trail map.
Plant checklist.
Bird checklist.
Mammal checklist.
Arboretum map, keyed for tree identification.
Pinellas County tree guide.
Turtle identification guide.
Pamphlets on shells, alligators, manatees, bees.

HEADQUARTERS: 7400 25th Street North, St. Petersburg, FL 33702; (813) 527-3814.

SEBASTIAN INLET STATE RECREATION AREA
Division of Recreation and Parks
578 acres.   Map 96, B-3.

On SR A1A north of SR 510.

The site is on a barrier island straddling Sebastian Inlet. The central portion is developed for intensive use. Whenever we've passed, the parking lots were well occupied. Day visitors number more than a million per year, campers about 35,000.

On the Indian River side are coastal hammocks fringed by mangroves. These natural areas make for good birding, but they can be seen only from the perimeter. No trails penetrate. A shallow lobe on the north side of the inlet is frequented by shore and wading birds.

The principal attraction is 3 miles of ocean beach backed by dunes. Access points are limited, so one can escape from congestion by walking. The beach is a turtle nesting area.

The park manager told us 40 percent of visitors come to fish. North of the inlet is an excellent surfing area, and 30 percent of visitors are surfers. We were surprised that swimming, boating, picnicking, and birding each account for 5 percent or less of visitor activity.

Because of this pattern, the park has no pronounced off season. The campground is often full from November through April. January–April tend to have the most day visitors, but day use is heavily influenced by weather.

ACTIVITIES

Camping: 51 sites. Telephone reservations accepted: (407) 589-9659.
Fishing: Surf, jetty, and catwalk.
Swimming: Miles of beach. No lifeguards. Wading in the inlet.
Boating: Ramp on Indian River.

PUBLICATIONS
Leaflet with map.
Bird checklist.

HEADQUARTERS: 9700 South A1A, Melbourne Beach, FL 32951; (407) 984-4852.

SEMINOLE RANCH WILDLIFE MANAGEMENT AREA
Florida Game and Fresh Water Fish Commission
6,000 acres.   Map 81, D-2.

From SR 50 at Christmas, north 2 miles on SR 420, Fort Christmas Road, then right 2 miles to entrance.

The site was purchased by the St. Johns River Water Management District and leased to the Commission. It adjoins the St. Johns River and the west shore of Cone Lake.

Along the lake and river are marshes, with oak/cabbage palm hammock adjoining. On slightly higher ground are pasture, hardwood swamp, and pine flatwoods.

As of our latest information, the District had vetoed construction of a marsh road because of drainage problems, and the site had no improved road. The WMA map shows about 7 miles of the Florida Trail, in two loops.

Deer hunting is the principal visitor activity, but hunting pressure seems to be light. The trail isn't closed in hunting season.

PUBLICATION: WMA leaflet.

HEADQUARTERS: Florida Game and Fresh Water Fish Commission, Central Region, 1239 SW Tenth St., Ocala, FL 32674; (904) 732-1225.

SOLDIERS CREEK PARK
Seminole County
1,500 acres.   Map 80, C-2.

From Sanford, southwest on US 17/92; south on SR 419; east on Osprey Trail.

Open 8 A.M.–5 P.M., Monday–Friday.

The Park was a passive greenbelt from US 17/92 to Lake Jessup. Now an Environmental Study Center, nature trails, and Big Tree Park are on about half of the upland acreage.

The big tree was discovered in the nineteenth century, a huge bald cypress in a swamp that was and is now usually under water. In the late 1880s, visitors reached it by leaping from log to log. President Calvin Coolidge may have leaped in 1929 when he made a dedication speech and a plaque was placed. A path was built in the 1930s.

According to a core sample, the tree is 3,500 years old. Its diameter is 17½ feet. Its height was 165 feet before a 1925 hurricane damaged the top. Another huge bald cypress is nearby.

Around the Nature Center, near the entrance, are an observation, wind, and solar energy tower; picnic area; and study sites.

The Florida Trail passes nearby. This is the northern terminus of its 27.4-mile Lake Jessup Section. A 3-mile loop trail passes through wet and dry hardwood hammocks and oak/palmetto scrub, leading to a freshwater swamp at the tip of the lake. A catwalk crosses the wet hammock. A boardwalk crosses a freshwater swamp to the big tree.

Nature Center programs staffed by teachers and volunteers are planned for school groups. Other visitors are welcome.

PUBLICATIONS
Nature Center leaflet.
Trails map.
Big Tree information.

HEADQUARTERS: Big Tree Park/Soldiers Creek Park, 3000A Southgate Road, Sanford, FL 32773; (407) 323-9615.

SOUTH HUTCHINSON ISLAND
Florida Power & Light Company
500 acres (estimated).   Map 103, B-1.

On SR A1A, about 7 miles south of Fort Pierce Inlet, just north of the St. Lucie Power Plant. The gate is near a metal shed.

We discovered this site 20 years ago. Revisiting in 1991 we were delighted to see few changes. We had just visited Jack Island (see entry, Fort Pierce Inlet State Recreation Area) and saw a marked resemblance. Years ago a dike was built for mosquito control. It formed a U-shaped impoundment that has become a dense mangrove swamp. It has two entrances on A1A about a half-mile apart.

The dike is broad, the top about 25 feet wide. Until recently one could drive around the dike. Fishermen, who seem to be the principal visitors, complain the entrances are now gated, so they must walk to their favorite spots. We estimated the trip around the impoundment to be about 2½ miles.

At two places, short catwalks penetrate the mangrove swamp. Farther on, we noticed a slender post stuck in the ground, decorated with red and yellow ribbons. Written on the post was the legend "AERIAL TARGET #12." We were neither strafed nor bombed.

As at Jack Island, the environment is favorable for a great variety of birds, and we saw many. Raccoon tracks were numerous, and a fisherman said he'd seen a young raccoon playing with a young gray fox. We counted more than 250 butterflies of five species. Golden-silk and crab spiders had built many webs over the trail.

It seemed to us on our first visit that this was a natural area worth preserving. We wrote to the Florida Nature Conservancy suggesting they investigate. In 1991 the St. Lucie County Property Appraisers office told us the power company owns it. The county manages the dike, roadway, gates, and catwalks as part of its mosquito control program, but doesn't control public use.

The power company doesn't encourage public use but permits it. That could change, but until then it's a delightful, quiet place for birding, walking, and fishing. We still believe it should be preserved.

TENOROC STATE RESERVE
Florida Game and Fresh Water Fish Commission
Division of Recreation and Parks
6,000 acres.   Map 84, D-3.

From US 92 east of Lakeland, north 3.4 miles on SR 33A, then right on Tenoroc Mine Road.

Open daylight hours, Thursday–Sunday only. All visitors must register.

Like nearby Saddle Creek Park (see entry), this was a phosphate mine. It was donated to the State in 1982. The large pits, now filled with water, have become fishing lakes of 20 to 250 acres; the total water surface is about 1,000 acres. Its full name is Tenoroc State Reserve Fish Management Area, and most visitors are fishermen. A small but increasing number of birders, hikers, and horseriders have been attracted. Our birding friends go there often. A campground is in future plans.

The uplands, flat to slightly rolling, are a mixture of grasslands and brush with scattered trees. The four largest lakes are beyond the site office and the fork in Tenoroc Mine Road. Other lakes are across SR 33A, with boat ramps on Old Combee Road and Lake Parker Drive.

ACTIVITIES

Hiking, backpacking. We were told a trail map is available, but it couldn't be found when we stopped at the office. A primitive campsite is provided for backpackers. We were told it's seldom used.

Fishing: Commission biologists are experimenting with management methods, chiefly to enhance the largemouth bass fishery. Special regulations require reservations and daily licenses, govern fishing methods, and require fishermen to report their catches. One lake is for fly rod fishing only. Some are for catch-and-release. Bass fishing is said to be outstanding.

Boating, canoeing: Ramps are on the largest lakes. Gasoline motors up to 10 hp are permitted on two lakes.

Horse riding: On designated trails. Proof of Coggins test is required.

Pets must be leashed.

PUBLICATIONS
Fishing leaflet with map.
Hiking trail map.
Horse trail map.

HEADQUARTERS: 3829 Tenoroc Mine Road, Lakeland, FL 33805; (813) 499-2422.

THREE LAKES WILDLIFE MANAGEMENT AREA
Florida Game and Fresh Water Fish Commission
53,503 acres, including Prairie Lakes.   Map 94, A-3.

From Kenansville on US 441 (Map 95), 9 miles north to entrance.

In 1974 the State acquired 51,285-acre Three Lakes Ranch. The unit has frontage on Lakes Kissimmee, Jackson, and Marian. The Prairie Lakes Unit, 8,200 acres, which we found the more interesting tract, lies between Lakes Kissimmee and Jackson. It was initially leased to the Division of Recreation and Parks for management, the balance of the property to the Commission. No recreation facilities were developed and visitation was light. In 1988 the area was recombined under the Commission's management. Hunting is now permitted throughout. Except in hunting season, it remains a quiet, attractive area for enjoyment of nature.

In the early 1900s, the Kenansville area had a brief boom while all the mature pine and cypress were cut. Thereafter most of it was used for grazing. Grazing continued, unauthorized, after it became State land.

Drainage also altered natural conditions. The Jackson Canal, which skirts Lake Kissimmee, lowered the level of Lake Jackson. Blocking the canal would restore the lake but inundate several hundred acres of exposed fertile land that ranchers claim. The State may have to buy it.

Recovery of the area began in 1976. The terrain is flat, the range of elevations only 20 feet. The principal plant communities are dry prairie, pine flatwoods, prairie hammocks, wet prairie, and scattered marshes. While scenic values, other than the lakes and proliferating wildflowers, are modest, the recovering ecosystems support abundant wildlife. Over 100 bird species have been observed, ranging from waterfowl and wading birds to wood warblers. Hikers often see sandhill cranes, caracaras, and bald eagles. Many reptiles and amphibians inhabit the site, as well as 16 known mammal species.

ACTIVITIES

Camping: Except in hunting season, camping is limited to primitive sites on the Florida Trail. In the Prairie Lakes Unit, a permit from the Ocala office is required.

Hiking, backpacking: The Florida Trail traverses the area, skirting Lakes Kissimmee and Jackson, exiting on SR 523. Also hiking on unmarked trails and unimproved roads.

Fishing: Lakes.

Canoeing, boating: The site has no improved ramp. Hand-carried craft can be launched at Lake Jackson.

PUBLICATIONS: WMA leaflets with maps: Three Lakes and Prairie Lakes.

HEADQUARTERS: Florida Game and Fresh Water Fish Commission, Central Region, 1239 SW 10th St., Ocala, FL 32674; (904) 732-1225.

TIGER CREEK PRESERVE
The Nature Conservancy
4,500 acres.   Map 94, B-1.

From Lake Wales, about 7 miles east on SR 60. South on Walk-In-Water
Road. Right on Wakeford Road to parking.

Open daylight hours.

Edward Bok, founder of Bok Tower Gardens, knew the Tiger Creek area
in the 1920s and hoped to save it. When development threatened, The Nature Conservancy acquired the first 900 acres in 1968. Many contributions
have supported subsequent acquisitions.

The Preserve is on the Lake Wales Ridge, part of the sand ridge that extends down the center of the Florida peninsula. Its centerpiece, Tiger Creek,
and tributary Patrick Creek are pristine blackwater streams flowing to Lake
Weohyakapka. The site is almost entirely forested: hardwood swamps and
hammocks beside the streams, sand pine and oak scrub, pine flatwoods,
and sandhill on higher ground. The range of elevations is 50 feet.

Logging of the uplands occurred in the past, but natural succession has
produced maturing woodlands. The wet forest is largely pristine, with huge
pignut hickories and maples.

A major reason for the Conservancy's commitment is that these natural
communities have 24 of Florida's rarest species, including the scrub jay,
scrub lizard, and sand skink. Among the rare plants are the pygmy fringe
tree and bonamia.

We were introduced to the Preserve a dozen years ago by environmentalist Ken Morrison, then director of Bok Tower, leader of the preservation
campaign. He and his wife Helen stopped every few feet to point out a bird,
tree, flower, or fungus. The Preserve wasn't yet open to the public, but there
was usually a Conservancy or Audubon volunteer willing to be escort and
guide. The trails were then unmarked, and some had yet to be cleared. When
we came to the creek, it seemed small but attractive. Ken assured us he had
canoed it, no doubt by dragging the broad shallows and tight maneuvering
in swifter-running narrows. Officially it's not canoeable, and canoeing isn't
permitted.

Now there is a resident land steward and guided hikes are offered on first
Saturdays, October–May, or to groups by reservation. Some trails have been
cleared, but most are short, in the northeast quadrant, and not well marked.
("Trail marking has recently been improved," wrote the land steward.) Volunteers of the Florida Trail Association are constructing a 12-mile route through

the principal natural communities. The first 2-mile section, beginning at the Pfunstein Road entrance, was open in April 1991. More should be complete when this book is published.

Flowering plants: 423 species have been identified in the Preserve, many of them spectacular. The peak blooming season is September to early November, but there's always something to see.

Wildlife: Observations are being recorded and checklists will be forthcoming. Thus far 130 bird species have been logged. The 20-plus mammal species seen include raccoon, river otter, armadillo, rabbit, opossum, and whitetail deer, with tracks of bobcat and fox. The list of reptiles and amphibians is far from complete, but someone with a special passion has recorded 43 species of ants.

No vehicles are permitted beyond parking areas.
Pets are prohibited.
The Preserve has no rest rooms or water.

PUBLICATIONS
Folder with map.
Trail map.

HEADQUARTERS: Lake Wales Ridge Office, The Nature Conservancy, P.O. Box 1319, Lake Wales, FL 33859; (813) 678-1551.

TOSOHATCHEE STATE RESERVE
Division of Recreation and Parks
28,800 acres.   Maps 81, D-2; 87, A-2.

From SR 50 at Christmas, 3 miles south on Taylor Creek Road.

Open 8 A.M. to sunset.

Crossing Florida on the Beeline Expressway, SR 528, one doesn't notice the Reserve. The highway crosses it but there's no exit. (One can exit west of the Reserve on SR 520, turning right on Taylor Creek Road.) The State acquired the land in 1977 as part of its Environmentally Endangered Lands Program, thus saving one of Florida's pristine forest and wetland areas. It remains pristine, with no development other than trails.

For a time the site wasn't open to the public and it is still not well known. Four out of five visitors are local residents. About one-third of them come to hunt or fish, about half for sightseeing, backpacking, hiking, and birding. On weekdays, except in hunting season, one can hike in solitude.

The site has 19 miles of frontage on the west side of the St. Johns River. Dikes along the river offer a hiking route and vantage point for wildlife observation. Wetlands adjoin the river and its tributaries, with swamps, marshes, and hardwood hammocks. Uplands are chiefly pine flatwoods. Throughout the site are many species of wildflowers, including the purple wild iris. Spring is the peak of the blooming season. Along Jim Creek is a 900-acre old-growth cypress swamp that has somehow escaped the chain saw. Logging trails show that portions of the site were cut, but some old-growth slash pines still stand.

Birds: An annotated checklist of 140 species is available. It includes a great assortment of waterfowl, shorebirds, and wading birds, birds of prey, and songbirds, most of them permanent or winter residents.

Mammals: Species observed include fox squirrel, river otter, gray fox, bobcat, and whitetail deer. Black bear and itinerant panther have been reported.

ACTIVITIES
Hiking, backpacking: A 40-mile section of the Florida Trail enters the site on SR 50 at the Christmas RV Park. The south trailhead (which may be changed) is on SR 520 one mile west of the St. Johns River Bridge. Trailside camping is permitted at designated sites, by reservation. The trail passes through pine flatlands, oak forests, and along river dikes. A network of intersecting trails begins at the two parking areas. Trail map and compass are advisable. So is insect repellent.

Horse riding: About 23 miles of horse trails are marked with fluorescent orange diamonds. Horses are not permitted on foot trails or Reserve roads. Camping is permitted at the designated site. Coggins test is required.

Dogs are permitted on leash, daytime only.

PUBLICATIONS
Leaflet with map.
Bird checklist.
Wildlife Management Area leaflet with map.

HEADQUARTERS: 3365 Taylor Creek Road, Christmas, FL 32709; (407) 568-5893.

UPPER ST. JOHNS RIVER MARSH
St. Johns River Water Management District
89,000 acres.   From Map 87, B-3 to Map 95, C-3.

Seven recommended access points west of I-95 between SR 520 and SR 60. Site map is necessary.

The site is a strip about 50 miles long, generally less than 3 miles wide. The southern third is a huge freshwater marsh, the headwaters of the St. Johns River, Florida's longest and largest. The river flows northward through a series of lakes, ultimately emptying into the Atlantic Ocean at Jacksonville.

The District acquired the area to protect and restore the river and its marshes, which were threatened by drainage, pollution, and development. A cooperative project with the U.S. Army Corps of Engineers will ultimately restore 125,000 acres of marshlands. The site is also a Wildlife Management District; hunting is regulated by the Florida Game and Fresh Water Fish Commission.

The area is 80 percent freshwater marsh. The 20 percent forested is hammock and swamp, with cypress, red maple, bay, live oak, and cabbage palm.

Wildlife has not been cataloged, but the following species are common.

Birds: Waterfowl, wading birds, other marsh species. Wood stork and Everglades kite are often seen. When we sent this entry to the District for checking, we were urged to emphasize that birding is excellent.

Mammals: Bobcat, river otter, raccoon, wild hog, deer.

Reptiles and amphibians: alligator, turtles, cottonmouth moccasin.

LAKES

The largest lakes within the site, from south to north, are

Blue Cypress Lake, 6,555 acres. County park. Access by Blue Cypress Lake Road, off SR 60.

Lake Washington, 4,362 acres. Road access. No ramp.

Lake Winder, 1,496 acres. Boat access.

Lake Poinsett, 4,334 acres. Access from SR 520.

ACTIVITIES

The District plans to increase nonconsumptive recreational opportunities.

Camping: 14 campgrounds. One is a county park on Blue Cypress Lake at the south end of the site. The others are primitive sites planned for hunters but available to all. Few have road access. Most are accessible by boat or canoe. Camp in campgrounds only.

Hunting: By permit. Deer, wild hog, small game, turkey, waterfowl.

Fishing: Largemouth bass, crappie, panfish.

Boating, canoeing: The river is navigable by small craft from a few miles south of US 192. The site map shows put-ins. The District advises that all craft carry a blaze orange flag on a 6-foot staff.

Dogs are permitted on leash.

PUBLICATION: Folder with map.

HEADQUARTERS: St. Johns Water Management District, P.O. Box 1429, Palatka, FL 32178; (904) 329-4404.

UPPER TAMPA BAY COUNTY PARK
Hillsborough County Parks and Recreation Department
596 acres.   Map 83, D-1.

In Tampa, west on SR 580 beyond the airport and canal. Left on Double Branch Road.

On a peninsula in Old Tampa Bay, the park includes pine flatwoods, hardwood hammock, freshwater ponds, salt marsh, mangrove swamp, salt barren, and tidal creek. This remnant of the natural areas that once surrounded Tampa Bay has been little changed since Indians gathered shellfish here. Threatened by development in the 1960s, it was saved by regulations protecting wetlands and by land purchase.

Go first to the Nature Center. It's one of the best we've seen anywhere, with excellent exhibits, dioramas, aquariums, and more. We followed two groups of young people. They were as fascinated as we were. The center and classrooms are housed in attractive modern buildings. An upper observation deck overlooks the tidal creek.

Go to the center first because the nature trails and boardwalks are not yet provided with interpretive signs or pamphlets. The Eagle Trail takes the visitor through each of the natural communities, but without guidance. Exhibits at the center describe and illustrate the flora and fauna of each. The Park leaflet also explains much of the site's natural history.

ACTIVITIES
Hiking: Three nature trails with boardwalks.
Fishing: Salt water.
Canoeing: Canoe launch is near the nature center. Canoeing in protected waters around the mangroves.

Pets must be leashed. Not allowed on boardwalks or in buildings.

PUBLICATION: Leaflet with maps.

HEADQUARTERS: 8001 Double Branch Road, Tampa, FL 33615; (813) 855-1765.

WEEDON ISLAND STATE PRESERVE
Division of Recreation and Parks
627 acres.   Map 91, B-1.

From Tampa, on US 92, cross the Gandy Bridge over Tampa Bay. Beyond the causeway, just before the dog track, turn left on San Martin Blvd. and follow signs.

Open 8 A.M. to sunset.

Weedon Island was Florida's first land purchase under the Environmentally Endangered Lands Act, in 1974. One wonders how so abused a bit of real estate qualified. Under State management, it's recovering, attracting fishermen, canoeists, and birders.

Shell mounds indicate Indians lived here as early as 10,000 B.C. (Some archaeologists raise eyebrows at that dating.) Later named "The Bayou," it was owned by a Colonel Henderson, who gave it to his daughter, Mrs. Leslie Weedon, in 1889. The Weedons made it a weekend resort.

In 1923 promoters built a gambling casino and a 2,000-foot boardwalk to Benjamin Island. In 1930 it became the planned site of "Grand Central Airport." The plan called for facilities to accommodate seaplanes as well as conventional aircraft, with an industrial park adjoining. Casino, airport, and industrial park were casualties of the Depression years. The casino saw a brief renaissance as a film studio, but it burned in 1963.

All this impacted heavily on a small island. Only 127 acres are uplands, and these acres are flat and subject to occasional flooding. Most of the area is tidal mangrove swamp. This was cut with a network of mosquito control drainage ditches. The spoil banks from these ditches provided a favorable site for Australian pine, an undesirable interloper. Other disturbances, such as a road built on fill, encouraged invasion by Brazilian pepper.

Enough? Not quite. Weedon and associated small islands, with their bays, lagoons, and shallows, are an important estuarine environment, providing food and habitat for fish, shellfish, and crustaceans. Motorboats dashing through the shallows damaged beds of sea grasses.

Now there is a new regime. The pavement ends at the entrance. Beyond is a broad white shell road. All other roads have been closed for revegetating. At road's end are a long wooden fishing pier, bulletin board, and canoe-launching area. The nearby waters are shallow, with tidal mud flats. Young mangrove shoots were growing on some flats.

Upland vegetation, chiefly a pine flatwood and scrubby flatwood community, looks young but vigorous. The island is an important natural area because of its 5½-mile shoreline rimmed by mangroves, red, white, and black. It is one of the few remaining mangrove communities fringing Tampa Bay. The smaller Weedon islands—Googe, Ross, Christmas, Snake, and Benjamin islands—are accessible only by boat and are relatively undisturbed. The surrounding waters have been designated an Aquatic Preserve. Soon after our visit the Department of Natural Resources published a rule banning power boats from the shallows around the Weedon islands. The rule was adopted to prevent further damage to sea grasses and to protect fishermen and canoeists.

Birding is excellent. The islands have an abundance of shore and upland species. One biologist inferred a large population of small mammals by noting the abundance of diamondback rattlesnakes. We saw a small rattlesnake, dead.

No trails are marked. Dense vegetation discourages venturing off the road. Along the road is a small picnic site with two tables.

ACTIVITIES

Fishing: Near the fishing pier we saw eight fishermen working the shallows, knee-deep to waist-deep.

Canoeing: A marked 4-mile canoe trail with a picnic stop opened in October 1990. The loop passes between Weedon and the smaller islands. Launching at the road's end.

HEADQUARTERS: 1500 Weedon Island Dr., St. Petersburg, FL 33702; (813) 570-5146.

WEKIVA RIVER–ROCK SPRINGS RUN CANOE TRAIL; LITTLE WEKIVA RIVER CANOE TRAIL

Division of Recreation and Parks
16 miles.   Map 80, B-1.

Put-ins at Kings Landing and Wekiwa Springs State Park. Downstream and on the Little Wekiva at marinas, outfitters.

The Wekiva is a canoeist's delight, an easy paddle through a natural area of lush wetlands, hardwood hammocks, pine flatwoods, and sand pine scrub. Wildlife is abundant, human intrusions few.

The river rises at Wekiwa Springs, in Wekiwa Springs State Park (see entry). (The springs and Park are spelled with a *w*, the river with a *v*.) It is soon joined by Rock Springs Run (see entry). About 3½ miles downstream is the Little Wekiva River, fed in part by Sanlando Springs, Palm Springs, and Sheppard (Starbuck) Springs. Continuing north a little less than

4 miles, the river passes under SR 46. Then it's about 5 miles to the end of the St. Johns River.

The river drops 1.6 feet per mile, rather steep for Florida. Because its flow is largely spring-fed, it can be canoed in periods of drought when some other rivers can't be. Commercial boats once carried passengers and freight from the St. Johns River to Wekiwa Springs, but the river has become too shallow for that. Indeed, some shacks upstream from SR 46 were abandoned as access even by outboard craft became difficult. We occasionally meet a slow-moving jon-boat. In places we pole instead of paddling, but this is a minor nuisance compared with the blessed absence of motor craft. Outboards are more common downstream, but we have seldom met more than a half dozen, and running at full throttle would invite damage to their propellers.

The river drains a 130-square-mile basin. Its wide, often-inundated floodplain has deterred development. In only a few places, chiefly near SR 46, are opportunities for riverside construction. Land at both ends of the river is now State-owned. More State acquisitions are impending. The last time we made the run, a crew from the Department of Natural Resources was demolishing riverside shacks on State-owned land.

In recognition of the Wekiva's natural qualities, the Florida legislature adopted the Wekiva River Protection Act. It has been designated an Outstanding Florida Water, a Wild and Scenic River, and an Aquatic Preserve.

The 16-mile canoe run begins at the Wekiwa Marina on Wekiva Spring Road. (One mile east of the Wekiwa Springs State Park entrance, turn north on Miami Springs Road.) At the end, after passing through the Lower Wekiva River State Preserve, the nearest take-out is 2 miles downstream on the St. Johns River, at High Banks Landing.

Local Sierra Club groups and other associations often sponsor shorter outings that begin at Katie's Wekiva River Landing and Campground. (From I-4, 5 miles west on SR 46; turn right on Wekiva Park Drive; 1 mile.) Canoes are transported to a private put-in on the Little Wekiva. It's then about four hours downstream to the Landing.

The upper portion of the Little Wekiva is narrow and winding. A few alternate channels require making the right choices. Sometimes one must push through floating masses of water hyacinth. Except for a few homes, the bordering land is wild, with good stands of cypress, oak, and pine.

On the main river, the run is more open. One can find places to go ashore for lunch or to stretch legs. Paddlers should save some energy for the 2 miles before Katie's. Here the river is wide, the current slow, and head winds common. Thereafter the channel narrows and the current quickens.

Flowering plants make the run colorful, in season such species as Florida bonamia, spring coralroot, butterfly and other orchids, spider lily, cardinal flower, and swamp honeysuckle.

We always see many birds here, including an exceptional number of limpkins, as well as various herons, osprey, wood stork, egrets, sandhill crane, and bald eagle.

This is black bear country, but we've never seen one. Manatees are seasonally common in the St. Johns River and may occasionally wander up the Wekiva. One always sees alligators and turtles.

REFERENCES

Wekiva River/Rock Springs Run Canoe Trail. (Folder with map.) Division of Recreation and Parks.

The Wekiva River, Scenic and Wild. (Booklet, 36 pages, illustrated.) Written, edited, and published by the Wekiva River Writers. Available locally.

WEKIWA SPRINGS STATE PARK

Division of Recreation and Parks

6,396 acres.   Map 80, C-1.

From I-4 north of Orlando, exit 49, west on SR 434 to Wekiwa Springs Road.

Open 8 A.M. to sunset.

Our introduction to this park was a Florida Audubon Society conference. Facilities available to environmental organizations include cabins, meeting hall, and dining building. This cluster is apart from other Park facilities.

It's one of the State's largest parks. Across Rock Springs Run is an 8,749-acre State Reserve. The scenic 16-mile canoe run down the Wekiva to the St. Johns River is through wetlands and forests, largely undeveloped, much of the adjoining land State-owned. (See entry, Wekiva River Canoe Trail.)

It is also one of the State's most popular. To avoid crowds in the developed area, visit before 11 A.M. summer or fall. The loop trail always offers quiet hiking.

Wekiwa Springs, in the southeast corner of the Park, is the principal source of the Wekiva River, a scenic attraction, and a popular swimming hole. From Rock Springs, in the northwest, Rock Springs Run loops northeast and south to the river, forming the Park's north and east boundaries, adding to the river flow.

All facilities are at the south end of the Park. The northern three-fourths is accessible only by a 13-mile trail loop. The several natural communities of this area have been little changed since the Timucuan Indians lived here.

The Park is on the east side of the long sand ridge that extends down the center of peninsular Florida. From river swamps characterized by bald cypress, tupelo, and ash, the land rises gradually to wet forest dominated by sabal and needle palms, laurel and water oak, and sweet bay. Pileated woodpecker and barred owl are typical inhabitants.

Slightly higher are the pine flatwoods, seldom flooded but with wet spots where ground water seeps to the surface. Saw palmettos, associating with pond and slash pine here, diminish on the sandhill region of the upper ridge, where longleaf pine dominates. Along the ridge are areas of sand pine scrub, a vanishing community that harbors the endangered scrub jay.

Numerous sinkholes are scattered through the uplands. The largest, now water-filled, is Lake Prevatt.

Birds: A checklist of 161 species notes seasonality and abundance. Permanent and winter residents are most numerous. Included are many species of waterfowl, shorebirds, and wading birds, and 21 species of wood warblers.

Mammals: Checklist of 24 species. Black bear are seen occasionally. Deer, bobcat, and typical small mammals.

Reptiles and amphibians: The exceptionally long list of 25 species of snakes says as much about the quality of observations as about the habitat. Also included are many species of turtles, lizards, salamanders, frogs, and toads.

ACTIVITIES
Camping: 60 sites. Telephone reservations accepted. The campground is often full on weekends, especially from Christmas to April.
Hiking, backpacking: The 13-mile loop is a section of the Florida Trail. Two trailside campsites are available, by permit.
Swimming: Spring and adjacent basin.
Canoeing: Launch site. Rentals.
Horse riding: An 8½-mile trail is available. Proof of Coggins test is required.

INTERPRETATION: *Nature trail* is near the spring. Guide ropes and Braille signs are provided.

PUBLICATIONS
Leaflet with map.
Checklists of vertebrates.

HEADQUARTERS: 1800 Wekiwa Circle, Apopka, FL 32712; (407) 884-2009.

WILDERNESS PARK
Hillsborough County Parks and Recreation Department
16,000 acres.   Map 83, D-3.

For access points, see the following.

The Lower Hillsborough Flood Detention Area is owned by the Southwest Florida Water Management District. It was acquired as part of a plan to protect downstream urban areas from floods. The area lies along the Hillsborough River, south of Hillsborough River State Park, east of I-75, north of US 301.

By agreement with the District, Hillsborough County is developing a cluster of recreation sites giving access to the 16,000 acres. They are as follows:

- *Trout Creek:* Morris Bridge Road at the Tampa Bypass Canal, just east of I-75 bypass. Canoe launch; boardwalk; fishing.
- *Morris Bridge:* Morris Bridge Road at the Hillsborough River. Hiking; boardwalks; boat launching.
- *Flatwoods:* On Morris Bridge Road 1 mile north of the Hillsborough River. Under construction: interpretive center, campgrounds, trails.
- *Dead River:* US 301 and Dead River Road, 1 mile south of Hillsborough River State Park. Hiking; fishing.
- *John B. Sargeant, Sr., Memorial:* US 301 and Stacy Road. Boardwalk; boating; fishing.
- *Veteran's Memorial Park:* US 301 at Tampa Bypass Canal, south of SR 574. Hiking, bank fishing along 0.7 miles of the canal.

The Water Management District's rules permit foot travel throughout the 16,000 acres. Thus far only a few maintained trails have been developed. We saw informal trails along the river, used by fishermen. Some old logging roads and tram trails can be used.

Canoeing is one of the best ways to see the flora and fauna of the wilderness. The Sargeant site is the farthest upstream put-in. The river current is slow enough to make round trips feasible.

It is possible to put in at Hillsborough River State Park and Dead River, upstream. However, between Dead River and Sargeant the run is designated "primitive," meaning that one can expect portages, pullovers, and downed trees.

Until more trails are developed and better maps provided, this is not a prime site for the casual one-time visitor. It provides a splendid wilderness opportunity for those who can take time for pathfinding and exploration.

PUBLICATION: Leaflet with area map.

HEADQUARTERS: Parks and Recreation Department, 1101 East River Cove Street, Tampa, FL 33604; (813) 272-5840.

WITHLACOOCHEE RIVER PARK
Pasco County
406 acres.   Map 84, B-1.

At Dade City, northbound on US 301 Truck Bypass, turn right just before it rejoins US 301. See sign. Proceed 4.7 miles, turning right at County Park sign.

Open dawn to dusk.

This small riverside park was dedicated shortly before our visit. It became riverside when the Southwest Florida Water Management District added 146 acres to the county land.

It looked new, attractive, immaculate. The paved entrance road passes through a forest of mature oaks, including many live oaks, with an understory of palmetto. At the first parking lot is a paved walkway to the canoe launch. This is also the beginning of the nature trail, not yet equipped with labels or markers. Beyond the first lot, the forest is open and much younger. Longleaf pines have been planted among spindly young oaks, so this will become a pine forest.

It was surprising to see several unusually large picnic shelters in a small park. Perhaps group picnics and class visits are its chief anticipated uses.

The river can be seen from the canoe launch dock and from a tower at the end of the nature trail. The banks are lined with large cypress trees, banks and shallows studded with cypress knees. The current is sluggish here, barely moving.

ACTIVITIES

Camping: Walk-in primitive campground. We saw no sign saying permits are required.

Hiking: The Florida Trail Association has been asked to add to the present hiking trail. We believe the new trail will provide river overlooks.

Canoeing: The river was about 3 feet below its normal level. It looked canoeable, but we can't say how far. We considered the possibility of paddling from here downstream to Silver Lake, where a popular run to Nobleton begins. Maps say it can't be done; the river becomes a marsh between Dade City and Lacoochee.

Dogs are permitted on leash.

HEADQUARTERS: Pasco County Parks and Recreation Department, 6520 Ridge Road, Port Richey, FL 34668; (813) 847-8118.

WITHLACOOCHEE RIVER (SOUTH) AND CANOE TRAIL

103 miles; canoe trail 83 miles.   Maps 84, A-1, to 71, D-2.

First put-in is at Coulter Hammock Recreation Area in the Richloam Tract, Withlacoochee State Forest (see entry). From US 301 west of Lacoochee, SR 575 east to Coit Road. Turn south 2½ miles.

Not to be confused with the other Withlacoochee River in northern Florida (see entry, Zone 2), this one rises in the Green Swamp (see entry) and wanders generally west and northwest to the Gulf of Mexico near Yankeetown. The 83-mile canoe trail ends at the Dunellon wayside park beside the US 41 bridge. Along the way are State lands and many recreation sites, public and private. The river continues through Lake Rousseau.

The river drains a basin of over 2,000 square miles. The upper section winds through wetlands and sandhills, often bordered by hardwood forests with saw palmetto and cabbage palm understory. Portions of the channel are narrow, between high banks. Here there is little development, much of the land State-owned.

At mile 23 the river enters Silver Lake, a Recreation Area in the Withlacoochee State Forest (see entry). Below the lake is a primitive camping zone, followed by swamp forest and, above Nobleton, an area of private cottages. On the east side near Nobleton is a privately owned game preserve. Silver Lake to Nobleton is a popular 9-mile canoe run. *(You can't enter the Silver Lake Park with a dog, even for immediate transfer to a canoe.)* We often put in at Nobleton, paddle upstream to Silver Lake and back.

Below Nobleton the river widens, with wetlands on both sides, and enters a remote section of the river. On the east side is the Jumper Creek Tract of the Withlacoochee State Forest (see entry) and, just beyond, Outlet River, a channel to Lake Panasoffkee. A short distance downstream is Gum Slough (see entry), discharging water from Gum Springs. On the west is Flying Eagle (see entry) and the Tsala Apopka chain of lakes. Several other tracts in this region have been listed for State purchase.

Although numerous springs contribute to the river's flow, it is subject to droughts. In the summer and fall of 1990, for example, we found the section from Silver Lake to Nobleton too shallow for even light outboard craft, and canoeists had to drag over shoals.

Exotic aquatic plants such as hydrilla, water hyacinth, and water lettuce have become established on some sections. They can impair fish habitat and impede water flow, as well as being an occasional nuisance to boaters.

It's possible to canoe the river from the first put-in to the Gulf. Finding overnight campsites is easy. Most canoeists choose shorter cruises.

PUBLICATION: *Withlacoochee River (South) Canoe Trail.* Division of Recreation and Parks.

WITHLACOOCHEE STATE FOREST
Division of Forestry
123,240 acres.   Maps 77, 78, 84.

Four principal tracts:
* *Citrus,* 42,613 acres, southwest of Inverness.
* *Jumper Creek,* 10,068 acres, northwest of Bushnell.
* *Croom,* 21,359 acres, northeast of Brooksville.
* *Richloam,* 49,200 acres, east of Lacoochee.

The smaller Headquarters Tract is on US 41 north of SR 476 (map 77, C-3).

More than half a million people, mostly Floridians, enjoy the recreation resources of the Forest annually. The prospective visitor should get a copy of the *Withlacoochee State Forest Mapguide.* No other map shows the Forest roads, trails, and recreation centers.

By the 1930s most of this area had been cut over, burned, grazed or farmed, and virtually abandoned. Between 1936 and 1939, the federal government bought it for an average price of $4.20 per acre. In 1954 it was transferred to the U.S. Forest Service, which began rehabilitation. Four years later, it was transferred to the State. The Jumper Creek Tract was purchased by the State in its Environmentally Endangered Lands Program in 1978.

The Division of Forestry has developed management plans based on the characteristics of each Tract. The sandy soils of Citrus and Croom are marginal for commercial timber production. Here recreation takes precedence; wildlife and timber management are important but secondary. Grazing was stopped in 1958. Pines were planted and controlled burning begun.

At Richloam, timber production has priority, with wildlife, recreation, and grazing included in management plans. Ecosystem preservation has first place at Jumper Creek, compatible recreation second.

Most of the Forest is open to hunting, under management by the Florida Game and Fresh Water Fish Commission.

All four Tracts are attractive. We have backpacked in Richloam, making camp beside the Withlacoochee River. Some of the trails in Citrus are hilly, a relief from flatland hiking. From the Silver Lake Recreation Area in Croom, one can canoe to the Jumper Creek Tract and beyond. When there's enough water in the river, one can begin the cruise at Richloam.

CITRUS TRACT

The highest point in the Forest is 215-foot Tillis Hill, one of Citrus's three Recreation Areas with campgrounds. Within the Tract are 44 miles of hiking trails with primitive campsites along the way. Unimproved roads offer additional hiking routes. A separate network of horse trails is blazed with blue bands. The only stable in the Forest is at Tillis Hill.

The trails pass through sandhill scrub, oak thickets, sand pine and longleaf pine forest, and hardwood forest. Some natural stands of longleaf pine/turkey oak are over 60 years of age. In the northern part of the tract, individual pines exceed 200 years.

This is one of the few places where the fox squirrel is abundant. Deer are also numerous. Other species often seen include fox, raccoon, red-tailed hawk, and quail.

ACTIVITIES

Hiking trails: Begin at Holder Mine and Mutual Mine recreation areas. *Hiking is prohibited during the general gun hunting season.*

Camping: Three camp areas; no facilities.

Fishing: At Mutual Mine Recreation Area.

Horse riding: Trails begin at Tillis Hill Recreation Area.

JUMPER CREEK TRACT

Access is from exit 64 on I-75; northwest on CR 470; west on CR 479; south on CR 416; entrance by Kettle Island Road. Most visitors come to hunt. After hunting season, it's a quiet area for hiking, birding, fishing, and horse riding.

The Withlacoochee River is the northwest boundary. North-flowing Jumper Creek bisects the Tract. The area includes cypress/hardwood swamps, freshwater marshes, live oak/cabbage palm hammocks with islands of pine flatwoods and upland hardwood forests. Wildlife is abundant.

There are no facilities. Boat landings are nearby.

CROOM TRACT

Silver Lake, a wide place in the Withlacoochee River, is the most popular attraction here. Many canoeists put in at the lake and make the easy half-day run to Nobleton. The Tract has 29 miles of hiking trails. A primitive canoe camp is on the river one mile north of Silver Lake.

Recreation Areas are at Silver Lake, River Junction, Iron Bridge, and Hog Island.

The area is similar to the Citrus Tract, with sandhill scrub, oak thickets, and stands of pine. Cypress trees are along the river and around small ponds. The northern section is hilly. A deep ravine is near the center of the Tract, another near the Tucker Hill tower on the west.

A former phosphate mine site has been set aside as the Croom Motorcycle Area, used by motorcycles and all-terrain vehicles.

ACTIVITIES

Camping: Three campgrounds with 131 sites, plus two primitive sites along the hiking trails. Also 50 sites in the Motorcycle Area.

Swimming: No designated areas.

Horse riding: Designated loop trail. Current Coggins test required.

Hiking is prohibited during the general gun hunting season.
Dogs may not be brought into Silver Lake even for immediate transfer to canoe.

RICHLOAM TRACT

Here the soil is fertile and well suited to timber production. The terrain is flatter than at Citrus or Croom, and wetlands are more extensive. Some trails are wet after a heavy rain and may require a bit of wading.

The Florida Trail makes a 31-mile loop within the Tract, close to the Withlacoochee River in the southwest and the Little Withlacoochee in the north. Little-traveled dirt roads are also hiking routes with 5- to 10-mile loops. A connector trail links with trails in the Green Swamp (see entry).

Plant communities include pine flatwoods, pine plantations, cypress ponds, and hardwood hammocks. The sabal (cabbage) palm is common. Wildlife is often seen, especially along the river.

The Tract has no campground; primitive campsites are designated by white bands on trees.

Hiking is prohibited for the first nine days of the general hunting season.

HEADQUARTERS TRACT

This 1,230-acre tract includes McKethan Lake, popular with fishermen. A paved road around the lake is used by distance runners. About 2 miles southwest on US 41, a sign marks the access road for the Colonel Robins Nature Trail. The road leads to a picnic area with rest room. The Trail has three loops, of 0.8, 0.75, and 1.0 miles through open pine forest. A trail guide is available on site.

Pets are prohibited in recreation areas, day-use areas, and campgrounds. Pets on leash are permitted on trails.

PUBLICATIONS

Mapguide. Map and information.
Citrus Hiking Trail.
Citrus Horse Trails.
Mutual Mine Recreation Area.
McKethan Lake Nature Trail.
Colonel Robins Nature Trail.
Croom Hiking Trail.
Croom Motorcycle Area.
Richloam Hiking Trail.
From the Florida Game and Fresh Water Fish Commission:
Richloam Wildlife Management Area.
Citrus Wildlife Management Area.
Croom Wildlife Management Area.
Jumper Creek Wildlife Management Area.

HEADQUARTERS: Withlacoochee Forestry Center, 15019 Broad St., Brooksville, FL 34601; (904) 796-5650.

ZONE 4
SOUTH FLORIDA

ZONE 4
SOUTH FLORIDA

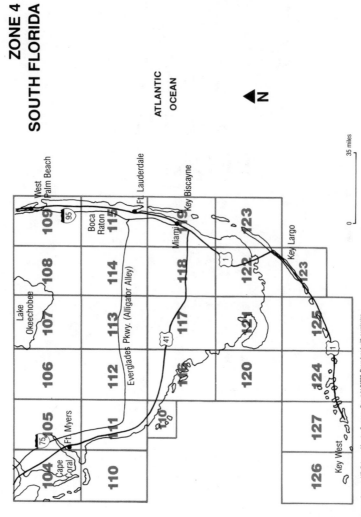

ATLANTIC
OCEAN

N

0   35 miles

104	105	106	107	108	109
110	111	112	113	114	115
	116		117	118	119
		120	121	122	123
126	127	124	125		123

Cape Coral
Ft Myers
Lake Okeechobee
West Palm Beach
Boca Raton
Ft Lauderdale
Miami
Key Biscayne
Key Largo
Key West
Everglades Pkwy. (Alligator Alley)

ENTRIES IN ZONE 4

The number preceding the natural area entry refers to the map number in the DeLorme *Florida Atlas & Gazetteer.*

Z ONE 4 IS SOUTH FLORIDA, from Lake Okeechobee to Key West and the Dry Tortugas. This is the meeting place of subtropical Florida and the true tropics.

We looked for natural areas on the Atlantic Coast from Jupiter to Key Biscayne and found a few, notably the Blowing Rocks Preserve and John D. MacArthur State Park. The State, counties, and private groups are hastily buying whatever fragments of the coast remain undeveloped.

Development on the Gulf Coast is reasonably heavy from Punta Gorda to Naples, but it's limited to the coastal fringe, including islands accessible by causeways.

The inland region from Okeechobee to the southern tip of the peninsula is the least populated part of Florida. This is the land of the Big Cypress and the Everglades, vast wetlands that have been degraded but may yet be salvaged. At the Corkscrew Swamp Sanctuary, Collier-Seminole State Park, Loxahatchee National Wildlife Refuge, and Everglades National Park visitors can see many aspects of these wetlands. Wilderness experience is available to those who travel on foot or by canoe.

Biscayne National Park and adjacent John Pennekamp Coral Reef State Park offer coral reef adventures to scuba divers and swimmers with snorkels. Nonswimmers can patronize glass-bottomed boats. From Key Largo to Key West, the islands linked by the Overseas Highway are threatened by popularity. We have entries for a few bits of nature along the way.

Offshore islands offer opportunities for solitude, if one has a seaworthy boat. Fort Jefferson National Monument on the Dry Tortugas is accessible by charter boat and seaplane. Florida Bay has dozens of islands, the Ten Thousand Islands region many more. Boat camping is permitted on some islands.

COMMON BIRDS OF ZONE 4
by Chuck Geanangel

Several places in south Florida are mandatory stops for birders: the Arthur R. Marshall Loxahatchee National Wildlife Refuge, Everglades National Park, Corkscrew Swamp Sanctuary, and the J. N. "Ding" Darling National Wildlife Refuge on Sanibel Island. Those seeking additions to life lists should find transportation to Fort Jefferson National Monument for noddies, boobies, tropicbirds, bridled terns, and cave swallows. The zone has much more.

Everglades National Park has the longest bird checklist of any in Florida, 347 species. A few, once recorded, are now extinct. Some are "accidentals," wanderers or storm-carried from other habitats. Populations of many, especially the wading species, have declined sharply since water was diverted from the Everglades.

Lists like these are at best a rough guide in trip planning. "Winter residents" will almost certainly be present in winter, but fall arrivals and spring departures vary from species to species and year to year. It was tempting to mention specialties and rarities that attract birders from afar, but one can't be sure of seeing them. When you visit a park or refuge, ask for a bird list. Then ask for the news: What special birds are present? When and where can they be seen?

WATER HABITATS, FRESH, BRACKISH, AND SALT
Permanent residents, here all year

Double-crested	Black-crowned Night-	Purple Gallinule
Cormorant	Heron	Common Moorhen
Anhinga	White Ibis	Limpkin
Great Blue Heron	Glossy Ibis	Killdeer
Great Egret	Wood Stork	Black-necked Stilt
Snowy Egret	Fulvous Whistling-	American Avocet
Little Blue Heron	Duck	Least Sandpiper
Tricolored Heron	Mottled Duck	Laughing Gull
Green-backed Heron	Osprey	Black Skimmer

Permanent residents of the coastal region

Brown Pelican	Wilson's Plover	Ruddy Turnstone
Reddish Egret	Semipalmated Plover	Red Knot
Yellow-crowned	Piping Plover	Sanderling
Night-Heron	Willet	Royal Tern
Clapper Rail	Whimbrel	Sandwich Tern
Black-bellied Plover	Marbled Godwit	

Transients, spring and fall

Semipalmated	Pectoral Sandpiper	Common Tern
Sandpiper		

Winter residents, fall to spring

Pied-billed Grebe	Blue-winged Teal	Lesser Scaup
American White	Northern Shoveler	Sora
Pelican	American Wigeon	American Coot
Green-winged Teal	Ring-necked Duck	Greater Yellowlegs

Lesser Yellowlegs
Spotted Sandpiper
Western Sandpiper
Dunlin
Stilt Sandpiper

Dowitcher
Common Snipe
Ring-billed Gull
Herring Gull
Caspian Tern

Forster's Tern
Red-breasted
   Merganser
Belted Kingfisher

Summer residents, spring to fall
Least Tern   Black Tern   Gray Kingbird

LAND HABITATS
Permanent residents, here all year

Cattle Egret
Black Vulture
Turkey Vulture
Bald Eagle
Northern Harrier
Red-shouldered Hawk
Red-tailed Hawk
Crested Caracara
Sandhill Crane
Rock Dove
White-crowned Pigeon
Mourning Dove
Ground Dove
Barn Owl
Eastern Screech Owl

Great Horned Owl
Barred Owl
Red-bellied
   Woodpecker
Northern Flicker
Pileated Woodpecker
Blue Jay
Scrub Jay
American Crow
Carolina Wren
Eastern Bluebird
Northern Mockingbird
Brown Thrasher
Loggerhead Shrike

European Starling
White-eyed Vireo
Yellow-throated
   Warbler
Pine Warbler
Prairie Warbler
Common Yellowthroat
Northern Cardinal
Rufous-sided Towhee
Red-winged Blackbird
Eastern Meadowlark
Boat-tailed Grackle
Common Grackle
House Sparrow

Transients, spring and fall

Chimney Swift
Ruby-throated
   Hummingbird
Great Crested
   Flycatcher
Eastern Kingbird

Purple Martin
Barn Swallow
Veery
Yellow Warbler
Cape May Warbler

Black-throated Blue
   Warbler
Blackpoll Warbler
Hooded Warbler
Indigo Bunting

Winter residents, fall to spring

Sharp-shinned Hawk
Broad-winged Hawk
American Kestrel
Yellow-bellied
   Sapsucker
"Empidonax"
   Flycatcher
Eastern Phoebe
Tree Swallow
House Wren

Blue-gray
   Gnatcatcher
Hermit Thrush
American Robin
Gray Catbird
Solitary Vireo
Northern Parula
Yellow-rumped
   Warbler
Palm Warbler

Black-and-white
   Warbler
American Redstart
Ovenbird
Northern Waterthrush
Painted Bunting
Savannah Sparrow
Swamp Sparrow
Brown-headed Cowbird
American Goldfinch

Summer residents, spring to fall

Swallow-tailed Kite	Gray Kingbird	Yellow-throated Vireo
Yellow-billed Cuckoo	Northern Roughwing	Black-whiskered Vireo
Common Nighthawk	Swallow	Red-eyed Vireo
Chuck-will's-widow		

ARTHUR R. MARSHALL LOXAHATCHEE NATIONAL WILDLIFE REFUGE

U.S. Fish and Wildlife Service

145,666 acres.   Maps 108, 109, 114, 115.

Entrance on SR 441 south of US 98.

Open sunrise to sunset, hours changing seasonally. Visitor center is open daily, mid-October to mid-April, 9 A.M. to 4 P.M. weekdays, to 4:30 P.M. weekends; closed Monday–Tuesday rest of the year.

On a map the Refuge looks unexciting: 221 square miles of flat wetlands surrounded by a pentagon of levees and canals. In fact, it's a place to be visited more than once. Its reputation is widespread; of half a million visitors a year, a growing number are from Europe and Japan.

This was once part of the natural Everglades, the "river of grass." It is one of three huge water storage areas built by the U.S. Army Corps of Engineers. The Refuge was established in 1951. Water retention and release are controlled by the South Florida Water Management District, not the Refuge.

Only a small bit of the Refuge is accessible to the causal visitor who enters at the headquarters area. One should go first to the visitor center for orientation. Outdoors is a kiosk with Refuge map, posted schedule of events, and other information. Inside are exhibits, dioramas, and slide show. Exhibits explain that southern Florida began to emerge from the sea only 20,000 years ago, the Everglades region becoming a shallow sea. Grasses colonized about 5,000 years ago.

Two nature trails and the beginning of a canoe trail are in the headquarters area. One can also walk on several dikes beyond the designated Marsh Trail route. This area, however, lies outside L-40, the boundary canal and levee. To visit the main body of the Refuge requires a boat. There is a ramp.

The northern half of the Refuge is closed to public use, except for the boundary canals. The southern half is open to boat traffic.

Although artificial and ruler-straight, the canals have much of interest. The banks have naturalized and birding is good.

Most of the area within the dikes is wet prairie, covered with 1 to 16 inches of water, with emergent vegetation, notably sawgrass. Sloughs are places with deeper water, the waterways of the Everglades. Scattered throughout the area are hundreds of tree islands, ranging in size from a few square yards to 300 acres and more. These tree islands are nesting areas for many birds and provide food and shelter for raccoons, bobcats, snakes, and other wildlife.

Birds: An annotated checked list of 250 observed species is available. Many species nest here. For some it's their farthest south. The greatest number of species is here in fall and winter, but birding is good in any season.

Mammals: We saw raccoon tracks on the Marsh Trail, droppings on the Cypress Swamp Boardwalk. Bobcat, otter, skunk, and deer are more likely to be seen on tree islands. Panther sightings have been reported.

Reptiles and amphibians: No checklist is available. Alligators are common, and 19 snake species have been recorded, as well as numerous turtles, lizards, salamanders, frogs, and toads.

OTHER ACCESS POINTS
Hillsboro Recreation Area is at the south end of the Refuge on SR 827, 8 miles from US 441. It has interpretive displays, boat ramp, bank fishing. A concessioner offers airboat tours, rental boats, fishing guides, fishing supplies.

Twenty-mile Bend is at the north tip of the Refuge, off US 441/98. Boat ramps, bank fishing.

ACTIVITIES
Hunting: Waterfowl, by permit, in designated area. Hunting is less than 1 percent of visitor activities.

Fishing attracts 30 percent of the visitors. It is permitted in all waters except at the headquarters management area and where marked by signs.

Canoeing on the 5.5-mile trail that begins in the headquarters area, canals, and sloughs in the southern half of the Refuge.

Boating is permitted in all waters except where posted. Rentals are available at the Hillsboro Recreation Area. Guided airboat tours are provided by a concessioner at the Hillsboro Recreation Area.

Pets are prohibited.

INTERPRETATION
Visitor center has information, exhibits, shows, bookshop.

Calendar of Events has schedules and information about *guided walks, lectures, guided canoe trips, slide shows,* and other events. Some require reservations. Tour guides are volunteers.

The *Cypress Nature Trail,* a 0.4-mile boardwalk, begins at the visitor center. Extensive cypress swamps once bordered the Everglades. This is one of the few remaining.

The *Marsh Trail* begins at a parking area beyond the visitor center. It is routed over a series of dikes. These enclose impoundments where water levels are managed to improve habitat for wading birds and migratory waterfowl. The success of this management is evident in the number and variety of birds present. We were surprised that little and great blue herons and anhingas did not take flight when we passed a few feet away. Several large alligators were basking. An observation tower is at the far end of the loop.

PUBLICATIONS
Leaflet with map.
Visitor's Guide. $0.25.
Calendar of Events.
Bird checklist.

HEADQUARTERS: Route 1, Box 278, Boynton Beach, FL 33437; (407) 732-3684.

BAHIA HONDA STATE PARK
Division of Recreation and Parks
635 acres.   Map 124, C-2.

In the Florida Keys. On US 1 at mile marker 37.

Open 8 A.M. to sunset. In the busy season, may be closed briefly when parking is full.

Like other islands in the chain, Bahia Honda is founded on an ancient coral reef. Only one-third of its acreage is above the mean high-water line, and only one-twentieth has been developed for recreation. Even before State acquisition in 1961, Bahia Honda beach was popular, the only one in the Keys resembling a barrier island: sandy, with primary and secondary dunes.

Most visitors come for swimming, snorkeling, scuba diving, wind surfing, and boating. In addition to its campground, the Park has six cabin units and a marina with 19 rental slips for boat campers. While most come by car, many day visitors are boaters.

The principal natural associations are the beach, tropical hardwood hammock, mangrove forest, and submerged shallows. In the southeast, a depression between the primary and secondary dunes holds fresh water in the rainy season; water, cattails, sedges, and grasses here attract a variety of birds.

Because of their location and exposure, the Keys have a unique vegetation, many species transported here by wind, wave, and birds from the West Indies. Among the unusual species are the satinwood tree, spiny catesbaea, and dwarf morning glory. Specimens here of the yellow satinwood and silver palm are U.S. Champions. Other trees of the key include gumbo limbo, Jamaican dogwood, seven-year apple, and coconut palm.

Birds: An annotated checklist is based on observations in a single year, 1979. Winter appears to be the best birding season.

Other wildlife: The same folder lists only two terrestrial mammals — raccoon and evening bat — plus a few reptiles and amphibians. Turtles nest on the beach in summer; nests are recorded and monitored.

Camping: Three campgrounds, 80 sites. Telephone reservations accepted.

INTERPRETATION: *Silver Palm Nature Trail* passes through the several plant communities.

PUBLICATIONS
Leaflet with map.
Checklist of plants.
Checklist of vertebrates.
Nature trail guide.

HEADQUARTERS: Rt. 1, Box 782, Big Pine Key, FL 33043; (305) 872-3897.

BIG CYPRESS NATIONAL PRESERVE
National Park Service
Acreage, federal, 716,000;
nonfederal, 181,361.   MAPS 112, 113, 116, 118.

I-75 and the Tamiami Trail (US 41) cross the Preserve. Headquarters is on the trail east of Carnestown. (I-75 replaced Alligator Alley.)

The Big Cypress Swamp lies north and west of Everglades National Park, 1.5 million acres of freshwater swamps, marshes, wet and dry prairies, forested islands, hammocks, and estuarine mangrove forests. In 1974 Congress authorized the purchase of about one-third of the area, adding 146,000 acres in 1988.

Acquisition was a massive undertaking. There were hundreds of individual owners. Many had bought parcels from speculators and never seen them. Owners of backcountry hunting camps were often unwilling to sell. It has taken years of work by a staff of lawyers to locate owners and conclude purchases. The work continues.

Federal acquisition caused a storm of controversy. The 1974 act authorized the Secretary of the Interior to "limit or control" hunting, fishing, trapping, motorized vehicles, mineral exploration, grazing – anything, in fact, the Secretary deemed necessary to carry out the purposes of the act. Hunters feared the National Park Service might restrict or even prohibit hunting. They and others wanted no restrictions on airboats and off-road vehicles; conservationists urged the Park Service to prohibit both because of their swaths of destruction and impact on wildlife. Owners of backcountry tracts argued that airboats and ORVs provide their only means of access.

Some of the most vociferous objections came from squatters who had built illegal hunting camps on government land. Most of the camps were shacks, but they included mobile homes and a few modern houses, some with landing strips. The squatters fought a delaying action in court, but most have been ousted.

Hunting is permitted, managed by the Florida Game and Fresh Water Fish Commission and National Park Service. In 1991 the National Park Service had a limit of 2,500 off-road vehicle permits. The area surrounded by the Loop Road was closed to ORVs. ORV trails and areas have been designated. Users are now required to follow the applicable signs and maps.

This wild area is not within the primary Everglades watershed, but does supply a significant amount of slow-flowing water to the western portion of Everglades National Park. Drainage has not affected it as disastrously as diversion of the natural water supply affects Everglades National Park. Receiving an average 60 inches of rainfall, chiefly in summer, the Big Cypress is wet six to eight months of the year, tinder-dry in winter, the normal dry season.

Many threats to the Big Cypress have come and gone. Old logging roads are overgrown, drainage canals clogged. A jetport proposed in 1968 was one of the threats that prompted creation of the Preserve. Few giant cypress remain and even fewer panthers, but the balance is now tilted in favor of nature undisturbed.

Visitors who want to sample the Preserve can see some of it from the few unpaved interior roads. Turner River Road, CR 839, is a ruler-straight route from I-75 to the Tamiami Trail. In the southeast, a loop road, SR 94, provides a scenic 24-mile drive. A few road spurs penetrate the swamp. Use caution on unpaved roads.

A more adventurous way to explore the Big Cypress is hiking all or part of the 38-mile Florida Trail, which crosses the Preserve north to south. We suggest first-time visitors park at the Oasis Ranger Station on US 41, check in, get a trail map, and hike north. Be prepared to do some wading.

Plants: No botanical inventory has yet been published. About one-third of the swamp is dominated by dwarf pond cypress surrounding wet prairies, in strips beside sloughs, and on occasional domes. Hammocks are occupied by hardwoods, sandy islands by slash pine. Mangroves grow densely along brackish waterways. Prairies are characterized by cabbage palm and saw palmetto. These are only the most prominent of several hundred species:

countless bromeliads and vines in the trees, giant ferns, several dozen species of orchids, aquatic plants such as pickerel weed and arrowhead, prairie wildflowers.

Birds: No checklist is yet available. It will include many species of wading birds, red-cockaded woodpecker, swallow-tailed kite, wild turkey, sandhill crane, bald eagle, and many more. Birding is best in winter.

Mammals: In this region are the few remaining Florida panthers, perhaps already doomed by inbreeding. How to save them has been the subject of acrimonious debate among scientists and animal rights advocates. Black bears, reduced in number, seem secure. Denizens include bobcat, river otter, raccoon, mink, gray and fox squirrels, marsh rabbit, cottontail, opossum, armadillo, whitetail deer. Manatees are sometimes seen in canals south of US 41.

Reptiles and amphibians: The swamp is fine habitat. No checklist is yet available, but it will include numerous frogs and toads, anoles, turtles, and alligator; as well as garter, ribbon, mud, and rat snakes; kingsnake, racer; pygmy and diamondback rattlesnakes.

ACTIVITIES

Camping: Primitive campgrounds only, most on the Florida Trail, a few on unpaved roads; inquire at headquarters. One private campground is near headquarters.

Hiking, backpacking: Chiefly on the Florida Trail.

Hunting: Florida Game and Fresh Water Fish Commission regulations.

Fishing: Chiefly in canals.

Canoeing: The principal canoe trail begins in the Turner River canal, on US 41 at the CR 839 intersection, and continues south through the Turner River, entering Everglades National Park and joining the Wilderness Waterway.

PUBLICATIONS

Illustrated folder with map.

Big Cypress Wildlife Management Area leaflet.

Turner River, Halfway Creek canoe trail map.

Off-road vehicle trails and areas system maps.

HEADQUARTERS: Star Route Box 110, Ochopee, FL 33943; (813) 695-2000.

OASIS RANGER STATION: (813) 695-4111.

BISCAYNE NATIONAL PARK
National Park Service
181,500 acres of land and water, mostly water.   Maps 119, 123.

Islands and reefs east of Homestead.

The Park encompasses, from west to east, a narrow strip of mangrove coast, shallow Biscayne Bay, a chain of 40 low-lying Florida Keys islands and outer coral reefs, including giant-coral patch reefs. These living reefs, magnets for countless brilliant fishes, lobsters, sponges, anemones, and other marine organisms, are the Park's outstanding feature.

The same reef formations extend into the John Pennekamp Coral Reef State Park, adjoining on the south. Established in 1959, Pennekamp was the first underwater park. No one expected it to become so popular. The reefs the Park was established to protect are endangered by too many boats and divers.

The Pennekamp experience was instructive. Biscayne National Park, authorized in 1968 and expanded to its present size in 1980, was planned for preservation. There's no mainland base for boat launching and only occasional public boat transportation to the islands. A single concessioner operates two tour boats that carry sightseers and divers to the reefs. Private boats visiting the islands and reefs are monitored to assure boaters' compliance with safety and resource protection regulations.

Birds: An annotated checklist of 179 species is available. It includes pelagic species of the Gulf Stream, among them such rarities as Audubon's shearwater, masked booby, and pomarine jaeger. Storm winds often carry species from distant habitats. The mangrove coast and islands both offer fine birding all year.

Bring insect repellent and sunscreen.

HOW TO VISIT THE PARK

Headquarters and visitor center are 9 miles east of Homestead on North Canal Drive (SW 328th Street), adjacent to Dade County's Homestead Bayfront Park. (A new visitor center is scheduled to open in 1994.)

Glass-bottomed tour boats visit the reefs daily for bottom viewing and snorkeling or scuba diving. Departures are from Park headquarters. For schedules and other information, call or write Biscayne Aqua-Center, P.O. Box 1270, Homestead, FL 33030, (305) 247-2400.

Canoes, rented from the concessioner, are suitable for exploring the mangrove coast and creeks, fishing and birding.

Power boats, necessary for visiting the islands and reefs, aren't available at the Park but can be rented at nearby marinas. Ramps are available at two Dade County parks within the boundaries. The Intracoastal Waterway traverses Biscayne Bay. Boat operators should consult marine charts.

THE COAST

Development has eliminated mangroves from much of Florida's coast to the detriment of wildlife and water quality, making the shore vulnerable to storms. The mainland strip of the Park is an almost unbroken belt of mangroves.

THE BAY

The sheltered waters of the Bay are ideal for cruising, fishing, swimming, and water skiing.

THE ISLANDS

Most of the 40 islands are small, with no visitor facilities. Most are covered with such trees as gumbo limbo, Jamaican dogwood, strangler fig, and satinleaf, with a dense understory of tropical shrubs and vines.

Elliott Key, largest of the islands, is due west of headquarters. It has boat docks. A visitor center is open intermittently. No reservations are required at the campground or for overnight mooring. Only Elliott Key has showers and drinking water. A hiking trail about 7 miles long runs the length of the island. Another parallels the shoreline and winds through a hardwood hammock.

Adams Key, a small island south of Elliott, has boat dock, picnic area, rest rooms, and nature trail. Day use only.

Sands Key, north of Elliott, has backcountry camping, by permit, and a popular anchorage.

Boca Chita Key, north of Sands Key, has an ornamental lighthouse, boat dock, picnic pavilion, rest rooms, and a primitive campground.

The Arsenicker Islands, at the south end of Biscayne Bay, and the islands in Sandwich Cove, near the Adams Key visitor center, are closed to visitors.

THE REEFS

Most of the reefs are in the south half of the Park. Visiting boaters should have all safety equipment, weather forecast, navigation charts, and copies of Park regulations. We recommend a stop at Adams Key. The best access to the reefs, the marked channel of Caesar Creek, is nearby.

Anchoring on the reefs is prohibited. Some mooring buoys have been placed. Otherwise anchor on sandy bottom, away from seagrass beds.

Cruising at more than idling speed risks bashing your hull on a coral head.

PUBLICATIONS

Illustrated folder with map.
Bird checklist.
Tour boat information.
Guide to the Patch Reef.

Information pages:
Boating.
Camping.
Coral Reefs.
Endangered Species.
Geology.
Threats to the Natural and Cultural Resources.

HEADQUARTERS: P.O. Box 1369, Homestead, FL 33090; (305) 247-7275.

BLOWING ROCKS PRESERVE
The Nature Conservancy
73 acres.   Map 109, A-3.

From US 1 at SR 706, 1 mile north; right on Beach Road, SR 707, for 2½ miles.

Open 6 A.M. to 5 P.M.

On Jupiter Island, the site extends from the Intracoastal Waterway to the ocean, with over a mile of Atlantic beach. The Nature Conservancy acquired it in 1969, largely as a gift from local residents who wanted to preserve its unusual geology, fauna, and flora.

The parking lot has an 18-car capacity, limiting crowding. (Roadside parking is prohibited.) An attractive walkway leads over the dunes. In the strip between road and beach, the Conservancy has removed intrusive exotic plants, chiefly Australian pine and Brazilian pepper. More than 50,000 plants of native species replaced them, their early growth assisted by irrigation. Similar restoration is under way between the road and the Intracoastal Waterway.

The site has Florida's largest outcropping of Anastasia limestone, a rugged, gray stone wall against which waves dash. Erosion has worn caves, tide pools, and blowholes. At high tide, when seas are rough, waves crash through the blowholes, sending plumes of water high in the air. The north end of the beach is sandy, suitable for swimming. This is a critical nesting area for loggerhead, green, and leatherback turtles. In the summer of 1990, 743 nests were observed.

Plants: More than 235 species have been identified. The fragile dune vegetation includes sea oats, panic grass, cordgrass, railroad vine, beach bean, saw palmetto, sea grape, beach star, beach creeper, and bay cedar, several of them rare species. About three-fifths of the land area is coastal strand, principal species being sea grape, saw palmetto, and myrsine, with a ground cover of beach sunflower. Black, white, and red mangroves fringe the Waterway, with buttonwood and cordgrass. About 7 acres are tropical hammock with gumbo limbo, mastic, pigeon plum, redbay, cabbage palm, willow bustic, and sea grape, with an understory of wild coffee, wild olive, marlberry, Jamaica caper, and necklace pod.

Wildlife: Bird and mammal checklists have not yet been completed. Birds observed include many shore, wading, and upland species. Of special interest: pileated woodpecker, osprey, brown pelican, loon. Raccoons are common; manatees are often seen in the Waterway. Reptiles recorded include black racer, corn snake, kingsnake, coral snake. Divers may see jacks, butterfly fish, parrotfish, tang, surgeons, nurse shark, barracuda, angelfish, wrasse, squirrelfish, squid.

INTERPRETATION
Naturalists are on site all year.
Visitor center has exhibits, talks, literature. Open 9 A.M. to 5 P.M.
Guided hikes are offered October–May, Sundays at 11 A.M., Wednesdays at 2 P.M. Special field trips can be arranged. By reservation: night walks to turtle nesting sites, June–July.

No food, coolers, beverages, or pets.

PUBLICATIONS
Leaflet with map.
Newsletter.

HEADQUARTERS: P.O. Box 3795, Tequesta, FL 33469. Office: (407) 575-2297. Preserve: (407) 747-3113.

CARL JOHNSON REGIONAL PARK
Lee County Department of Community Services
278 acres.   Map 111, A-1.

On SR 865 between Ft. Myers Beach and Bonita Beach.

SR 865 crosses a chain of islands enclosing the Estero Bay Aquatic Preserve. Estero Island, north of the Park, is heavily developed. The Regional Park is within a mangrove estuarine bay system. Visitors ride a tram through dense mangroves and over a tidal basin to Lovers Key State Recreation Area

(Inner Key and Black Island) a complex of estuary, mangrove, and hammock, where birding is good.

Good shelling, fishing, birding. There's a launching ramp.

HEADQUARTERS: 24340 Estero Boulevard, Fort Myers, FL 33931; (813) 585-2438.

CAYO COSTA STATE PARK
Division of Recreation and Parks
2,132 acres.   Map 104, C-1.

12 miles west of Cape Coral. Access by private or cruise boat only.

Open 8 A.M. to sunset.

The Park is part of a chain of barrier islands shielding Charlotte Harbor and Pine Island Sound. It includes Lacosta Island, North Captiva Island, and a number of smaller islands. Except for visitor facilities on Lacosta Island, the Park islands are undeveloped. Nearby are the islands of the Pine Island National Wildlife Refuge.

Acquisition of Cayo Costa began in 1976. Thanks to past land speculators, it was a prodigious task. There were over 700 separate ownerships. Fortunately, few owners had attempted to build or otherwise alter their holdings.

On a limestone base, the island soils are a mix of sand, shell, marl, and peat. A beach and dune system is on the Gulf side, the foredunes five to eight feet high. Tidal currents and storms have greatly changed the shapes of the islands over many years. The islands have over 10 miles of shoreline on the Gulf.

The islands are almost entirely forested, pine forests and oak/palm hammocks in the interior, mangrove swamps on the bay side. Lacosta Island has small freshwater marshes but no perennial freshwater ponds.

One dock is on the Bay side, another on the Gulf. Two commercial ferry services operate: Kingfisher Cruise Lines from Punta Gorda, (813) 639-0969; Tropic Star Cruises from Pineland (813) 283-0015. Docks on the Gulf side are for day use only. Overnight dockage is on the Bay side.

Most visitors come by private boat and most come to swim and picnic. One in five stays overnight. Summer is the peak season.

Birds: A checklist is available. Almost all Gulf barrier islands have excellent birding.

ACTIVITIES
Camping: Primitive campground one mile from the dock. The Park has 12 rental cabins.
Fishing is said to be excellent.
Swimming: Gulf beaches.

PUBLICATIONS
Leaflet with map.
Shelling at Cayo Costa.
Bird checklist.
Ferry information.

HEADQUARTERS: P.O. Box 1150, Boca Grande, FL 33921; (813) 964-0375.

CHARLES DEERING ESTATE

Metropolitan Dade County Park and Recreation Department
358 acres.   Map 119, D-1.

From US 1, east on 152nd St. (Coral Reef Drive). Turn right on 72nd Avenue.

Open Saturdays and Sundays only, 9 A.M. to 5 P.M.

A natural area in Miami? With bobcats? We took a second look. The park is on the southern outskirts of Miami, with a mile of frontage on Biscayne Bay, just outside Biscayne National Park. It includes Chicken Key, a rookery.

Two historic bayfront homes are within the park, but most of the site is coastal mangrove, hardwood hammock, and pineland forest, habitats that have had little past disturbance. An extensive list of plants is available. Flowering plants include morning glory, seaside mahoe, railroad vine, rose mallow, dwarf lantana, blazing star, pineland allamanda, firebush.

Wildlife: The checklist of birds records 161 species. Mammals the visitor might see include river otter, raccoon, opossum, spotted skunk, cotton mouse, cotton rat, manatee, dolphin. Bobcat and fox are present but seldom seen. Other species often seen include gopher tortoise, common snapper, anole, Everglades racer, red and yellow rat snakes, kingsnake, green treefrog, five-lined skink.

The emphasis is on history and nature interpretation. Historical and archeological exhibits, films, and lectures are offered in a new classroom; programs at 10, 12, 2, and 4 o'clock. One nature trail visits the mangrove habitat, another the uplands. Interpretive activities include tram tours, guided walks, and guided canoe trips.

Pets are prohibited.

PUBLICATIONS
   Park leaflet.
   Bird checklist.
   List of plants.
   Trail maps.

HEADQUARTERS: 16701 SW 72nd Ave., Miami, FL 33157; (305) 235-1668.

CHEKIKA STATE RECREATION AREA
Division of Recreation and Parks
640 acres.   Map 118, D-2.

15 miles north of Homestead; 6 miles west of Krome Avenue (SR 997)
on SW 168th St.

We suggest stopping here if you are nearby, but not on a warm weekend.
The site has become a popular picnic and swimming place for nearby residents. The interpretive program is disappointing.

This mile-square SRA at the western edge of metropolitan development
is a small sample of the East Everglades. Most of the area is sawgrass wetlands, a wet prairie 3 to 5 feet above sea level dotted with tree islands. Rising in the center is a typical Everglades hammock, a rocky outcropping 10
to 12 feet above sea level, colonized by tropical hardwoods: gumbo limbo,
Jamaican dogwood, poisonwood, strangler fig. The hammock extends westward, bisecting the SRA.

The campground is at the edge of the hammock. At the campground exit
the entrance road turns south to the parking area. Here are two artificial
ponds, the larger used for swimming. Nearby is a small interpretive center
and a nature trail which includes a boardwalk into the sawgrass.

Plants: A list of trees, shrubs, and flowering plants typifies the flora of
the Everglades.

Birds: A checklist of 69 species is available. It includes both yellow-
crowned and black-crowned night-herons, wood stork, roseate spoonbill,
swallow-tailed and Everglades kites; king, clapper, and Virginia rails.

Mammals: Recently, says a Park document, this has become part of the
range of the endangered Florida panther. More common are raccoon, bobcat, eastern gray squirrel, armadillo, opossum, red fox, marsh rabbit, and
river otter.

Reptiles and amphibians: The checklist includes 7 turtle species, 5 lizards, and 18 snakes, including eastern diamondback and dusky pygmy rattlesnakes and water moccasin. Also alligator and several frogs.

ACTIVITIES
Camping: 20 sites. No reservations.

PUBLICATIONS
Leaflet with map.
Wildlife checklists.

HEADQUARTERS: P.O. Box 1313, Homestead, FL 33030. (305) 252-4438.

COLLIER-SEMINOLE STATE PARK
Division of Recreation and Parks
6,423 acres.   Maps 110, C-2; 111, D-3.

Off US 41, 17 miles southeast of Naples.

Open 8 A.M. to sunset.

West of the Everglades, south of the Big Cypress, the Park is a meeting place of tropical forest and swamp. Its southern portion is a mangrove swamp cut by tidal waterways leading to the Gulf of Mexico, a 4,760-acre wilderness preserve accessible only by boat.

Just past the entrance station is the unique Bay City Walking Dredge used in the 1920s to construct the Tamiami Trail, a road many said couldn't be built. Beyond are two campgrounds. The Park road then turns south to the picnic area, boat ramp, boat basin, and nature trail.

Across US 41 is a roadless area, its entrance east of the Park gate. Here a 6.5-mile trail loops through slash pine and scrubby pine flatwoods, with cypress heads. The western part of the trail is usually wet, the eastern higher and drier.

Wilderness Preserve. Almost three-fourths of the Park is swamp with a thick growth of white, black, and red mangroves and buttonwood. Tidal waterways with many side creeks meander through the swamp, sometimes widening into bays. Only 30 canoes, three people each, are allowed to enter in a day. In half a day of paddling, we met only two other canoes.

Grocery Place, a primitive campground in the wilderness, is limited to five canoes per night, by permit. It and Old Grove, presumed to have been homesteads, are strips of high ground, islands in the marsh. Otherwise there are almost no places to go ashore and no visitor facilities.

A concessioner offers narrated boat tours of the wilderness.

Birds: An annotated checklist of 122 species is available. The great majority are permanent or winter residents.

Mammals: Bottlenose dolphin and manatee are sometimes seen in the waterways. Florida panther has been reported in the hammocks. Black bear is present but seldom seen. Often seen are opossum, armadillo, marsh rabbit, gray squirrel, cotton mouse, cotton rat, raccoon, bobcat, river otter, and whitetail deer.

ACTIVITIES

Camping: 130 sites. No reservations. The busy season is from Thanksgiving to Easter.

Hiking, backpacking: Collier-Seminole Trail, 6.5 miles, is also a segment of the Florida Trail. Campers must register to use the backcountry campsite.

Fishing: Saltwater species.

Canoeing: Rentals are available.

Boating: Ramp and boat basin. Access to the Gulf and Ten Thousand Islands.

Winter visits are preferable; biting insects can be fierce in summer. Canoeists should be aware of strong tidal currents. Also, it's easy to become lost among the mangrove islands.

INTERPRETATION

Royal Palm Hammock Trail, 0.9 miles, passes through tropical hammock, white mangrove forest, and salt marsh.

Museum in the style of a Seminole War blockhouse has natural history and cultural exhibits.

Guided pontoon boat tour, concession-operated. Call (813) 642-8898.

Guided walks and *campfire programs* are offered occasionally. Ask for schedules.

PUBLICATIONS

Leaflet with map.
Park information page.
Wilderness leaflet with map.
Hiking trail information and map.
Wildlife checklists.
Boat tour information.

HEADQUARTERS: Rt. 4, Box 848, Naples, FL 33961; (813) 394-3397.

CORKSCREW SWAMP SANCTUARY
National Audubon Society
10,560 acres.   Map 111, B-3.

From US 41 9 miles north of Naples, east 21 miles on SR 846. Left at sign. Or exit 17 from I-75 (Naples Park), east 17 miles.

Open 9 A.M. to 5 P.M.

The Sanctuary protects the nation's largest remaining stand of old-growth bald cypress. Many of the trees are over 500 years old, some of the oldest trees in eastern North America. The largest are 130 feet tall.

The habitats are typical of the Big Cypress swamp. Trees include bald cypress, slash pine, cabbage palm, maple, bay, and holly. The swamp has many ferns, bromeliads, orchids, hibiscus, and swamp lily. A treeless central marsh has arrowhead, pickerel weed, sawgrass, and willow.

The first stop for arrivals is the visitor center. Beyond it is a two-mile boardwalk loop trail through the heart of the Sanctuary. What you see here depends on the season, the time of day, and rainfall. Water level in the swamp normally fluctuates by about 4½ feet, low in winter, the dry season, higher after summer rains.

One of our visits to Corkscrew was at a time of record nesting and hatching for the rare wood stork. Hundreds of adults and young were in the trees, the young clattering noisily. Stork numbers dropped in the following years. We assumed that, like the Everglades, the Sanctuary had experienced disruption of its natural water supply by drainage and development. We had also thought drought would inhibit wood stork nesting and hatchings. Both assumptions were wrong.

"The Sanctuary's hydrology is *perfect,*" the manager-biologist responded. "The cypress forest is as healthy as ever. The wood storks do fly as far as 30 miles (each way) on a daily basis to feed. It is water diversion *outside* our watershed that has reduced their feeding areas."

As for those occasional dry years: "Some of the greatest food supply and most intensive and spectacular feeding congregations of birds and other animals occur during drought years. . . . Food is concentrated in drying waterholes and available in abundance."

The wood storks may nest as early as November or as late as March. They feed on fish, and it seems high water is necessary to maximize fish reproduction, while receding water makes them more available for feeding. However, explanations of stork behavior are often prefaced by "apparently." If you want to see and hear the young, telephone to learn what's happening.

Many plants and aquatic animals depend on high-water periods for nutrition and reproduction. Most birds and mammals reproduce in winter. There's always much to see from the boardwalk: an alligator just below your feet, an anole on the railing, a green treefrog on a leaf, webs of orb spiders in the lower branches, birds almost anywhere. We've never spotted a bobcat but once did see a large diamondback rattlesnake. A platform at the far end of the boardwalk overlooks a large treeless marsh where wading birds can usually be seen.

The boardwalk trail is self-guiding, but there is usually a staff member on patrol to point out and identify things of interest and to answer questions. The slower you walk, the more you'll see.

Birds top the list of visitors' interests. Nearly two hundred species have been recorded, more than 60 nesting here.

Efforts to preserve this remnant wilderness began in 1954. Donations of land and money brought the Sanctuary to its present size in 1968. About 70 percent of the visitors come between Christmas and Easter, about equally divided between Florida residents and others, many of the latter from overseas.

PUBLICATIONS
Leaflet with access map.
Bird checklist.
Boardwalk tour guide, loaned with payment of admission.
Wood Storks.

HEADQUARTERS: Rt. 6, Box 1875 A, Sanctuary Road, Naples, FL 33964; (813) 657-3771.

DUPUIS RESERVE
South Florida Water Management District
21,875 acres.   Map 108, A-2.

From SR 710 at Indiantown (map 102, D-3), 6 miles west on SR 76. Gate and trailhead are on the south side.

Open dawn to dusk except on scheduled hunt days.

The Reserve, 2 miles from the east shore of Lake Okeechobee, includes pasture, pine flatwoods, cypress forest, wet prairies, and numerous ponds, also a remnant of Everglades marsh. Canals are on its north and south, the J. W. Corbett Wildlife Management Area (see entry) on the east.

Since acquiring the former ranch, the District has been restoring it, removing trash and unwanted structures, reflooding wetlands, eliminating exotic plant species, and using prescribed burning to promote growth of native plant communities.

The Division of Forestry is assisting in restoring native flora. Wildlife management is a responsibility of the Florida Game and Fresh Water Fish

Commission. The Florida Trail Association has developed hiking trails, the DuPuis Horsemen's Association equestrian trails.

ACTIVITIES

Camping: Only horse riders with permits may camp with tents or self-contained vehicles at the equestrian trailhead.

Hiking, backpacking: Four trail loops. Distances from trailhead are 4.3, 6.8, 11.5, and 15.5 miles. The DuPuis grade can also be hiked. A primitive campsite is near the beginning of loop 4. Camping permits must be requested in writing from the Save Our Rivers Division of the District at its headquarters.

Orange blazes mark the trail, not the usual white blazes of the Florida Trail.

Hunting: Special rules and schedules. Inquire.

Horse riding: Three loops extending 7.2, 12.2, and 16.5 miles from trailhead parking at gate 3. Riders must obtain and carry permits from the District's Department of Land Management.

PUBLICATIONS

Hiking trails information and map.
Equestrian trails information and map.

HEADQUARTERS: P.O. Box 24680, 3301 Gun Club Road, West Palm Beach, FL 33416; (407) 686-8800. Information on hunting schedules can also be obtained from the Florida Game and Fresh Water Fish Commission regional office: (407) 683-0748.

THE EVERGLADES

See entries: Everglades Water Conservation Areas; Everglades National Park, Arthur R. Marshall Loxahatchee National Wildlife Refuge.

Once upon a time, the Everglades watershed began near Orlando. The Kissimmee and other streams drained to Lake Okeechobee. In periods of heavy rainfall, water flooded over the lake's southern rim into the Everglades basin. This broad basin, extending to Florida Bay, also received about 60 inches of rainfall a year, most of it in summer and fall. On the basin's gentle slope, water moved too slowly to cut channels. Here was the unique "river of grass," flowing to what became Everglades National Park. Vast expanses of sawgrass, some 10 feet tall, were dotted with tree islands. This was the domain of the alligator, Florida panther, and innumerable herons, egrets, waterfowl, and other birds. Centuries of vegetation decay had built a thick bed of peat.

Disruption of the great natural system began in the early 1900s. Lake Okeechobee was diked and its water diverted. 700,000 acres of adjacent land were drained and diked for farming. Levees were built to protect the fast-developing east from floods. South of Okeechobee, huge engineering works – canals, ditches, levees, and pumping stations – checked the natural water flow.

Conservationists protested that loss of water was a disaster for wildlife, both prey species and the predators dependent on them. Salt water was permeating deeper into the National Park. For years the protests failed to move the decision makers. Agriculture and development dominated Florida's political system. Then came a dry year in which no water was released to the Park. The ecological catastrophe got national attention. Congress ordered that the Park be guaranteed water. Water managers complied, but mandatory water releases didn't simulate the natural wet–dry cycle. Release of water during natural dry periods was damaging, disrupting nesting and feeding patterns, drowning alligator and apple-snail eggs. The very existence of some wildlife species was threatened.

Water management measures were only part of the disruption. Natural water flow was blocked or restricted by the Tamiami Trail and other roads, pipelines, and landfills. Pesticides and nutrients draining from farmland are another problem. Exotic plants such as melaleuca, Australian pine, Brazilian pepper, and hydrilla invaded the area. Only vigorous opposition blocked construction of a large jetport.

In 1989 the Everglades Expansion Act authorized expansion of the National Park's boundaries to the east, adding 107,600 acres. The State of Florida will pay part of the cost and also donate 36,000 acres. Florida had bought 17,000 acres and federal funds hadn't been appropriated when we went to press.

So the controversy continues. Politicians and administrators are caught between the conflicting demands of farmers, municipalities, developers, hunters, fishermen, environmentalists, and the National Park.

Other factors complicate the debate. Drained and exposed to the air for cultivation, peat beds have oxidized and dwindled. Alarming concentrations of mercury found in wildlife have been attributed to various sources. Governors have made promises. The federal government has sued the State. To solve the problem of pollutants draining from farmland, it has been proposed that government buy the land and naturalize it.

The Everglades can never again be what they were. If all the promises are fulfilled, the system can be stabilized, normal wet and dry periods restored to whatever part of the area remains, and threats to wildlife alleviated.

EVERGLADES WATER CONSERVATION AREAS
South Florida Water Management District
860,000 acres.   Maps 108, 109, 114, 115, 117, 118.

From SR 80 south to US 41; west of US 441.

Three Water Conservation Areas and the Everglades National Park are most of what remains of the Everglades, about half of the original acreage. The three adjoining Water Conservation Areas are surrounded by canals and dikes equipped with pumps, gates, and other water control devices. Area 1, on the north, has become the Arthur R. Marshall Loxahatchee National Wildlife Refuge (see entry). Areas 2 and 3 have been combined as the Everglades Wildlife Management Area, its wildlife managed by the Florida Game and Fresh Water Fish Commission. Management of water remains the responsibility of the South Florida Water Management District.

Although the National Park has attracted the greatest attention and concern, the three Water Conservation Areas were and are a vital part of the Everglades ecosystem. Their sawgrass marshes, tree islands, and sloughs are still there. So is the extraordinary Everglades wildlife, although greatly reduced in numbers.

Providing for public recreation here is one of the mandates to the managing agencies. The opportunities are limited. No roads or trails penetrate Areas 2 and 3 except SR 84, which crosses Area 3, and US 27, which runs between the two. Trails could be built on some of the dikes. One was proposed along Levee 28, at the eastern edge of the Big Cypress National Preserve (see entry), but the Florida Trail in the Preserve is a parallel route. Airboats and swamp buggies are the only practical means of travel within the swamp, plus marginal use of outboard craft during high water. Canoes and motorboats operate in the peripheral canals and several that cross the Areas.

The South Florida Water Management District is endeavoring to ban tracked and wheeled vehicles, shut down illegal hunting camps, and control illegal dumping.

Along the public roads are two dozen launching ramps, several marinas, and a few public and private campgrounds.

We suggest that first-time visitors go to Area 1, the Arthur R. Marshall Loxahatchee National Wildlife Refuge (see entry). The visitor center and dike trails are a fine introduction to the eastern Everglades. The next step is to bring or rent a canoe or outboard craft and begin exploring the canals and sloughs.

PUBLICATIONS
Map and list of recreation facilities.
Wildlife Management Area leaflet.

HEADQUARTERS: South Florida Water Management District, P.O. Box 24680, 3301 Gun Club Road, West Palm Beach, FL 33416; (407) 686-8800.

EVERGLADES NATIONAL PARK
National Park Service
1,398,653 acres, including
625,000 acres of water.

Maps 116, 117, 121,
122, 123, 125.

The southern tip of mainland Florida. The principal entrance is SR 9336 from Homestead. Shark Valley entrance is on US 41; west entrance at Everglades City.

November–April is the best season for a visit. Mosquitos are a serious problem in summer.

It's the largest National Park in the East, the nation's only large subtropical wilderness, the only such everglades in the world. From the beginning, its life has been uneasy. Now it's dying of dehydration and other ailments.

Before it became a Park, the area's wildlife was decimated by market hunters. Development encroached on the perimeter. Conservationists urged establishment of a National Park, and in 1929 Congress asked the Secretary of the Interior to investigate. Five years later Congress authorized the Secretary to acquire over two million acres of land but for the next 12 years provided no money for the purpose. Florida's legislature appropriated the first land purchase money in 1946. Congressional funds began coming only in 1958.

At first the Park had only a small constituency. In 1948 only 7,500 visitors came. The only Park road was rough gravel and dirt—or mud. Opening a good road to Flamingo marked the beginning of the Park's popularity. Wayside developments such as the Anhinga Trail and Pa-hay-okee Overlook gave the growing number of visitors appreciation of the Park's unique qualities.

Soon the Park became world famous. Today almost a third of the visitors come from other nations. Most visitors come for the day. The only overnight accommodations inside the Park are the Flamingo Lodge and Outdoor Resort and two campgrounds. A modest but increasing number of visitors are finding their way into the watery Everglades Wilderness.

The Wilderness Area, 1,296,500 roadless acres, is 93 percent of the Park. Only a few short foot trails penetrate it. However, almost half of the Park's land area is a lacework of rivers, bays, and tidal creeks, many miles navigable by motor craft, many more by canoes. On the south, the boundaries include Florida Bay, with over a hundred islands; on the west the Ten Thousand Islands.

The Park has two principal ecosystems. Sweeping in from the north is the vast expanse of the "river of grass," tall sawgrass dotted with tree-covered hammocks. When water flowed freely in wet seasons, a river 40 miles wide and a few inches deep moved almost imperceptibly through the grass. The land was naturally drier in winter except for sloughs and waterholes. Plants and animals were adapted to this seasonal pattern. The mortal threat to them and the Park is disruption of the natural cycle.

Where fresh water meets saline tidewater, the mangroves begin. Dense mangrove forests line every waterway, and mangroves grow densely on many islands that seem to have no soil, only a tangle of roots. As the seasonal flow of fresh water has diminished, salty water has moved farther inland, causing ecological change.

A chief symptom of the Park's plight is the frightful collapse of its populations of wading birds. Since the 1930s the number of herons and egrets has declined from 265,000 to 18,500. Nesting wood storks declined from 6,000 to 500.

Also striking is the outspoken way in which the Park Superintendent and his staff declare the Park's ailments will prove terminal unless decisive action comes soon. The looming disaster is explained in Park publications and by rangers who meet the public. One leaflet concludes,

> The support of citizens, legislators, and public officials is needed to assure that public policy is enacted to save this great park. The quality of life and the survival of a national heritage are at stake. Just as we share the enjoyment of this natural resource, we share the responsibility for finding solutions to these problems.

Share the enjoyment! However changed, it's still a great park, a great place to go. Back in the 1960s a friend advised us to hurry to East Africa if we hoped to see its wildlife. We've been there several times since, most recently in 1988. True, the losses of species and habitat are tragic. Most of the black rhinos have been slaughtered. But we saw five in the Mara, another five in the Ngorongoro Crater, and thousands of wildebeeste, zebra, topi, gazelle, and other species. Those who see are the most determined that it shall not be lost.

We notice grim changes in the Everglades, but the visitor still sees many birds and other wildlife. Indeed, from December through February there are concentrations around waterholes.

Birds: The annotated checklist of 347 species is by far the longest we've had from any Florida site. It includes every category. Some of those listed are released or escaped exotics. Some are birds that have wandered or been storm-blown far from their usual haunts. 85 species are known to nest here. Winter is the best season for birding, but there's plenty to see even in summer.

Where's the best birding? Thinking back over our visits, the answer seems to be "everywhere." The most conspicuous eagle nests are around Whitewater Bay. The eagles aren't shy; we've photographed eagles raising chicks in a nest overhanging a busy boat channel.

Mammals: A checklist of 40 species is available. Only 14 of these are species that visitors might see were they at the right place at the right time. In our visits, we have seen deer, raccoon, otter, and marsh rabbit. Once a manatee in Buttonwood Canal.

Reptiles and amphibians: We asked for a current checklist and didn't receive it. The list in our file is dated 1968. It includes a large assortment of frogs and toads, turtles, lizards, snakes, and, of course, the alligator.

FEATURES

Entering the Park from Homestead, allow at least half a day for stops on the 38 miles from the entrance to Flamingo. High spots are as follows:
Royal Palm Visitor Center, Anhinga Trail, and Gumbo Limbo Trail. Excellent wildlife viewing. Anhinga Trail is a birding hot-spot and always has alligators.
Pinelands Trail.
Pa-hay-okee. Boardwalk and observation platform.
Mahogany Hammock. Boardwalk.
Paurotis Pond. Rare palms.
Nine Mile Pond.
West Lake. Boardwalk into a mangrove swamp.
Flamingo is the principal center, with ranger station, lodgings, restaurant, store, marina, boat livery, and nearby campground. From here boats travel up the Buttonwood Canal to Whitewater Bay and beyond, or out into Florida Bay.
Buttonwood Canal and Whitewater Bay are the principal access to the interior waterways. The 99-mile Wilderness Waterway from here to Everglades City traverses several rivers and bays. In and around Whitewater Bay are countless islands, creeks, and channels where it's easy to become lost.
Shark Valley Information Center is on US 41, at the northern boundary of the Park. A 15-mile loop road penetrates the grassy Shark River Slough, past tree islands and hardwood hammocks. It's a prime area for wildlife viewing. Tram tours are available. The road is open to hikers and bikers. An observation tower is at the end.
Gulf Coast Ranger Station is near Everglades City, at the northwest corner of the Park. This is the end of the Wilderness Waterway and the gateway to the Ten Thousand Islands.
Florida Bay and its islands are about a third of the Park area. The southeast boundary is the Intracoastal Waterway, close to the Florida Keys. A ranger station is on Key Largo. The Bay is shallow, most of it less than 6 feet deep.
Everglades City, at the northwest corner of the Park, has a visitor center. Food, lodging, marina, and other facilities here are commercially operated.
Ten Thousand Islands, off Everglades City, are popular with fishermen, canoeists, boaters, and campers.

ACTIVITIES

Camping: Two campgrounds; 403 sites, 60 of them walk-in. First come first served. The main visitor center has information on whether and where sites are available. Campgrounds are usually full in winter, especially Christmas through February. Commercial campgrounds are at Homestead and Everglades City.

Backcountry camping: Boat-access sites are around Whitewater Bay, along the Wilderness Waterway, in Florida Bay, on the coast, and in the Ten Thousand Islands. Many of these are "chickees"—wooden platforms. All require permits. None have water. Mosquito repellent, fine-mesh no-see-um netting, sun block, hat, raingear, and flashlights are essential.

Hiking, biking, backpacking: Hiking-biking trails in the Flamingo area are from 4 to 13 miles. All are for day use. Hiking-biking trails in the Pinelands area are up to 11 miles one way; backcountry camping requires a permit from the main visitor center. The 15-mile hiking-biking loop at Shark Valley is for day use only.

Fishing: Fresh and salt water. Some waters are closed, and special rules apply within Park boundaries. Inquire.

Boating: Marinas and launching at Flamingo and Everglades City. Ramps are also at Little Blackwater South, Paurotis Pond, and West Lake. Skiffs, houseboats, and pontoon boats can be rented at Flamingo. Boaters should obtain a copy of *Fishing and Boating Regulations,* as some areas are closed. Also marine charts, compass, and emergency gear.

Exploring backcountry mangrove rivers and creeks in an outboard runabout, we have wondered what we'd do if the motor quit. One couldn't travel on foot through the mangroves. Paddling would be difficult at best, futile in a headwind. How soon might another adventurer come this way?

The 99-nautical-mile Wilderness Waterway can be navigated by motor craft; only boats of 18 feet or less, without cabins or high windshields, should try it. Look out for manatees and mud flats.

Canoeing, canoe camping: More of the National Park and its wildlife can be seen by canoe than any other way. Canoe trails are at Noble Hammock (3 miles), Hells Bay (4 miles), Nine Mile Pond (5 miles), West Lake (8 miles), and Bear Lake (12 miles), all beginning near Flamingo. There's unlimited canoeing around Whitewater Bay, Florida Bay, and the Ten Thousand Islands. Campsites are available, by permit.

Canoeing the Wilderness Waterway, usually a seven-day trip, is for the experienced and well equipped. Some who make the journey say, "Never again!" Others are delighted. There's no public transportation, so one must arrange a shuttle. Especially on weekend mornings, be alert for motor craft in the Buttonwood Canal.

Canoes can be rented at Flamingo and Everglades City.

Pets must be under physical control. They are not allowed on trails, in the backcountry, or in amphitheaters.

Airboats, swamp buggies, and off-road vehicles are prohibited.
Don't smoke on trails.

INTERPRETATION
   Visitor centers and information are at the main entrance, Royal Palm, Flamingo, Shark Valley, and Everglades City.
   Ranger-guided activities are scheduled daily in winter. They include hikes, talks, boat and tram tours, campfire programs, demonstrations, and more. Schedules are available at information centers.
   Guided boat tours from Flamingo to Whitewater Bay are offered daily. Tours of the Ten Thousand Islands and mangrove swamps from Everglades City.
   Exhibits are at many places through the park.

PUBLICATIONS
   Everglades National Park folder with map.
   Visitors Guide. Published seasonally.
   Birds of Everglades National Park.
   Mammals of Everglades National Park.
   Fishing and Boating Regulations.
   Information pages:
       Flamingo Canoe and Hiking Trails.
       Hiking & Biking Trails of the Pinelands.
       Your Park in Danger.
       Returning the Flow; East Everglades Restoration.
       Mercury Found in Everglades Bass.
       Endangered Species in Everglades National Park.
   Sales Catalog of Publications & Related Products.
   Concession information:
       Scenic boat tours.
       Shark Valley tram tours.
       Flamingo Lodge; Marina and Outpost Resort.
       Everglades guided canoe trips.

HEADQUARTERS: Box 279, Homestead, FL 33030; (305) 247-6211.

FAKAHATCHEE STRAND STATE PRESERVE
Division of Recreation and Parks
46,703 acres; more being acquired.   Map 116, A-1.

   Jane's Scenic Drive, west from SR 29, 2½ miles north of US 41. Boardwalk on US 41, behind Indian village, 7 miles west of SR 29.

The Fakahatchee Strand adjoins the Big Cypress National Preserve (see entry). A "strand" is an elongated depression through which water drains slowly in the rainy season. The Fakahatchee, 3–5 miles wide and 20 miles long, is at the southern end of a broad drainage basin. Like the Everglades, it is dependent on flow from the northern basin.

State acquisition of the Strand began in 1974. The goal is about 74,000 acres. Before State acquisition, the area had been affected by logging, drainage, and fires. Hunters roamed the area in swamp buggies. Some had built shacks. Poaching, including orchid poaching, was a serious problem. The Fakahatchee Strand has the nation's greatest concentration and variety of orchids, at least 44 species, several of which grow nowhere else.

The State's objective is to restore the natural qualities of the Strand, and provide a wilderness experience for hiking and primitive camping.

The loggers cut many of the giant cypress trees that formed a closed canopy over the swamp. Commercial logging ended in the 1950s, and cypress is making a comeback. A stand of old-growth cypress can be seen from the boardwalk.

We first entered the Strand with a ranger in 1979. We waded most of the day in water sometimes ankle deep, occasionally hip deep. Now and then we came to a dry hammock where we could rest or eat lunch. Although he knew the Strand well, the ranger often consulted his compass. It's wild country with dense vegetation, no trails, and few landmarks.

One reason for strict resource protection is that this region has the last known resident population of the Florida panther. Although panthers occasionally wander far, it is only here that they still breed and raise cubs. A team of federal and State wildlife specialists has been studying how best to assure the survival of the species.

Orchids and panthers are evidence that the Strand has exceptional qualities. There are many more. The world's largest concentration of the handsome royal palm is here, and a unique royal palm/bald cypress association. Many species of bromeliads, ferns, and vines grow in profusion, including species known only here. Wildlife includes black bear, wood stork, and bald eagle. Insects, too! The biting varieties are most troublesome in spring and early summer.

The Strand swamp itself is the largest of the several natural communities. Others include sloughs, swamp lakes, marl prairies, hammocks, and cypress domes. Tidal swamps and estuarine marshes are in the south.

HOW TO SEE THE STRAND

Jane's Scenic Drive is built on an old logging grade. We were told poachers once posted lookouts at the entrance.

The boardwalk, 2,000 feet long, on US 41, is at present the only daily access to the Strand for visitors.

Guided wades, not walks, are offered once a month between November and April. One must make a reservation at least two weeks in advance. Wades last several hours. Boots and protective clothing are required.

Fakahatchee Hiking Trail, 10 miles, is on an old logging grade. Primitive camping is permitted. Call for information.

Canoe trail is an unmarked wilderness route on the East River. Call for information.

PUBLICATIONS
  Leaflet, no map.
  Boardwalk trail guide.

HEADQUARTERS: P.O. Box 548, Copeland, FL 33926; (813) 695-4593.

FLORIDA KEYS NATIONAL WILDLIFE REFUGES
U.S. Fish and Wildlife Service
23,851 acres.   Maps 123, 124, 126, 127.

Scattered islands in and near the Florida Keys. A few are on Keys crossed by US 1, the Overseas Highway. Others are accessible only by private boat.

The complex includes four National Wildlife Refuges:
  • *Key Deer NWR*, 7,902 acres; Map 124, C-2.
  • *Great White Heron NWR*, 7,408 acres; Map 127, C 2-3.
  • *Key West NWR*, 2,019 acres; Map 126, D 2-3.
  • *Crocodile Lake NWR*, 6,522 acres; Map 123, B-1.

Most of the islands are small and typical of the Keys: based on old coral reefs, fringed with red and black mangroves, tropical and subtropical trees, and other plants on higher ground.

KEY DEER NWR
  The Key Deer refuge was established in 1957 to protect the critically endangered Florida Key deer, a diminutive form of the mainland whitetail. (Bucks weigh 60 to 90 pounds, does 50 to 70.) Hunting, poaching, and loss of habitat to development had reduced the herd to less than 50 individuals. With protection the herd increased to between 350 and 400 individuals in the late 1970s, then declined to 250–300.
  The deer are most often seen early morning and late afternoon along Key Deer Boulevard (Big Pine Key) and on adjacent No Name Key. We saw nine of them at dawn one misty morning on Big Pine Key. They regarded us with mild curiosity. We resisted the temptation to feed and pet.

Both Big Pine and the Torch Keys have substantial residential and commercial development. Too many residents and visitors don't resist the temptation to feed the deer, thus putting them at risk. Dependence on food that people provide reduces natural foraging and causes nutritional problems. Food attracts the deer to developed areas, including roads. Since hunting and poaching have stopped, road kills are the chief cause of death. Loss of habitat is still a threat. Only a few days ago plans for a new road were shelved after protests.

Nature trail on Big Pine Key is 1.5 miles north of the Key Deer Boulevard and Watson Boulevard intersection.

Blue Hole, 1.25 miles north of the same intersection, is an old rock quarry. Alligators are often seen.

Feeding the deer violates federal law.

GREAT WHITE HERON NWR AND KEY WEST NWR

Extending from East Bahia Honda Key to the Marquesas, the islands and surrounding waters of the Key Deer, Great White Heron, and Key West refuges were brought into the federal system to protect migratory and nesting bird species, among them the roseate spoonbill, mangrove cuckoo, white-crowned pigeon, magnificent frigatebird, smooth-billed ani, brown pelican, and "great white heron," now considered a color phase of the great blue heron. Several of the species are rare.

CROCODILE LAKE NWR

The Crocodile Lake NWR, on North Key Largo, was established to protect the endangered American crocodile.

Fishing, snorkeling, and diving in Refuge waters are not forbidden, but there are numerous federal and State regulations. Before visiting any of the offshore islands, we suggest stopping at Refuge headquarters on Big Pine Key for information.

PUBLICATIONS

Refuge leaflet with map.
Maps of the four units.
Bird checklist.
Checklist of mammals, reptiles, and amphibians.
Public Use; National Key Deer Refuge.
The Facts on Public Feeding.

HEADQUARTERS: P.O. Box 510, Big Pine Key, FL 33043; (305) 872-2239.

FORT JEFFERSON NATIONAL MONUMENT
National Park Service
39 acres of land, 64,000 of water.   Map 126, A–B, 1–2.

Private boat, charter boat, or air taxi from Key West.

These are the Dry Tortugas, a cluster of tiny islands and reefs due west of Key West. "Dry" because they have no fresh water.

The only visitor facilities are on Garden Key, largest of the seven islands. Its centerpiece is Fort Jefferson. If less imposing than Mayan pyramids, it is nonetheless surprising: six-sided, a half-mile around, stone walls 8 feet thick, its construction materials barged here. Construction began in 1846. The idea was to aid U.S. control of the Gulf of Mexico and Caribbean. It was never quite finished, but it was used. Union forces garrisoned it in the Civil War, but no shots were fired except at passing privateers. It became a military prison, its most distinguished inmate being Dr. Samuel A. Mudd, who was convicted of complicity in the assassination of President Lincoln. He was pardoned after he saved many lives when yellow fever struck. The fever killed the prison doctor, among others. Decommissioned as a fort and prison, it saw later service as a coaling station, seaplane base, and radio relay station.

Some visitors come out of curiosity, some to be able to say they have set foot on the Dry Tortugas. Birders come to see the great number of sooty and noddy terns that nest here and the great variety of migrants that pass, including some species seldom seen on the mainland and unusual numbers of frigatebirds. Those who come by boat may see bridled tern, Audubon's shearwater, and roseate tern on the way.

Many visitors come to snorkel and scuba dive on the coral reefs. The warm, clear water is ideal for viewing the countless colorful fishes of the reef, as well as sea fans, anemones, and sponges.

ACTIVITIES
Camping: Grassy area. Bring everything, including water.
Fishing: Special regulations; inquire.
Swimming: Snorkeling and scuba diving for the experienced.
Boating: Seaworthy craft, charts, and navigating skill are essential. Rough water is common. Mooring at docks or piers is limited to 2 hours. No overnight mooring to docks or piers.

INTERPRETATION: Video program, self-guiding tour, and guided activities.

PUBLICATIONS
Leaflet with map.
Birds of Fort Jefferson National Monument.
Guide to Bird and Plant Life of Garden Key.
Walking the Seawall.
Charter boat and air taxi information.

HEADQUARTERS: P.O. Box 6208, Key West, FL 33041; (305) 247-6211.

HUGH TAYLOR BIRCH STATE RECREATION AREA
Division of Recreation and Parks
180 acres.   Map 115, C-3.

On East Sunrise Boulevard in Fort Lauderdale.

If you're in Fort Lauderdale, visit this remnant of the old Florida coast. When Hugh Taylor Birch first visited this area in 1893, only one other building was on this long stretch of barrier island. He gave his last 180 acres of the original 3-mile-long property to the State in 1942 to protect it from development.

The barrier island beach of which this is a segment lies between the ocean and the Intracoastal Waterway. The site includes ocean beach, dunes, tropical hardwood hammocks, live oak hammocks, freshwater lagoons, and mangrove swamps.

Plants: Annotated checklist. More than 500 plant species have been recorded. Most of the original native flora survives despite competition from exotic species such as melaleuca, Australian pine, and Brazilian pepper. Melaleuca and Brazilian pepper have been controlled.

Birds: Checklist of 173 species.

INTERPRETATION
Visitor center is the Birch home built in 1940. Exhibits, audiovisual presentations. Open weekends and holidays, 10 A.M.–5 P.M.
Nature trail begins at south end of beach parking lot.

PUBLICATIONS
Leaflet with map.
Plant checlist.
Bird checklist.
Terramar Visitor Center.

HEADQUARTERS: 3109 East Sunrise Boulevard, Fort Lauderdale, FL 33304; (305) 564-4521.

J. N. "DING" DARLING NATIONAL WILDLIFE REFUGE
U.S. Fish and Wildlife Service
5,030 acres.   Map 110, A 1-2.

On Sanibel Island (see entry). Entrance to Wildlife Drive is on the Sanibel–Captiva Road.

Wildlife Drive is closed on Fridays; visitor center and Indigo Trail are open.

When we visit Sanibel Island, every day begins at dawn on Wildlife Drive, and we're there again as the sun sets. This 5-mile drive offers some of the best birding one can find anywhere.

The Refuge occupies most of Sanibel's north side, a maze of mangrove islands and flats, shallow lagoons and sloughs. The northern half of the Refuge is a Wilderness Area accessible only by boat. Wildlife Drive, an auto route on dikes, passes a series of brackish and saltwater impoundments.

Birds: An annotated checklist of over 200 species is available. Birding is especially good at low tide, when great numbers of wading birds are feeding in the shallows. One great sight is a flock of roseate spoonbills coming in against the setting sun.

Bring binoculars, a bird guide, and insect repellent. In some refuges, an automobile is a useful blind. Here you park and walk. The birds don't mind. For photographing with a 35-mm camera, a 300-mm lens is about right for most bird scenes.

A visitor center is at the beginning of the Drive. Here you view an orientation slide program, obtain the Drive Guide, trail map, and bird checklist. On the Drive is an observation tower.

Bailey Tract is a disjunct part of the Refuge off Tarpon Bay Road. Almost 2 miles of trails encircle small impoundments that attract wading and shorebirds. Many upland species frequent the brush and trees. We have seen more alligators here than from Wildlife Drive, twice in the ditch beside Tarpon Bay Road. (The observation tower that once stood here is gone.)

SATELLITES

Four small satellite refuges are managed from here. They aren't mentioned in Refuge publications. Most are small, scattered islands. None have visitor facilities. If you're cruising and interested, inquire at Refuge headquarters.

- *Island Bay NWR,* 20 acres, on the north side of the Charlotte Harbor mouth.
- *Pine Island NWR,* 404 acres. Islands in Pine Island Sound.
- *Matlacha Pass NWR,* 244 acres. Islands in Matlacha Pass.
- *Caloosahatchee NWR,* 40 acres. Wetland on the Caloosahatchee River.

ACTIVITIES

Hiking: The 2-mile Indigo Trail begins near the visitor center. Shell Mound Trail is a short loop near the end of the Drive.

Fishing, salt and fresh water, is permitted along Wildlife Drive and in Tarpon Bay.

Canoeing: The 1½-mile Commodore Creek Canoe Trail wanders through mangrove forest and Mullet Lake. One need not stay on the marked trail but should remember where it is. Canoes can be rented or launched at a commercial marina at the north end of Tarpon Bay Road. Head due west from the marina to find the beginning of the trail.

Birding is better at low tide, but parts of the canoe trail are impassable when the tide is out. Check the tide table and watch the flow.

Canoeing in the Wilderness Area is possible by paddling through Tarpon Bay to San Carlos Bay and entering at MacIntyre Creek. Better have a nautical chart and a weather forecast.

The Refuge leaflet shows a 4-mile Buck Key Canoe Trail off Captiva Island. We haven't canoed there. Canoes can be rented at a nearby marina.

PUBLICATIONS
Refuge leaflet with map.
Wildlife Drive guide.
Commodore Creek Canoe Trail guide.
Bird checklist.

HEADQUARTERS: 1 Wildlife Drive, Sanibel, FL 33957; (813) 472-1100.

J. W. CORBETT WILDLIFE MANAGEMENT AREA
Florida Game and Fresh Water Fish Commission
57,892 acres.   Maps 108, A-3; 109, A-1.

From North Palm Beach, west on SR 809 and 809 A. Cross SR 710. In 8.1 miles, turn north on Seminole Pratt–Whitney Road, about 3 miles to entrance.

This is one of only two WMAs where every visitor or family must have a $25 wildlife management stamp. Hikers are included.

The WMA is a few miles east of Lake Okeechobee. Pine flatwoods have a heavy understory of palmetto. There is much standing water in the rainy season. The best wildflower season is late spring to early summer. Wildlife is abundant.

Backpacking: A 14-mile segment of the Florida Trail crosses the site. Trailhead is at the Youth Camp, near the WMA entrance. No public road is at the west end. Camping at designated sites. A camping permit is required.

PUBLICATION: Leaflet with map.

HEADQUARTERS: Florida Game and Fresh Water Fish Commission, Everglades Region, 551 North Military Trail, West Palm Beach, FL 33415; (407) 640-6100.

JOHN D. MACARTHUR BEACH STATE PARK
Division of Recreation and Parks
225 land acres; 535 acres submerged.   Map 109, B-3.

On SR A1A east of North Palm Beach.

Open 8 a.m. to sunset. Nature Center open 9 a.m.–5 p.m. Wednesday–Sunday.

The new nature center is one of the finest we've seen anywhere, State or federal, outstanding in architecture, displays, and a staff that includes more than 60 highly trained volunteers. The excellent motion pictures shown in the auditorium can't be called a "film"; it's the first we'd seen produced with new disk technology.

The Park is on a barrier island between the ocean and Lake Worth. It looks like two islands separated by Lake Worth Cove, but they join at the north end. Parking and the nature center are on the inner arm. The paved walk from the parking area comes first to a kiosk with exhibit panels on the flora and fauna of the area. A panel on weather has instruments recording current wind speed and direction, temperature, and barometric pressure. Written on the panel is the schedule of tides and the weather forecast: for our day, "Sunny, cool, beautiful!"

A wide boardwalk a quarter-mile long crosses the Cove to the outer beach. A tram carries handicapped visitors across. The Park has 1.8 miles of ocean frontage.

Such excellence indicates a larger budget than the State can allocate to a small park. From the outset there have been generous gifts from the John D. and Catherine T. MacArthur Foundation, plus help from Palm Beach County and the community at large.

The plan has been carefully crafted to restore, preserve, and interpret a rare natural area hemmed in by fast-increasing commercial and residential construction. Looking back from the boardwalk, one sees a backdrop of high-rise office buildings and condominiums. On either side of the walk, the cove is populated by herons, gulls, and pelicans, with mullet and needlefish in the shallows.

The Park is a mixture of sand beach, well-vegetated dunes, coastal and tropical hammock, mangroves, salt marsh, and shallow lagoon. Sea turtles nest on the outer beach, as many as one nest every 10 feet in season. Management practices are eliminating such exotics as Australian pine and Brazilian pepper.

Because his fourth-grade class hadn't appeared, we were given a guided tour by one of the uniformed volunteers. He seemed to know not only the name of every plant but also something about its habits. He plucked one leaf so we could see salt crystals, another for us to smell. In the Nature Center, a staff member was teaching a volunteer how to feed fishes in the aquarium. Later she allowed us to hold her pet, a handsome corn snake. Staff and volunteers provide a lively schedule of talks, guided walks, and special exhibits.

PUBLICATIONS
    Leaflet with map.
    Activities schedule.

HEADQUARTERS: 10900 State Road 703, North Palm Beach, FL 33408. Office: (407) 624-6950. Nature Center: (407) 624-6952.

JOHN PENNEKAMP CORAL REEF STATE PARK
Division of Recreation and Parks
2,350 land acres; 53,661 acres of water.   Maps 122, 123.

US 1 at Key Largo.

This first underwater park was established in 1959. When we first visited in 1966, the campground was half full. Next morning we were among half a dozen boats heading for the reef. Since then the Park has been overwhelmed by visitors, almost 2 million a year. Fifty charter boats take swimmers, divers, and sightseers to the reef. Private craft swarm, from jon-boats to yachts.

Fragile living corals have been damaged by boat hulls and anchors, collectors, and pollution. State Park employees do their best to educate visitors and enforce the rules. They have placed mooring buoys along the reef. Boaters are asked to use the buoys instead of anchoring, to move on if all buoys are in use. When enough buoys have been installed, this may become a rule.

With so many visitors afloat, protecting people is as difficult as protecting the reef. We turned back once because of rough seas, but several craft less seaworthy than ours continued on. Operators of dive boats do much to assure that their clients understand scuba gear and procedures, but divers in private boats have no such supervision.

Ships traveling the Gulf Stream have been known to dump oily bilge water that drifts to the reefs. After several groundings on Gulf reefs, navigation rules have required ships to keep away. A developer's proposal to pump sewage effluent underground on a nearby key was defeated because of its anticipated effect on the corals.

It's a wonderful world down there! The intricate and diverse hard coral formations, waving sea fans, whips, and plumes, and schools of colorful fishes bring divers back again and again. All this, in clear, warm water, makes the Florida reefs world famous.

On shore are the visitor center, ranger station, a boardwalk in a mangrove swamp, a nature trail in a tropical hardwood hammock, swimming beaches, marina, boat ramp, dive shop, snack bar, and campground. Camping space is limited; only 1 visitor in 50 spends the night. Traffic on the reef is heaviest from December 15 to April 15.

Glass-bottomed boat tours from the Park dock offer a fine introduction to the reefs.

ACTIVITIES

Camping: 47 sites. Telephone reservations accepted. The campground is usually full November 15 to May 15 and all weekends.

Fishing: Special rules apply. Inquire. Spear fishing is prohibited.

Swimming: Beaches on Largo Sound.

Boating: Boaters should be familiar with all Park rules and safety precautions. Boaters should have nautical charts and required safety gear. They are advised to file float plans. Rentals are available.

A ramp on the other side of Key Largo, on Blackwater Sound, provides boat access to Florida Bay, within Everglades National Park.

Canoeing: In sheltered waters. Rentals are available.

PUBLICATIONS

Park folder with chart.

Florida's Coral Reefs.

Bird checklist.

Trees of John Pennekamp Coral Reef State Park.

Concession information: tours, rentals.

HEADQUARTERS: P.O. Box 487, Key Largo, FL 33037; (305) 451-1202.

JUNO BEACH

Palm Beach County   Map 109, A-3.

On SR A1A.

This is one of the least crowded fine beaches on this part of the coast. From the developed area of Juno Beach, drive north beyond Juno Beach Park. First are several developed beach accesses: paved parking and crosswalks over the dunes. Beyond, still County owned, are pull-off parking places with informal trails through the dunes. No signs prohibit dogs on the beach.

Early on a warm January morning we had the beach to ourselves, walking several miles without seeing anyone. By 9:30 a few walkers had appeared, but they stayed in the more developed area.

We were impressed by Palm Beach County's efforts to acquire every foot of undeveloped beachfront.

LAKE OKEECHOBEE
OKEECHOBEE WATERWAY
U.S. Army Corps of Engineers
448,000 acres.   Maps 101, 102, 107, 108.

Sometimes called "the liquid heart of Florida," this huge, shallow lake is the end of the Kissimmee River watershed (see entry) and the beginning of the Everglades (see entry). The St. Lucie Canal links it to the Intracoastal Waterway and Atlantic Ocean, the Caloosahatchee River to the Gulf of Mexico. Both are navigable. The Corps maintains dredged boat channels across the lake. The route is considered safe for all motor craft. One of the alternate routes hugs the south shore.

The lake provides water storage on which southern Florida depends, cities and farms as well as the Everglades and other natural areas. Massive changes have altered that function. The Kissimmee River entry describes how channelization of the river eliminated its wetlands, so the lake receives an excess of water in wet seasons, too little in dry. Channelization is one cause of the lake's serious pollution. Others are runoff from cattle pastures and fertilizer-enriched water from sugarcane fields.

One can drive around this huge lake without seeing it. Frequent flooding over its south rim was a natural water supply for the Everglades. By the 1920s, several thousand people, chiefly engaged in farming, had settled in Clewiston and Moore Haven. Hurricanes in 1926 and 1928 sent raging floodwaters into those communities, drowning hundreds. Okeechobee is now surrounded by a 35-foot dike. Surrounding the lake are many marinas, launching ramps, picnic areas, and campgrounds, public and commercial.

St. Lucie Canal: Two recreation areas are on this 25-mile route. A campground, ramp, and other facilities are at the St. Lucie Lock and Dam, a day-use area at the Pt. Mayaca Lock. A road paralleling the canal is seldom visible because of the overgrown banks. Birding is good.

Caloosahatchee River: The river has three lock-and-dam structures. It passes LaBelle, Fort Myers Shores, and Fort Myers. The lower reaches are highly developed and usually have much boat traffic. Several recreation areas, including three campgrounds, are along the way.

ACTIVITIES

Hiking: The 110-mile circuit of the lake has been called Florida's longest and driest loop route. We don't recommend it.

Fishing: Some say fishing isn't what it used to be, but the Bass Anglers Sportsman Society voted it the best bass lake in the nation. The Florida Game and Fresh Water Fish Commission calls it "a tremendous repository of speckled perch, largemouth bass, and panfish."

Hunting: Okeechobee is popular with duck hunters, too. Each fall approximately 300,000 waterfowl drop down into the extensive marshes.

PUBLICATION: Map of recreation facilities.

HEADQUARTERS: U.S. Army Corps of Engineers, Natural Resources Office, 525 Ridgelawn Road, Clewiston, FL 33440; (813) 983-3335.

LIGNUMVITAE KEY STATE BOTANICAL AREA
Division of Recreation and Parks
280 land acres; 101 acres submerged.   Map 123, D-2.

Boat access only. Off Indian Key Channel between Upper and Lower Matecumbe keys.

Closed Tuesdays and Wednesdays.

This pristine tropical hammock, a natural community once common in the Florida Keys, is carefully protected. A three-hour round-trip boat tour leaves Indian Key fill at 1:30 P.M. Thursday through Monday; telephone reservations are advisable. *Tour schedules may change. Call Long Key State Recreation Area, (305) 664-4815, for information.*

Private and charter boats may dock at Lignumvitae Key (except Tuesday and Wednesday), but visitors must wait in the dock area for a one-hour guided walk. These are offered at 10:30 A.M., 1 P.M., and 2:30 P.M.

Indians lived on the island before the voyages of Columbus. White settlers were here before the ill-fated railroad and the Overseas Highway were built. Someone built a 3,000-foot rock wall and two blockhouses, which still stand, unexplained. On our tour we were shown the Matheson mansion, built in 1919 and now restored. The tour was on quiet trails through the subtropical hardwood hammock.

Buttonwood and black and white mangroves fringe the tidal zone, punctuated by tidal mangrove forests and creeks. The surrounding shallows have sea grass beds and mud flats, with corals, sponges, and algae in deeper water.

We recommend the experience. The ranger who guided us knew the flora and fauna of the island and was obviously devoted to its protection. The tour is the more enjoyable because no visitors roam the island and one sees no litter or vandalism.

Nearby Shell Key State Preserve is closed to visitors. We cruised around it.

PUBLICATION: Leaflet with map.

HEADQUARTERS: P.O. Box 1052, Islamorada, FL 33036; (305) 664-4815.

LONG KEY STATE RECREATION AREA
Division of Recreation and Parks
849 land acres; 117 acres submerged.   Map 125, B-3.

Florida Keys at mile 67.5, Overseas Highway.

The SRA is on Long Key Point, which partially encloses Long Key Bight. The uplands are mostly tropical hardwood hammock, with gumbo limbo, Jamaican dogwood, poisonwood, mahogany, and crabwood. Because of the key's irregular shape, the SRA has over 10 miles of shoreline, much of it fringed with mangroves. Beaches are nesting sites for sea turtles, May to September.

Plants: A checklist is available at the ranger station. Guided walks are offered every Wednesday. Something is always in bloom.

Birds: 75 species have been recorded. Winter is the best season. A bird walk is offered every Thursday in winter.

ACTIVITIES
Camping: 60 sites. Telephone reservations accepted. From January to April sites are often booked weeks in advance.
Fishing: Includes bone fishing flats.
Boating: No ramp, but a commercial marina is nearby.
Canoeing: Trail. Rentals.

INTERPRETATION
A unique feature of the SRA is a canoe nature trail that winds through the tidal Long Key lakes. The trail guide spots good fishing holes.
The SRA also has two upland nature trails and a lagoon boardwalk.
Programs include illustrated talks, guided walks.

PUBLICATION: Canoe trail guide.

HEADQUARTERS: P.O. Box 776, Long Key, FL 33001; (305) 664-4815.

ROOKERY BAY NATIONAL ESTUARINE SANCTUARY, BRIGGS MEMORIAL NATURE CENTER
The Conservancy, Inc.
6,000 acres.   Map 111, D-2.

From US 41 about 7 miles southeast of Naples, south about 3 miles on SR 951, then right on Shell Island Road.

Open 9 A.M. to 5 P.M. Closed Mondays, July 4, Thanksgiving, Christmas, and New Year's Day.

We don't have entries for most Aquatic Preserves, areas of bays, estuaries, shallows, and coastal marshes selected for special protection. Most are accessible only by boat and have no headquarters. Rookery Bay is a special case.

Local citizens organized to protect Rookery Bay in 1966. Early land purchases of mangrove islands and shores by The Conservancy, Inc., which they founded, were aided by the National Audubon Society and The Nature Conservancy. In 1978 it was designated a National Estuarine Sanctuary.

Private donations created the Briggs Memorial Nature Center, dedicated in 1982. When we visited, a capable naturalist was at the Center and exhibits were being refurbished. From the Center a boardwalk passes through a number of distinct plant communities, maintained by a few inches of difference in their elevations. A platform at the end overlooks a brackish pond.

An excellent Boardwalk Guide introduces the visitor to the characteristic plants: red, black, and white mangroves; scrub oak, popcorn lichen, black rush, slash pine, saw palmetto, bromeliads, and others. It alerts visitors to wildlife species that may be seen.

It's a quiet place now, not well publicized. We were the only visitors on an October morning. Development along SR 951 will bring more.

Canoeing and a boat cruise are sometimes available. Call ahead.

PUBLICATION: Boardwalk Guide.

HEADQUARTERS: 401 Shell Island Road, Naples, FL 33942. (813) 775-8569.

SANIBEL ISLAND
See entry, J. N. "Ding" Darling National Wildlife Refuge
12 miles long; ½ to 2½ miles wide.   Map 110, A1-2.

From Fort Myers, SR 867 over causeway.

This crescent-shaped island encloses Pine Island Sound and San Carlos Bay. A short bridge at the west end is the access to Captiva Island.

We first visited Sanibel in 1957, before the causeway was built, crossing by ferry. We were producing a film, and Sanibel was a fine location. We pitched our tent near the lighthouse and fell in love with the island. By the time we decided to move to Florida, the love affair had ended. After the causeway opened in 1963, the County government approved virtually unrestricted development. High-rise condominiums and motels soon lined the splendid beach just above the high-tide mark. Shops were everywhere, once-quiet roads congested. The National Wildlife Refuge, occupying about one-third of the island, is as magnificent as ever, but Sanibel is no longer a place we'd choose to live. Friends who lived there for 20 years have left.

Like most barrier islands, Sanibel's shape changes with storms and tides. When friends planned a visit, we recommended a sand spit that had been our favorite swimming and picnicking site. They couldn't find it. A great storm had swept it away and deposited the sand elsewhere. A marina's dock was now 50 yards from the water, and several waterfront homes were no longer on the Gulf.

Sanibel's long Gulf beach is splendid for swimming but most famous for shells. It's the best shelling beach in our hemisphere. More shells are carried in on every tide, often accumulating in drifts. As the tide goes out, a parade of shell hunters patrols the beach, walking in the "Sanibel stoop." Hobbyists assemble shells in every conceivable pattern, from napkin rings to the Last Supper.

Our visits were memorable. One night we saw, far offshore, a giant manta ray leap into the air, briefly silhouetted against the full moon. We saw tens of thousands of robins royally drunk from feasting on the fermented fruit of Brazilian pepper. We filmed oyster drills destroying an oyster bed; in subsequent years we marked the succession: as the drills reached the far end of the bed, oysters were regenerating where the attack had begun.

There's no public campground on Sanibel. The County maintains 1,100-foot Bowman's Beach, 196 acres, at the west end of the island. An interesting nature center is on Sanibel–Captiva Road.

INDEX

NOTES

NOTES

NOTES

NOTES

NOTES

NOTES

NOTES

NOTES